PHYSICAL GEOGRAPHY

A Laboratory Manual

PHYSICAL GEOGRAPHY

A Laboratory Manual

Fourth Edition

John J. Hidore

University of North Carolina
Greensboro, North Carolina

Michael C. Roberts

Simon Fraser University
Burnaby, British Columbia

Prentice Hall
Upper Saddle River, New Jersey 07458

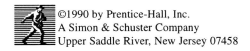©1990 by Prentice-Hall, Inc.
A Simon & Schuster Company
Upper Saddle River, New Jersey 07458

Printed in the United States of America
10 9 8 7 6 5 4 3

ISBN   0-02-354511-9

Prentice-Hall International (UK) Limited, *London*
Prentice-Hall of Australia Pty. Limited, *Sydney*
Prentice-Hall Canada Inc., *Toronto*
Prentice-Hall Hispanoamericana, S.A., *Mexico*
Prentice-Hall of India Private Limited, *New Delhi*
Prentice-Hall of Japan, Inc., *Tokyo*
Prentice-Hall of Southeast Asia Pte. Ltd., *Singapore*
Editora Prentice-Hall do Brasil, Ltda., *Rio de Janeiro*

PREFACE

This laboratory manual is designed to be used in an introductory course in physical geography where laboratory work is an integral part of the course. It can be used along with, and as a supplement to, any basic textbook in physical geography. The exercises are designed to acquaint the student with the kinds of materials and data with which the physical geographer works, such as topographic maps, aerial photographs, remote sensing imagery, weather maps, and numerical data.

One of the problems in incorporating a laboratory into an introductory physical geography course, as with any other teaching laboratory, is the assembling of the equipment and materials needed. This manual is intended to reduce the extent of this problem by including a series of weather maps, matched pairs of aerial photographs suitable for stereoscopic viewing, and field data pertaining to the environment. Some of the exercises are traditional in the topics covered, and others are directed at current environmental problems.

For many students in a college-level physical geography course, it will be their first formal academic exposure to the topic. Throughout their lives exposure to physical geography will continue, and the exercises contained here are designed to give the students a greater awareness and understanding of the environment in which they live. For those students continuing in the field, the exercises should serve as an introduction to methodology and some current problems.

The fourth edition differs from the three previous editions in several ways:
1. There are four entirely new exercises.
2. One of the exercises from the third edition has been deleted.
3. New material has been added to update some of the exercises.
4. Exercise 10 now relates to agricultural drought and involves calculating the soil moisture balance for three different areas of the United States.
5. Many of the exercises have been rewritten to make them easier for the student to understand.
6. A copy of *Topographic Map Symbols* (Department of the Interior, U.S. Geological Survey, National Mapping Division) is provided inside the back cover.

New exercises are the following: Exercise 2, written by John Oliver of Indiana State University, examines the vertical structure of the atmosphere in terms of temperature, pressure, and stratification. Exercise 39 is concerned with soil erosion and was written by Bradley Davis of the University of North Carolina at Greensboro. The Universal Soil Loss Equation is used to test the effects of the variation of slope steepness, slope length, and plant cover on soil loss. The exercise also provides current data on the rate of erosion in the Piedmont of the United States. Exercise 40, by Michael W. Mayfield of the Appalachian State University, and Exercise 41, by Jeffrey C. Patton of the University of North Carolina at Greensboro, bring an introduction to remote sensing to the manual. Exercise 40 uses visual examination to determine differences in surface features in part of Nigeria. The exercise illustrates how satellite images can be used to detect changes over a period of time. Two images are used, one from 1973, and the second from 1986. Exercise 41 takes the student through the procedure used in computer analysis of satellite images. In this exercise, the student will classify land use using two different bands of reflected radiation.

We invite users of this manual to forward suggestions on the content of the manual and to notify us of any errors that are detected.

CONTENTS

Name: _____

Laboratory Section: _____

Exercise 1

ISOLINE MAPS

One of the problems constantly faced by physical geographers is the need to graphically portray the data they have assembled. The medium most frequently used is the map, because it has great flexibility regarding the kinds of data that can be shown and the ways of portraying the data. One of the most effective maps is that employing the *isoline* (a line that joins points of equal value), which permits quantitative analysis to be carried out.

This exercise is placed first in this manual because isoline maps are frequently used in your textbook, in classes, and in later exercises in this laboratory manual. A thorough grasp of the isoline will prove to be of great value in comprehending many aspects of physical geography.

CONSTRUCTION OF ISOLINES

To construct an isoline map, a geographer must have locational coordinates for each datum so that it can be positioned on the map. Figure 1.1 illustrates the use of isolines by way of a partially completed map. The major difficulty facing the geographer is to make a decision on where to place an isoline between two points, a process called *interpolation*.

In the data above, the distance between the two points (36 and 42) should be divided into equally spaced divisions. On the right-hand side the correct location for a line with the value of 40 is shown. The other lines represent the integer values between 36 and 42.

Now study Figure 1.1 for the spacing and locating of isolines. The area between isolines can be shaded to emphasize the areas of high and low values on an isoline map. Traditionally, darker colors or heavier shading has been applied to the high values (Figure 1.2), and lighter colors to the low values.

PROBLEMS

As an introduction to the construction and interpretation of isolines, you are presented with the task of producing a map of average annual precipitation (in inches) for the state of Nebraska (Figure 1.3).

You will need the following items to do the exercise:

   Pencil and eraser
   Colored pencils
   Black felt-tip pen

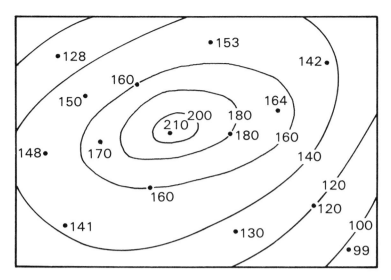

Figure 1.1.   Construction of isolines showing interpolation between data pairs

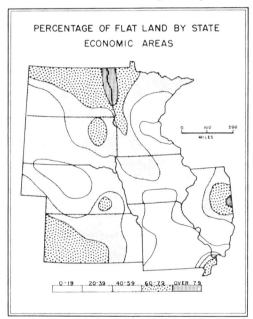

Figure 1.2.   Use of shading to emphasize the high and low values on an isoline map (From J. J. Hidore, 1963, "The relationship between cash-grain farming and landforms," *Economic geography,* **39: 87, Fig. 5)**

1. Draw the *isohyets* (lines of equal precipitation) using the following isohyet values: 15, 18, 21, 24, 27, 30, 33, and 36 inches. Use a pencil for all your initial work. Once the isohyets are drawn to your satisfaction, go over them with a black felt-tip pen.
2. The locations of the precipitation measurements are shown by the black dots.
3. Shade or color the map to emphasize the changing pattern of precipitation across the state.
4. Insert a title, scale, and legend. Make sure that you have identified the isohyets.
5. Produce an *isopach* map (lines of equal thickness of rock units) on Figure 1.4 of the depth of ash deposited by Mount Saint Helens' eruption of 18 May 1980. Draw the isopachs at the following intervals: 70, 60, 50, 40, 30, 20, 10, 5, and 1 millimeters (mm). Plot the 10 mm isopach first. By doing this you will be able to establish the pattern of the other isopachs.
6. Insert a title and legend.

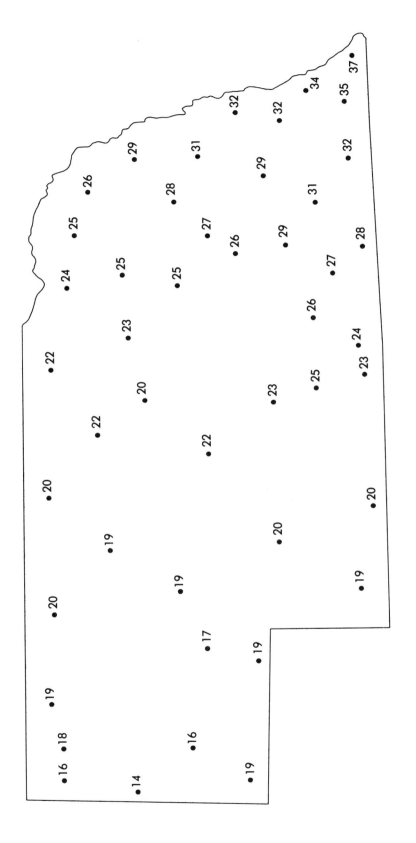

Figure I.3.

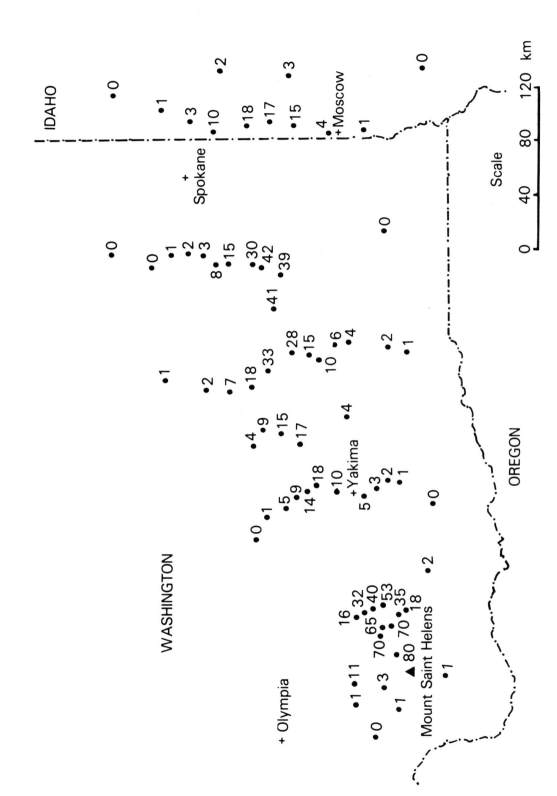

Figure I.4.

Name: _____

Laboratory Section: _____

Exercise 2

THE ATMOSPHERE: VERTICAL CHANGES IN TEMPERATURE AND PRESSURE

As early as the mid-nineteenth century, with the growing popularity of ballooning and mountaineering, it was realized that some standard was needed to provide information about changes in the atmosphere which occur with altitude.

Although a number of ideas were suggested, it was not until 1924 that a set of standard conditions for the atmosphere was adopted. At that time, the system proposed by the International Committee for Air Navigation was accepted. As more upper air data became available, this system was modified until today the atmospheric model proposed by the U.S. Committee on Extension of the Standard Atmosphere is widely used. The most recent version of this is the 1976 U.S. Standard Atmosphere.

The purpose of the *Standard Atmosphere* is to establish an idealized vertical distribution of atmospheric properties which, by international agreement, can be used for a variety of purposes including missile and aircraft design, performance calculations, and pressure calibration. The values given represent the year-round mean conditions in daylight hours for a midlatitude location. Variables provided include temperature, pressure, density, and electrical state.

Table 2.1 provides pressure data for the U.S. Standard Atmosphere up to a height of 70 kilometers (km). The unit for measuring pressure is the millibar (mb), which is equal to a force of 1000 dynes per square centimeter (a dyne is the force needed to accelerate a mass of 1 g by 1 cm/sec).

Table 2.1. U.S. Standard Atmosphere

Ht. (km)	Pressure (mb)	Ht. (km)	Pressure (mb)	Ht. (km)	Pressure (mb)
0	1013.2	5.0	540.4	18.0	75.65
.5	954.6	6.0	472.2	20.0	55.29
1.0	898.8	7.0	411.0	25.0	25.49
1.5	845.6	8.0	356.5	30.0	11.97
2.0	795.0	9.0	308.0	35.0	5.75
2.5	746.9	10.0	265.0	40.0	2.87
3.0	701.2	12.0	194.0	50.0	.79
3.5	657.8	14.0	141.7	60.0	.23
4.0	616.5	16.0	103.5	70.0	.06

PROBLEMS

1. At any altitude only the air molecules above that level can contribute toward the mass of the atmosphere. Thus pressure measurements can be used to describe how much of the atmosphere occurs below or above given altitudes.

    Use the data given in Table 2.1 to estimate the following:
    a. The altitude (to the nearest kilometer) below which approximately 50% of the atmosphere is found: _____ km
    b. The altitude (to the nearest kilometer) below which approximately 75% of the atmosphere is found: _____ km
    c. The percentage of the atmosphere below a transcontinental jet aircraft that is flying at 30,000 feet (approximately 9 km) _____ %

2. Use the data in Table 2.1 to determine the rate of pressure decrease between the following altitudes:

1 km Interval	**10 km Interval**
a. 0 and 1 km _____ mb	d. 0 and 10 km _____ mb
b. 5 and 6 km _____ mb	e. 20 and 30 km _____ mb
c. 9 and 10 km _____ mb	f. 60 and 70 km _____ mb

    In one or two sentences describe the rate at which pressure changes with altitude.

Figure 2.1 is a graphical representation of the Standard Atmosphere and shows temperature variations with altitude. These variations permit the atmosphere to be divided into sections or layers named the *troposphere, stratosphere, mesosphere,* and *thermosphere.* The boundary between each of these layers is represented by a zone where temperature is constant with height (an isothermal layer). These boundary zones are named for the sphere that occurs immediately below the isothermal layer. Thus the *tropopause* is at the top of the troposphere, the *stratopause* is above the stratosphere, and so on.

3. Use Figure 2.1 to estimate the following:
    a. The temperature at the tropopause _____
    b. The lowest temperature shown on Figure 2.1 is _____ °C and is found in the layer known as the _____ which occurs at an altitude of _____ km
    c. The altitudes at which the temperature of –20 °C is encountered are _____ km, _____ km, and _____ km.
    d. The temperatures of the isothermal layers referred to as:
        i.   The tropopause _____ °C
        ii. The stratopause _____ °C
        iii. The mesopause _____ °C

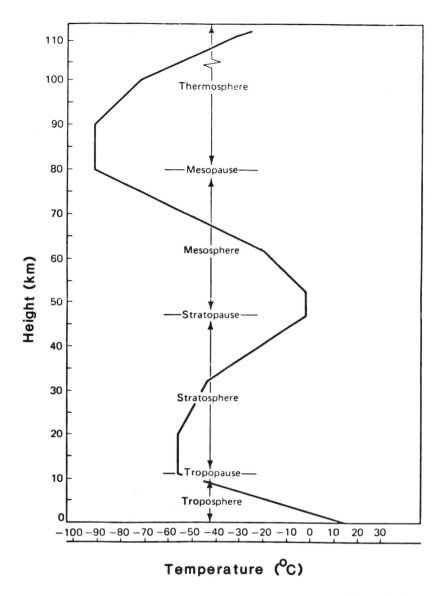

Figure 2.1. The Standard Atmosphere: temperature and vertical structure

4. As noted previously, the Standard Atmosphere is an idealized depiction or model for average midlatitude conditions. Variations from the standard conditions occur over space and time. The following questions relate to these variations. For example, soundings through the atmosphere at a city located at sea level and at 40 degrees north show that temperatures decline at an average rate (a *lapse rate*) of 6.5 °C/km. The surface temperature is 10 °C, while at the tropopause the temperature is found to be –55 °C. Enter the data for surface temperature and tropopause temperature in Table 2.2 and use the given lapse rate to find the height of the tropopause.

On the same day, a city near the equator records a surface temperature of 25 °C and soundings reveal a lapse rate of 6.5 °C/km. The height of the tropopause is found to be 16 km. Enter these data in Table 2.2 and from them estimate the temperature at the tropopause. In the

Table 2.2.

	Midlatitude location	Equatorial location
Temperature at tropopause	_____	_____
Surface temperature	_____	_____
Lapse rate	_____	_____
Height of tropopause	_____	_____

space below write a sentence or two about the height of the tropopause at the equator and in midlatitudes.

5. Figure 2.2 provides the temperature structure through the atmosphere for January and July at 40 degrees north latitude.
   a. Draw appropriate lines showing the tropopause at the two different times of the year.
   b. The decrease in temperature in the troposphere is known as the lapse rate. To estimate the lapse rate for the given set of conditions:
      i. Calculate the difference in temperature between the surface and the tropopause. Use the abbreviated table below.

	January	July
Surface temperature	_____	_____
Tropopause temperature	_____	_____
Temperature difference	_____	_____

      ii. These data represent temperature differences for the entire depth of the troposphere. This depth can be estimated by determining the height of the tropopause above the surface.
         Height of tropopause in January is _____ km
         Height of tropopause in July is _____ km
      iii. The lapse rate is usually expressed in terms of temperature decrease for each kilometer. Using the data you have obtained for the temperature difference and the height of the tropopause, calculate the lapse rates for January and July by dividing the difference in temperature by the height.
         The January lapse rate is _____ /km
         The July lapse rate is _____ /km
   c. Using the data you have calculated, describe the variations in temperature, height of the tropopause, and lapse rates for January and July.

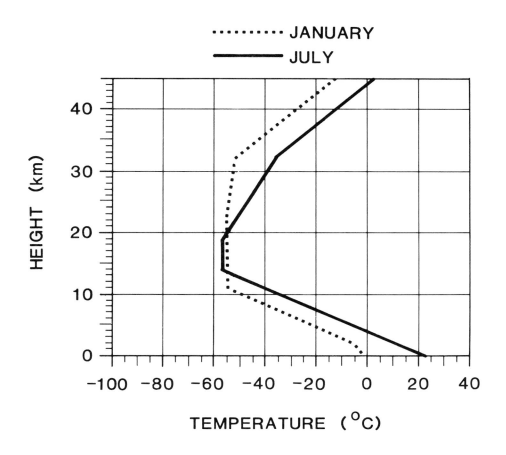

Figure 2.2   Temperature profiles of the atmosphere in January and July

Exercise 3

RADIATION AND TEMPERATURE

Solar radiation is the primary source of energy in the earth environment, although the Earth intercepts but a very small portion of the total radiation emitted by the sun. While the amount of radiation reaching the Earth is fairly constant throughout the year, the amount of radiation reaching any point on the ground varies greatly through time. The amount of solar radiation reaching the surface (*solar intensity*) is affected by the amount of radiation reflected and scattered back to space and by the amount of energy absorbed directly by the atmosphere. Each of these elements is a function of the angle the solar beam makes with the surface (*angle of incidence*). The difference in solar intensity, which is largely due to the angle of the solar beam, is the primary reason for the equator to pole variation in temperature.

To illustrate the effects of the angle of the solar beam on radiation intensity, Figure 3.1A shows the beam of one square unit perpendicular to the surface. It illuminates an area on the surface of one square unit. When the angle is reduced to 30 degrees, as in Figure 3.1B, a solar beam of one square unit illuminates a larger area—in this particular case, an area twice as large. Since the same amount of energy is being spread over a larger area, the intensity (energy per area) must be less. Since the area is twice as great in Figure 3.1B, the intensity must be just one half as great as in Figure 3.1A. Table 3.1 gives the intensity of the solar beam for various angles as a percentage of a perpendicular beam. Note that for an angle of 30 degrees, the radiation intensity is 50% of that of a perpendicular beam, which is in agreement with the illustration in Figure 3.1. The intensity of solar radiation varies as the sine of the angle of the sun above the horizon, and Table 3.1 is, in fact, a table of sines.

PROBLEMS

1. Figure 3.2 represents a cross section of the atmosphere. Measure the lengths of solar beam A and solar beam B. The ratio of the length of travel through the atmosphere of beam B to that of A is _____ :1. This greater length of travel increases the amount of reflection, absorption, and scattering of radiation back to space, making the actual radiation received at the surface even less than that due to solar angle alone.

   In Figure 3.3 the shaded area from A_1 to A_2 represents a solar beam with a diameter equal to that of the Earth. In the figure draw a line from point B_1 to B_2 and label it the circle of illumination. Extend line $C_1 C_2$ through the circle and label it the solar equator. Next construct a line from the center of the circle through D_1, a line tangent to the circle at D_1, and a line representing a ray of solar energy from D_2 to D_1.

   At any one time half the Earth is illuminated by solar radiation. The intensity of the radiation decreases as the distance from C_1 increases. The intensity of the radiation decreases as a result of the progressively lower angle of the beam and the greater distance the radiation

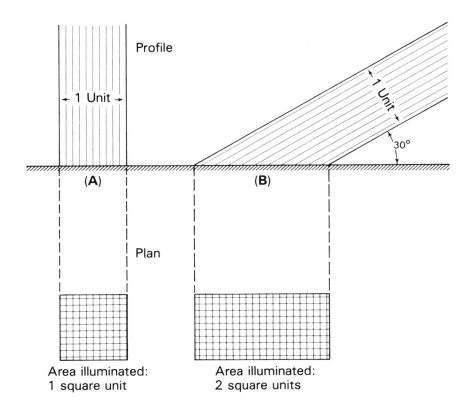

Figure 3.1. Effect of the angle of incidence on radiation intensity

Table 3.1. Intensity of Solar Radiation[a]

Angle of Beam	Degrees - units									
	0°	1°	2°	3°	4°	5°	6°	7°	8°	9°
0°	00.00	01.75	03.49	05.23	06.98	08.72	10.45	12.19	13.92	15.64
10°	17.36	19.08	20.79	22.50	24.19	25.88	27.56	29.24	30.90	32.56
20°	34.20	35.84	37.46	39.07	40.67	42.26	43.84	45.40	46.95	48.48
30°	50.00	51.50	52.99	54.46	55.92	57.36	58.78	60.18	61.57	62.93
40°	64.28	65.61	66.91	68.20	69.47	70.71	71.93	73.14	74.31	75.47
50°	76.60	77.71	78.80	79.86	80.90	81.92	82.90	83.87	84.80	85.72
60°	86.60	87.46	88.29	89.10	89.88	90.63	91.36	92.05	92.72	93.36
70°	93.97	94.55	95.11	95.63	96.13	96.59	97.03	97.44	97.81	98.16
80°	98.48	98.77	99.03	99.25	99.45	99.62	99.76	99.86	99.94	99.98

[a]Radiation intensity for given angles of solar incidence expressed as a percentage of that of a beam perpendicular to the surface. To determine the relative intensity of a solar beam with an angle of incidence of 53 degrees, read down the left-hand column to 50 and then across the row to 3. The relative intensity for an angle of incidence of 53 degrees is 79.86%.

has to travel through the atmosphere. The angle of the radiation with the surface at point D_1 is 30 degrees, the same as in the example in Figure 3.2. Hence, the solar radiation is less than half what it is at point C_1. The maximum intensity of the radiation is at point C_1, which is the solar equator.

2. For each of the cities in Table 3.2 determine the angle of incidence, the relative intensity of the solar beam, and the length of day at the time of the equinox (use Table 3.1). In Figure 3.3

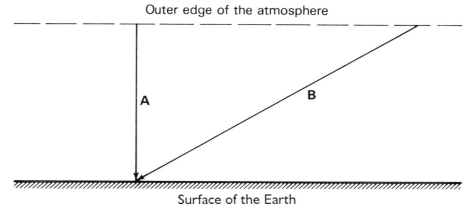

Figure 3.2.   Cross section of atmosphere

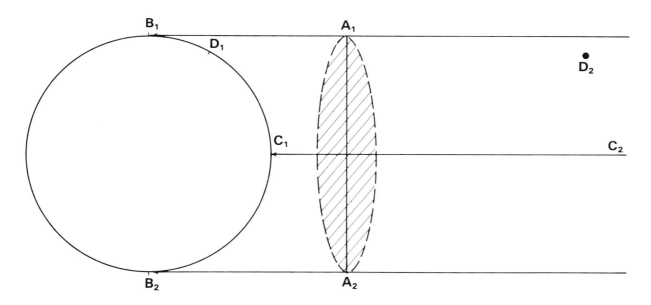

Figure 3.3.   Latitude and the angle of radiation

let B_1 represent the North Pole, B_2 the South Pole, and the extension of line C_1C_2 through the circle the geographical equator. Figure 3.3 and Table 3.2 now represent the Earth–sun relationship at the time of the equinox.

Table 3.2.   Effect of Latitude on Radiation Intensity

Location	Latitude	Angle of Incidence	Radiation Intensity (%)	Length of Day
Nome, Alaska	65°N			
Edmonton, Alberta	55°N			
Portland, Oregon	45°N			
Oklahoma City, Oklahoma	35°N			
São Paulo, Brazil	23½° S			
Punta Arenas, Chile	53° S			

Name: _____

Laboratory Section: _____

Exercise 4

THE SEASONS–I

The seasons of the year, which are such important regulators of life, are associated with temperature and moisture changes throughout the year. Seasonal changes in temperature result primarily from the inclination of the Earth on its axis and the revolution of the Earth about the sun. These two phenomena produce changes in the intensity and duration of sunlight at most points on the Earth's surface.

While the curvature of the Earth is partially responsible for the varying intensity of radiation, the problem is compounded as a result of the changing position of the heat equator. As the Earth revolves about the sun with its axis of rotation inclined 66½ degrees to the plane of the ecliptic, the perpendicular rays of the sun shift latitudinally over an angular distance of 47 degrees. This shifting of the perpendicular beam produces large imbalances of heating between the northern and southern hemispheres.

PROBLEMS

1. In Figure 4.1, draw in parallels at 23½ degrees north and south and at 66½ degrees north and south. Draw in the circle of illumination. Label the Tropic of Cancer, Tropic of Capricorn, Arctic Circle, and Antarctic Circle. Next, draw in several lines representing beams of solar radiation. Place two of these at right angles to the circle of illumination and tangent to the

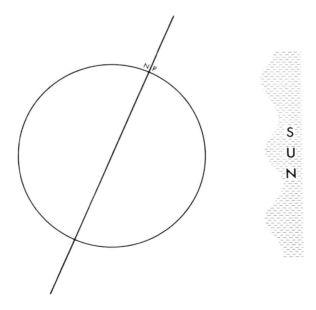

Figure 4.1   The Earth at the summer solstice

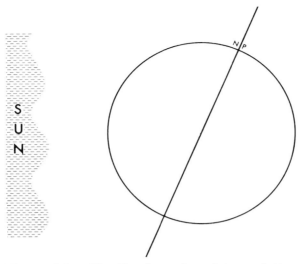

Figure 4.2.   The Earth at the winter solstice

surface. Place a third beam perpendicular to the Earth's surface at the Tropic of Cancer. This diagram represents the radiation conditions as they exist at the time of the summer solstice.

Repeat the process for Figure 4.2, which, when completed, represents the radiation conditions for the winter solstice. Now complete Table 4.1.

2. Between latitudes _____ degrees north and _____ degrees south, the sun is directly overhead twice each year. The latitudinal zone in which the noon sun is observed always to be south of the zenith is _____ degrees north to _____ degrees north, and the zone in which the noon sun is always observed north of the zenith is _____ degrees south to _____ degrees south. The maximum variation in the angle of the noon sun experienced at any point on the Earth's surface is 47 degrees. The latitudinal zone that experiences this variation extends from _____ degrees to _____ degrees on either side of the equator.

3. Based upon the angle of solar radiation, determine whether Indianapolis (40 degrees north) has more or less radiation than the equator on the following dates:
    a.   Spring equinox (March 21) _____
    b.   Summer solstice (June 22) _____
    c.   Fall equinox (September 23) _____
    d.   Winter solstice (December 22) _____

Table 4.1.   Angle of Radiation by Season

	March 21	June 22	September 23	December 22
Latitude of vertical rays of the sun	_____	_____	_____	_____
Tangent rays of the sun in the northern hemisphere	_____	_____	_____	_____
Tangent rays of the sun in the southern hemisphere	_____	_____	_____	_____
Name associated with each date	_____	_____	_____	_____

4. St. Louis, Missouri, is located at a latitude of approximately 39 degrees north. Using the data provided in Table 4.2, determine the date in the spring when the radiation intensity at St. Louis becomes equal to the intensity at the equator: _____. For a period of time after this date, the radiation intensity in St. Louis (barring the effects of atmospheric pollution) will be greater than at the equator. As the perpendicular beam of solar radiation moves southward again after the summer solstice, there will again occur a time when solar radiation at St. Louis is nearly the same as at the equator. That date is _____. There is thus a period of about _____ weeks when solar intensity in the latitude of St. Louis is greater than it is at the equator. A similar situation exists for all locations in the United States with latitudes south of 47 degrees north.

5. Latitudinal changes in insolation are also affected by the varying length of the day. At the times of the equinoxes, the length of the day is equal everywhere, 12 hr of daylight and 12 hr of darkness. During the rest of the year, there are inequities between the northern hemisphere and the southern hemisphere. Table 4.3 shows the lengths of the daylight period for the summer and winter solstices, the longest and shortest days of the year respectively. At the time of the summer solstice, determine the length of the daylight period for the equator and for Minneapolis.

   a. Equator _____
   b. Minneapolis _____

Table 4.2. Declination of the Sun on Selected Days of the Year

Day	January	February	March	April	May	June
1	− 23°04′	− 17°19′	− 7°53′	+ 4°14′	+ 14°50′	+ 21°57′
5	22 42	16 10	6 21	5 46	16 02	22 38
9	22 13	14 55	4 48	7 17	17 09	22 52
13	21 37	13 37	3 14	8 46	18 11	23 10
17	20 54	12 15	1 39	10 12	19 09	23 22
21	20 05	10 50	− 0 05	11 35	20 02	23 27
25	19 09	9 23	+ 1 30	12 56	20 49	23 25
29	18 08	-	3 04	14 13	21 30	23 17

Day	July	August	September	October	November	December
1	+ 23°10′	+ 18°14′	+ 8°35′	− 2°53′	− 14°11′	− 21°40′
5	22 52	17 12	7 07	4 26	15 27	22 16
9	22 28	16 06	5 37	5 58	16 38	22 45
13	21 57	14 55	4 06	7 29	17 45	23 06
17	21 21	13 41	2 34	8 58	18 48	23 20
21	20 38	12 23	+ 1 01	10 25	19 45	23 26
25	19 50	11 02	− 0 32	11 50	20 36	23 25
29	18 57	9 39	2 06	13 12	21 21	23 17

From U.S. Naval Observatory, 1950, *The American ephemeris and nautical almanac for the year 1950*, table by R. J. List (Washington, D. C.).

Table 4.3. Length of Daylight for Intervals of 1 Degree of Latitude[a]

	0°	1°	2°	3°	4°	5°	6°	7°	8°	9°
0°	12:07 12:07	12:11 12:04	12:15 12:00	12:18 11:57	12:22 11:53	12:25 11:50	12:29 11:46	12:32 11:43	12:36 11:39	12:39 11:36
10°	12:43 11:33	12:47 11:29	12:50 11:25	12:54 11:21	12:58 11:18	13:02 11:14	13:05 11:10	13:09 11:07	13:13 11:03	13:17 10:59
20°	13:21 10:55	13:25 10:51	13:29 10:47	13:33 10:43	13:37 10:39	13:42 10:35	13:47 10:30	13:51 10:26	13:56 10:22	14:00 10:17
30°	14:05 10:12	14:10 10:08	14:15 10:03	14:20 9:58	14:26 9:53	14:31 9:48	14:37 9:42	14:43 9:37	14:49 9:31	14:55 9:25
40°	15:02 9:19	15:08 9:13	15:15 9:07	15:22 9:00	15:30 8:53	15:38 8:46	15:46 8:38	15:54 8:30	16:03 8:22	16:13 8:14
50°	16:23 8:04	16:33 7:54	16:45 7:44	16:57 7:33	17:09 7:22	17:23 7:10	17:38 6:57	17:54 6:42	18:11 6:27	18:31 6:10
60°	18:53 5:52	19:17 5:32	19:45 5:09	20:19 4:42	21:02 4:18	22:03 3:34	- 2:46	- 1:30	- -	- -

[a]The upper figure in each pair of figures represents the longest day, and the lower figure represents the shortest day. To find the length of daylight for 37 degrees, read down to 30 degrees in the left column and across the row to 7 degrees. The longest day at 37 degrees is 14 hr, 43 min. Note that the two periods do not add up to 24 hr because daylight is measured when the rim of the sun, rather than the center of the sun, is visible.

Exercise 5

ATMOSPHERIC HUMIDITY

Atmospheric humidity is the result of the presence of water vapor in the atmosphere. Water in the gaseous state is one of the many gases that make up a given unit volume of air. The amount of water vapor that the air contains varies greatly. Since all gases exert pressure, the water vapor in the air contributes part of the total atmospheric pressure.

The maximum amount of water the air can hold (*saturated vapor pressure*) is associated with the temperature of the air. The saturated vapor pressure for temperatures from –59 °C to +49 °C is given in Table 5.1.

PROBLEMS

1. List the saturated vapor pressure for each pair of temperatures listed below and determine the differences in vapor pressure.

    –12 °C (10 °F) _____   10 °C (50 °F) _____   32 °C (90 °F) _____
    –18 °C (0 °F) _____   4 °C (40 °F) _____   26 °C (79 °F) _____
    Difference _____   Difference _____   Difference _____

2. As the temperature increases, the amount of water the air can hold per degree rise of temperature (*increases, decreases, stays the same*). As the temperature increases, the saturated vapor pressure increases at (a *geometric*, an *arithmetic*) rate. The amount of water the air can hold at 27 °C (80 °F) is _____ times that at –18 °C (0 °F).

CONDENSATION

If more water vapor is present than the air can hold, some of this water vapor will condense, or change from the gaseous to the liquid state. Since all air near the surface of the Earth contains water vapor, it can be made to yield this water if it can be brought to the saturation point. A parcel of air can be brought to the saturation point if cooled sufficiently, since the ability to hold moisture is reduced as the temperature goes down. The temperature at which air will become saturated if cooled sufficiently is known as the *dew point.*

PROBLEMS

3. Determine the dew point of the air for the conditions that follow. (Use Table 5.1.) Note that the temperature of the air is not needed to find the dew point. It is provided in the table to give more complete information for the examples.

Air temperature (°C)	Vapor pressure (mb)	Dew point (°C)
0	4.8	_____
21	14.9	_____
32	36.3	_____
35	37.8	_____

4. Relative humidity is defined as the ratio of the actual vapor pressure of the air to the saturated vapor pressure, expressed as a percentage.

$$\text{Relative humidity} = \frac{\text{actual vapor pressure}}{\text{saturated vapor pressure}} \times 100$$

If the actual vapor pressure of a parcel of air is 25 mb and the air temperature is 29 °C (85 °F), what are the saturated vapor pressure and the relative humidity?
   a. Saturated vapor pressure _____
   b. Relative humidity _____

5. One of the advantages of technology is being able to live in dwellings that are heated to comfortable temperatures while the temperatures outdoors may be very cold. Bringing cold air indoors and heating it change its character considerably. Not only is the air heated, but the relative humidity is altered to a great extent.
   Air at a temperature of –18 °C (0 °F) and 70% relative humidity is brought indoors and heated to 21 °C (70 °F). What will the relative humidity be indoors? _____ Compare the moisture conditions inside this house with atmospheric conditions at a desert site where air temperature is 38 °C (100 °F) and relative humidity is 12%. Which has the higher actual vapor pressure? _____ It has been demonstrated that such low humidity inside a house is not only hard on health but also very hard on the structure of the home and on wooden furniture. The wood tends to become brittle and crack. It is recommended that humidity be maintained above 20% and preferably above 40%. For this reason, many modern heating systems incorporate humidifiers.

6. On a clear spring evening the temperature drops at the rate of 1 °C/hr until the dew point is reached. It continues to cool at the rate of 0.5 °C/hr until 6 A.M. If the temperature at 5 P.M. is 10 °C and the relative humidity is 62%, condensation will begin at _____ (A.M., P.M.) in the form of (dew, frost) and the minimum temperature will be _____. If the temperature at 5 P.M. is 7 °C and the relative humidity is 57%, condensation will begin at _____ (A.M., P.M.) in the form of (dew, frost) and the minimum temperature will be _____.

7. Evaporation is the process of change in state of a substance from liquid to gas. This is a cooling process, and one means of measuring relative humidity uses this attribute of evaporation. A thermometer with the bulb wetted and with air circulated around it will have a different temperature than one with a dry bulb. The difference in the temperatures of the two thermometers is proportional to the relative humidity.
   Given the following atmospheric conditions:

   air temperature = 21 °C (70 °F)
   wet-bulb depression = 3 °C (5 °F)

   a. What is the relative humidity? (See Table 5.2)
   b. What is the saturated vapor pressure of the air? (See Table 5.1.) _____

Table 5.1. Saturation Vapor Pressure Over Water and Over Ice in Millibars[a]

Temperature in °C	Temperature in °C									
	0	1	2	3	4	5	6	7	8	9
40	73.777	77.802	82.015	86.423	91.034	95.885	100.89	106.16	111.66	117.40
30	42.430	44.927	47.551	50.307	53.200	56.236	59.422	62.762	66.264	69.934
20	23.373	24.861	26.430	28.086	29.831	31.671	33.608	35.649	37.796	40.055
10	12.272	13.119	14.017	14.969	15.977	17.044	18.173	19.367	20.630	21.964
+0	6.1078	6.5662	7.0547	7.5753	8.1294	8.7192	9.3465	10.013	10.722	11.474
−0	6.1078 (6.1078)[b]	5.623 (5.6780)	5.173 (5.2753)	4.757 (4.8981)	4.372 (4.5451)	4.015 (4.2148)	3.685 (3.9061)	3.379 (3.6177)	3.097 (3.3484)	2.837 (3.0971)
−10	2.597 (2.8627)	2.376 (2.6443)	2.172 (2.4409)	1.984 (2.2515)	1.811 (2.0755)	1.652 (1.9118)	1.506 (1.7597)	1.371 (1.6186)	1.248 (1.4877)	1.135 (1.3664)
−20	1.032 (1.2540)	0.9370 (1.1500)	0.8502 (1.0538)	0.7709 (0.9649)	0.6985 (0.8827)	0.6323 (0.8070)	0.5720 (0.7371)	0.5170 (0.6727)	0.4669 (0.6134)	0.4213 (0.5589)
−30	0.3798 (0.5088)	0.3421 (0.4628)	0.3079 (0.4205)	0.2769 (0.3818)	0.2488 (0.3463)	0.2233 (0.3139)	0.2002 (0.2842)	0.1794 (0.2571)	0.1606 (0.2323)	0.1436 (0.2097)
−40	0.1283 (0.1891)	0.1145 (0.1704)	0.1021 (0.1534)	0.09098 (0.1379)	0.08097 (0.1239)	0.07198 (0.1111)	0.06393 (0.09961)	0.05671 (0.08918)	0.05026 (0.07975)	0.04449 (0.07124)
−50	0.03935	0.03476	0.03067	0.02703	0.02380	0.02092	0.01838	0.01612	0.01413	0.01236

[a]To find the saturation vapor pressure for 13 °C, read down the left column to 10 °C and across that row to 3 °C. The saturation vapor pressure for 13 °C is 14.969 mb.
[b]Values over water at subfreezing temperatures in parentheses.

Table 5.2. Relative Humidity

Dry-Bulb Temperature in °C	Depression of the Wet Bulb in °C [a]																			
	1	2	3	4	5	6	7	8	9	10	11	12	13	14	15	16	17	18	19	20
32	93	87	80	74	68	62	57	51	46	41	36	31	27	23	20	16	12			
31	93	87	80	74	68	62	56	50	45	40	34	31	26	22	19	14				
30	93	86	80	74	67	61	54	49	43	38	34	29	25	21	17					
29	93	86	80	73	66	59	53	47	42	37	32	28	24	20						
28	93	86	79	71	65	57	51	45	41	36	32	27	23	18						
27	93	85	78	70	63	56	50	45	40	35	31	26	21							
26	92	84	76	68	61	55	49	44	39	34	30	25								
25	91	82	74	67	60	54	48	43	38	33	28									
24	90	81	72	65	58	52	47	42	37	33										
23	90	81	72	65	58	52	46	41	37											
22	90	81	72	64	58	52	46	41	36											
21	89	80	72	63	57	51	45	40	35											
20	89	80	71	63	57	51	45	39												
19	89	79	71	63	56	50	44	38												
18	89	79	70	62	55	49	44													
17	88	79	70	62	54	48	42													
16	88	79	69	61	54	48														
15	88	78	69	61	53															
14	88	78	69	61																
13	88	78	69																	
12	88	77																		
11	88																			

[a]The depression of the wet bulb is the difference in temperature between the dry thermometer and the wetted thermometer.

c. Knowing the saturated vapor pressure and the relative humidity, calculate the actual vapor pressure of the air.

Saturated vapor pressure $\times \dfrac{\text{relative humidity}}{100} =$ _____

d. What is the dew point of this air? (Use Table 5.1.) _____
   Note: Dew point is the temperature to which air must be cooled in order for saturation to occur.

8. Determine the relative humidity for each of the following conditions. Use Table 5.2.

Dry-bulb temperature (°C)	Wet-bulb temperature (°C)	Relative humidity (%)
32	30	_____
18	15	_____
16	10	_____

Name: _____

Laboratory Section: _____

Exercise 6

ADIABATIC PROCESSES IN THE ATMOSPHERE

The primary source for heating of the atmosphere is re-radiated energy from the surface of the Earth. Thus, temperatures in the atmosphere usually decrease with height. This change in temperature with height is referred to as the *lapse rate*.

PROBLEMS

1. The data in Table 6.1 represent the observed temperatures at different heights at two different times of day. Plot the data given in Table 6.1 on Figure 6.1, using a dashed line for the 7 A.M. data and a solid line for the 2 P.M. data. Draw a horizontal line across the graph at the height marking the top of the zone in which temperature increases (*temperature inversion*).

   What factors are responsible for the differences in the two lapse rates that have been plotted?

The unequal heating of the atmosphere at the surface is one of the factors producing atmospheric turbulence. As air rises from the surface, it expands because of decreasing pressure with height. This rate of cooling due to expansion in unsaturated air is approximately 1 °C per 100 m (5.5 °F per 1000 ft). This is called *adiabatic cooling* because no heat is lost to the system. It is an internal adjustment in energy distribution due to the expanding volume as the air rises.

Table 6.1. Sample Lapse Rates

Altitude (meters)	7 A.M.	2 P.M.
Surface	7 °C	24 °C
360	15	21
720	13	18
1080	11	15
1440	9	12
1800	7	9
2160	5	6

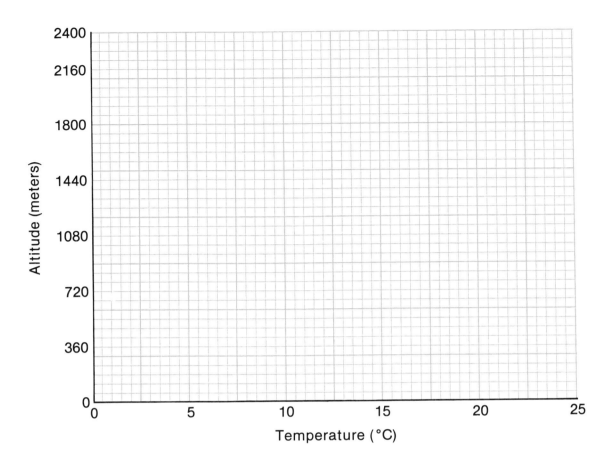

Figure 6.1. Graph on which to plot 7 A.M. and 2 P.M. temperatures

2. In Figure 6.2, *A* represents a parcel of air at the surface with a temperature of 7 °C and a dew point of 2 °C. If the air were to start to rise, it would cool by expansion at a dry adiabatic rate of _____ per 100 m. If the air were to rise until condensation began, the dew point would be reached at a height of _____ m. The altitude at which the dew point is reached is referred to as the *lifting condensation level.* This level is often visible in the atmosphere in the form of the flat base of cumulus clouds. In Figure 6.2, point *B* represents this level in the atmosphere. Insert the altitude and temperature for this level near point *B*. If the air continues to rise after condensation begins, theoretically it will continue to cool adiabatically at 1 °C per 100 m; however, the condensation of moisture that must occur releases heat into the air at a rate of 600 calories per cm^3. (This heat was acquired in the original evaporation of the water.) This addition of heat by the condensation cuts down the net rate of cooling with height. The net rate of cooling while condensation is occurring is known as the *wet adiabatic rate.* This rate will depend upon how much condensation takes place. The greater the condensation, the lower the net rate of cooling and the lower the wet adiabatic rate. Assume for this problem a wet adiabatic rate of 0.5 °C per 100 m for the parcel of air ascending from *B* to *C*. What would be the air temperature at point *C*? _____

    If an air parcel descends through the atmosphere, the air will heat at the dry adiabatic rate as it will necessarily be unsaturated. Thus while rising air cools at varying rates, descending air heats at a uniform rate. If the parcel of air were to settle back to the surface from level *C*, the resulting surface temperature would be _____ °C. The parcel of air has been heated _____ °C and the source of the heat was the process of _____.

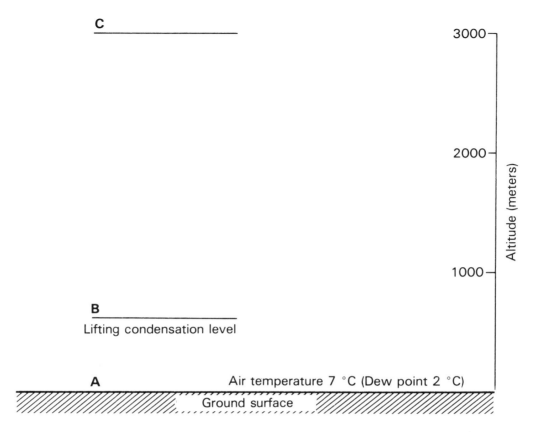

C _____

3000

Altitude (meters)

2000

1000

B _____
Lifting condensation level

A   Air temperature 7 °C (Dew point 2 °C)
Ground surface

Figure 6.2.   Graph on which to plot height and temperature of lifting condensation level

Chinook winds serve as a dramatic example of the effects of different rates in cooling and heating an air mass. Normally, air rising and flowing over the Rocky Mountains remains aloft downwind from the mountains. However, should the airstream descend the leeward slopes, it will warm at the dry adiabatic rate. When the chinook starts to blow in winter, dramatic increases of temperature have been recorded in the area flanking the Rockies in the United States and Canada; for example, in Spearfish, South Dakota, the temperature jumped from −20 °C to 7 °C during a 2-min period on 22 January 1943.

3.   On a July day the air temperature at the surface is 32 °C. The wet-bulb temperature is 31 °C. There is a broken layer of cumulus cloud present. Using Table 5.2, determine the dew point of the air. The dew point is _____ °C and the cloud base is at _____ m. If the cloud layer is 700 m thick, the temperature at the upper surface of the cloud layer is _____ °C. (Assume a wet adiabatic rate of 0.5 °C.)

Exercise 7

THE SEASONS–II

Over most of the Earth's surface the fundamental aspect of the seasons is not the change in temperature from summer to winter but the alternation of wet seasons and dry seasons. All life forms adjust to the rhythmic pattern of rainy and dry seasons. Throughout the zone from 30 degrees north to 30 degrees south, the change in temperature is small compared to the difference in moisture balance from summer to winter. The continent of Africa illustrates very well the seasonal imbalance in water availability. Table 7.1 contains mean precipitation data for the months of July and January along the meridian of 20 degrees east. The data extend along this meridian from 25 degrees north to 25 degrees south.

PROBLEMS

1. Plot the mean January precipitation on Figure 7.1 using a solid line and the mean July data using a dashed line.
2. Compare the area under the two curves. Does Africa receive the greater amount of rainfall south of the equator or north of the equator? _____ table
3. Africa extends over about 70 degrees of latitude. According to the completed graph, what is the width of the latitudinal zone that receives rainfall in both seasons? _____ Most of the continent of Africa experiences a dry season of several months.

SEASONAL DISTRIBUTION OF PRECIPITATION IN NORTH AMERICA

A wide variety of precipitation regimes exists in North America, but four regimes can be established on the seasonal distribution of precipitation. The temperature and precipitation data are given in Table 7.2 for four cities that are representative of the types of regimes. Figure 7.2 shows the areas of the United States that experience each type of regime and the location of a major city within each area. Your instructor may wish to provide in the blank lines in Table 7.2 the data for the city in which you live or some other city.

Table 7.1. Mean Precipitation in Millimeters from 25°N to 25°S at 20°E Longitude

| | Latitude | | | | | | | | | | |
| | North | | | | | | South | | | | |
Month	25°	20°	15°	10°	5°	0°	5°	10°	15°	20°	25°
July	Tª ≈ 0	20	120	160	135	90	30	10	T ≈ 0	T ≈ 0	T ≈ 0
January	0	0	T ≈ 0	5	20	50	130	210	260	140	20

ªT = trace

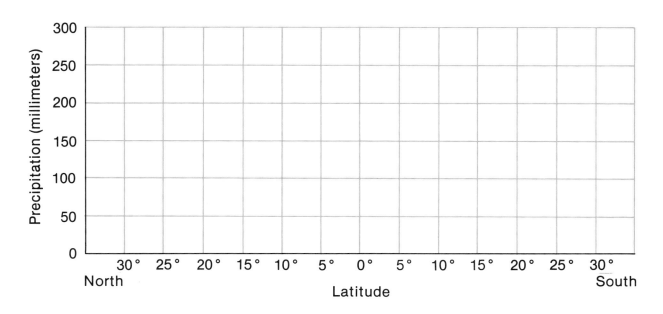

Figure 7.1. Graph on which to plot latitudinal distribution of precipitation in Africa

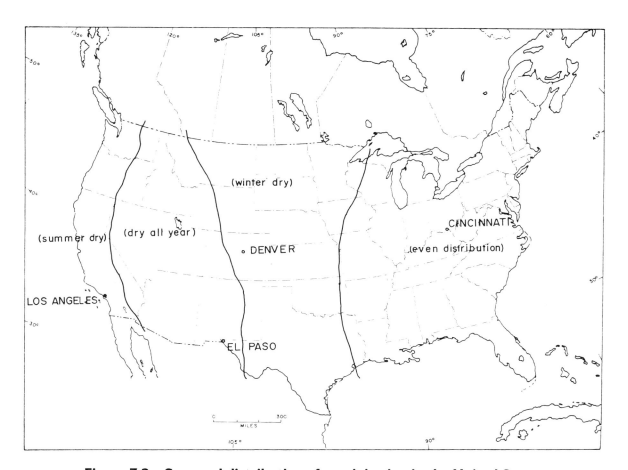

Figure 7.2 Seasonal distribution of precipitation in the United States

28

Table 7.2 Mean Temperature in °C and Precipitation in Millimeters for Selected Cities[a]

	Jan.	Feb.	Mar.	Apr.	May	June	July	Aug.	Sept.	Oct.	Nov.	Dec.	Year
Denver													
T	0.3	1.4	4.0	9.2	14.3	20.1	23.6	22.8	18.1	12.1	5.1	2.1	11.1
P	12	16	27	47	61	32	31	28	23	24	16	10	327
El Paso													
T	8.1	9.5	13.0	17.8	22.5	28.1	28.3	27.5	24.7	18.5	10.9	7.1	18.0
P	12	10	9	7	10	18	33	30	29	22	8	12	200
Cincinnati													
T	0.9	1.7	5.9	12.3	17.9	23.0	24.9	24.3	20.6	14.4	7.0	1.8	12.9
P	93	71	99	92	97	106	91	83	69	57	75	70	1004
Los Angeles													
T	13.2	13.9	15.2	16.6	18.2	20.0	22.8	22.8	22.2	19.7	17.1	14.6	18.0
P	78	85	57	30	4	2	T	T	6	10	27	73	373
Station _____													
T	—	—	—	—	—	—	—	—	—	—	—	—	—
P	—	—	—	—	—	—	—	—	—	—	—	—	—
Station _____													
T	—	—	—	—	—	—	—	—	—	—	—	—	—
P	—	—	—	—	—	—	—	—	—	—	—	—	—

[a]The upper figure in each pair of figures represents temperature and the lower figure represents precipitation.

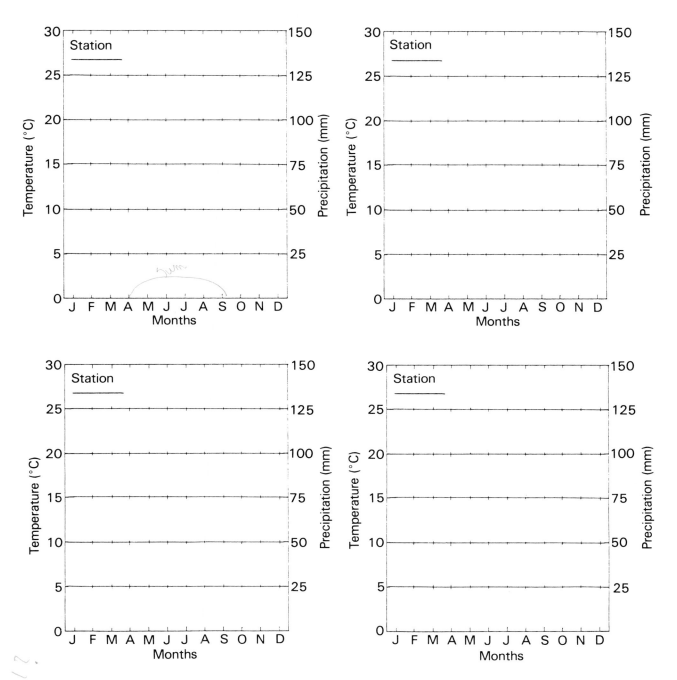

Figure 7.3 Graphs on which to plot seasonal variation in precipitation

PROBLEMS

4. Plot the temperature and precipitation data given in Table 7.2 on the graphs provided in Figure 7.3.
5. Which city has the least difference in the percentage of precipitation that falls in the summer six months and the winter six months? _A-S-O-M_
6. Which city has the greatest share of precipitation in the summer half-year? _more in summer_ _____
7. Which city has the greatest share of precipitation in the winter half-year? _____
8. Deserts are often defined as areas where the average precipitation is less than 250 mm (10 in.). Which of the cities would qualify as a desert city? _____ _annually_

one city only!?

_#1_

Name:_____

Laboratory Section: _____

Exercise 8

PROBABILITY AND INTENSITY OF PRECIPITATION

Precipitation varies widely over the surface of the Earth and throughout the year. Deserts are characterized by infrequent and widely scattered rainstorms. Humid areas, such as eastern North America or Great Britain, tend to have frequent precipitation. Two characteristics that provide a great deal of information about the climate of an area are the probability and intensity of precipitation. Probability is a statistical indication of the likelihood of an event occurring in any given period. The probability of precipitation on a given day of the year is expressed thus:

$$\text{Probability } (\%) = \frac{\text{number of rainy days}}{\text{number of days in the year}} \times 100$$

For example, London experiences an average of 164 precipitation days a year. The probability of precipitation on any given day is:

$$\text{Probability } (\%) = \frac{164}{365} = 45\%$$

It is for this reason that London has the reputation of being such a rainy place. It rains about every other day. Another site, Cherrapunji, India, has a similar probability. It rains about every other day. The average number of rainy days is 159 for a probability of 44%.

The frequency of precipitation tells only part of the story. Another aspect of the precipitation in an area is how much precipitation occurs with each event. *Intensity* of precipitation is a measure of the amount of precipitation per unit time.

$$\text{Intensity} = \frac{\text{total precipitation}}{\text{number of units of time}}$$

If the example of daily intensity is used, the data needed are mean annual precipitation and the number of days with precipitation. London averages 25 in. of precipitation per year.

$$\text{Intensity} = \frac{25 \text{ in.}}{164 \text{ days}} = 0.15 \text{ in./day}$$

Cherrapunji, India, averages 425 in. of precipitation each year, so intensity is considerably higher.

$$\text{Intensity} = \frac{425 \text{ in.}}{159 \text{ days}} = 2.67 \text{ in./day}$$

Cherrapunji is likely to receive nearly 20 times as much precipitation in each event. The very low intensity of precipitation in London contributes to the image of a cloudy, drizzly city. It is not a place where a visitor should expect long periods of sunshine.

Table 8.1 contains the amount of precipitation that occurred on each day during a year at French Lick, Indiana.

PROBLEMS

1. Carefully determine the number of precipitation days in each month and the total for the year.

Jan.	Feb.	Mar.	Apr.	May.	June	July	Aug.	Sept.	Oct.	Nov.	Dec.	Year
___	___	___	___	___	___	___	___	___	___	___	___	___

2. Calculate the mean probability of precipitation on any given day of the year.

$$\text{Probability} = \frac{}{365} \times 100 = \underline{\hspace{2cm}} \%$$

3. Calculate the average interval between precipitation episodes.

$$\text{Mean interval} = \frac{\text{number of nonprecipitation days}}{\text{number of intervals between episodes}} = \underline{\hspace{2cm}} \text{ days}$$

Using the data in Table 8.1, complete Table 8.2. Table 8.2 will then contain information needed to calculate the answers to problems 4–11. Use the following guidelines to complete the table.

1. In row A place the number of precipitation days in each month and the total for the year.

Table 8.1 Daily Precipitation at French Lick, Indiana
(inches)

Date	Jan.	Feb.	Mar.	Apr.	May	June	July	Aug.	Sept.	Oct.	Nov.	Dec.
1	.04	.60				.31						
2	.02		.32	.87	.02	.01					.04	
3	.07	.12	.18	.02		.92			.89		.31	.01
4	.02		.42	.01		.30	.03	.92	.13		.27	
5			.41			.33			.60			
6						.29						
7												
8		.33								.11		
9		.23					.38	.06		.35		
10	.08	.06			.09		.05		.20	1.27	.32	
11	.08				.10			.03				
12	.02				.48					.03		.48
13			.13	.59		.47			.14	.24		
14		.10		.04	.65	.07			.48	1.57		
15		.15	.01		.17	.40			.48	.15	.40	
16					.55	.03						.62
17	.06				.26	.36						.49
18	.01		.40									
19				.75			.22		1.25			
20				.54			.07	1.77		.40	.82	
21				.32		.03				.06		.47
22		.06									.02	.39
23	.07			.08			.05		.04			
24				2.12			.39					
25				.05		.19			.20			
26		.52										
27							.85		.75			
28				.68			.15				.03	.02
29	.48		.08	.32							.91	
30					.18							.01
31					.05		.90					

Table 8.2

	Jan.	Feb.	Mar.	Apr.	May	June	July	Aug.	Sept.	Oct.	Nov.	Dec.	Year
A	__	__	__	__	__	__	__	__	__	__	__	__	__
B	__	__	__	__	__	__	__	__	__	__	__	__	__
C	__	__	__	__	__	__	__	__	__	__	__	__	__
D	__	__	__	__	__	__	__	__	__	__	__	__	__
E	__	__	__	__	__	__	__	__	__	__	__	__	__

2. In row B place the number of days in each month. The data are for a year that is not a leap year.
3. In row C place the number of nonprecipitation days in each month and for the year.
4. In row D place the number of intervals between precipitation events. When determining the number of intervals for the year, note that an interval can wrap around the beginning or end of the month. For instance, the last interval without precipitation in February continues on through the first day of March. When counting intervals for the year, treat this is one interval.
5. In row E place the total amount of precipitation in each month and for the year.

PROBLEMS

4. Which month has the most precipitation days? _____ Which has the least? _____

5. What is the mean probability of precipitation on any given day of the year?

   Probability $= \dfrac{}{365} \times 100 =$ _____ %

6. What is the mean interval between precipitation episodes during the year?

   Mean interval $= \dfrac{\text{number of nonprecipitation days}}{\text{number of intervals between episodes}} =$ _____ days

7. What is the probability of precipitation on any given day in April? _____% What is the probability in December? _____%

8. What is the average precipitation intensity in inches per day for the year? _____

9. In which month does precipitation fall most intensely? _____ What is the mean intensity for the month? _____

10. In which month is precipitation of lowest intensity? _____ What is the average intensity? _____

11. How can you explain the difference in intensity between these two months?

٢

Name:_____

Laboratory Section: _____

Exercise 9

WIND SYSTEMS AND WINDCHILL

Wind is the result of pressure differences in the atmosphere and represents the movement of air to restore equilibrium in the system. Winds, or atmospheric circulation, serve two major functions in the environment: to transfer energy from low to high altitudes and to transfer moisture from the oceans to the land masses. Both functions are major ones in the operation of the Earth's environmental system.

PROBLEMS

1. A graphic device for illustrating the average wind conditions at a given location is the *wind rose*. A wind rose is a means of depicting the frequency and velocity with which the wind blows from different directions.

    On Figure 9.1 are the basic outlines for constructing wind roses with the major compass points marked. Complete the wind rose for the two months as follows, using the wind data for French Lick, Indiana, shown in Table 9.1.

    a. Construct lines perpendicular to the circle proportional in length to the frequency with which the wind blows from each direction. Let 1 mm represent each percentage point.

    b. Indicate the average velocity of the wind from each direction by attaching flags on the direction arrow according to the Beaufort scheme shown in Appendix B, part 9.

    c. In the center of each wind rose, write in the percent of time the wind is calm in each month.

Table 9.1. Wind Direction and Velocity for
French Lick, Indiana, in the Months of July and January

	Direction (degrees)								
	0	45	90	135	180	225	270	315	calm
July									
Average velocity (mph)	10	8	5	5	7	6	8	9	
% of time	2	2	10	14	24	22	12	9	5
January									
Average velocity (mph)	12	7	5	6	8	10	11	14	
% of time	10	2	2	7	10	22	19	18	1

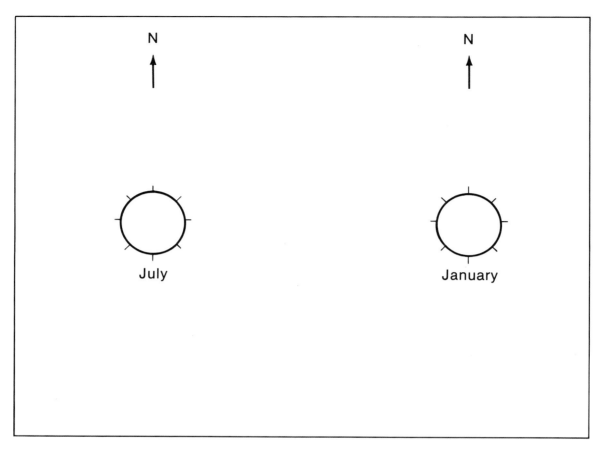

Figure 9.1. Outlines for wind roses

HUMAN PHYSIOLOGY AND WEATHER

A wide variety of factors besides actual temperature determine an individual's sensation of warmth or cold. One of the major factors is wind velocity. In midlatitudes in winter, and in polar areas, winds have a significant effect on the human body and hence on the amount of clothing that must be worn to protect oneself from the cold. The heat loss from the body depends on a variety of factors, such as the amount of the body covered by clothing, the thickness of the clothing, and the amount of physical activity. Normally in cold weather only the face or the face and hands would be exposed, accounting for some 3–10% of the surface area of the body. However, when the legs are uncovered, the percentage of exposed surface increases to 30% or more. An average layer of winter clothing will have a resistance to heat loss of about 1 calorie/m^2/sec compared to 0.5 calorie/m^2/sec for gloves or shoes and, of course, none for uncovered flesh. An additional source of heat loss is through the lungs, and it is very difficult to prevent this kind of heat loss. In fact, as much as 20% of the total heat loss of the body may occur in this fashion. Some of the heat loss is caused by the evaporation of water in the lungs and some by direct heating of the air. The cold air that is breathed in is heated to body temperature and the humidity increased almost to the saturation level.

EFFECTS OF WIND ON COMFORT

In calculating the effective temperature due to windchill, it is necessary to take into account that the wind speeds people normally experience are less than those reported at weather stations. Wind

Table 9.2 Sensible Temperature Scale for Various Values of Windchill Factor K

50	Hot
100	Warm
200	Pleasant
400	Cool
600	Very cool
800	Cold
1000	Very cold
1200	Bitter cold
1400	Exposed flesh freezes
2000	Exposed flesh freezes in 1 min
2500	Limit of tolerance

velocity is taken at a height of 33 ft (10 m) at North American weather stations. Wind velocity increases rapidly from the ground surface upward, being almost double at a height of 33 ft. At head height for a person 5 ft 6 in. tall, the wind velocity is only about 57% of reported velocity. An exception to this rule, of course, is when wind velocity is reported calm. A person walking at the rate of 3 mph would have an effective wind speed of 3 mph.

The windchill factor, or cooling due to wind, can be expressed as

$$K = (91.4 - t)(4\sqrt{v} + 5 - \frac{v}{4})$$

where K = windchill in kilocalories per square meter per hour
 t = temperature in degrees Fahrenheit
 v = wind velocity in miles per hour

The windchill factor increases as wind velocity increases and the temperature decreases. When heat loss becomes significant, injury may occur to the skin on the exposed areas, such as hands, feet, ears, nose, or even legs. In the table of values of windchill (Table 9.2), there are certain critical values that are of interest. For instance, at $K = 1400$, exposed flesh will freeze, and at $K = 2000$, exposed flesh freezes in approximately 1 min.

PROBLEMS

2. For the following wind and temperature conditions, determine the value of K, and whether or not the windchill is sufficient to cause frostbite.

Temperature (°F)	Wind (mph)	K	Frostbite potential
20	36		
10	36		
0	16		
−10	9		
−20	4		

Would any of the cases listed above be sufficiently severe to cause almost instantaneous tissue damage (damage in less than 1 min)? _____ If so, under which set of circumstances?

_____

3. Table 9.3 contains equivalent temperatures based on wind velocity.
 a. Utilizing the table, determine the equivalent temperature when there is an ambient air temperature of 22 °F and wind velocity of 20 mph. _____

Table 9.3   Windchill Equivalent Temperature (°F)

Temperature (°F)	Wind Speed (mph)								
	Calm	5	10	15	20	25	30	35	40
32	34	32	27	24	21	17	14	12	10
30	32	30	25	21	18	15	12	10	7
28	30	28	23	19	15	12	9	6	4
26	28	26	21	17	13	9	6	3	1
24	26	24	19	14	10	7	3	0	−3
22	25	22	16	12	8	4	1	−3	−6
20	23	20	14	9	5	1	−2	−6	−9
18	21	18	12	7	2	−2	−5	−9	−13
16	19	16	10	5	0	−4	−8	−12	−17
14	17	14	8	2	−3	−7	−12	−16	−20
12	15	12	6	0	−5	−10	−15	−23	−24
10	13	10	4	−2	−8	−13	−18	−26	−28
8	11	8	1	−5	−11	−16	−21	−30	−32
6	9	6	−1	−7	−13	−19	−24	−34	−36
4	7	4	−3	−10	−16	−22	−28	−38	−40
2	5	2	−5	−12	−19	−25	−31	−42	−44
0	3	0	−7	−15	−22	−28	−35	−46	−49
−2	1	−2	−10	−17	−25	−31	−39	−50	−54
−4	−1	−4	−12	−20	−28	−35	−42	−54	−58
−6	−3	−6	−14	−22	−30	−38	−46	−59	−63
−8	−4	−8	−16	−25	−33	−41	−50	−63	−67
−10	−6	−10	−19	−28	−36	−45	−54	−68	
−12	−8	−12	−21	−30	−39	−48	−58		
−14	−10	−14	−23	−33	−42	−51	−62		
−16	−12	−16	−26	−36	−45	−55	−66		
−18	−14	−18	−28	−38	−49	−59			
−20	−16	−20	−30	−41	−52	−63			
−22	−18	−22	−32	−44	−55	−66			
−24	−20	−24	−35	−47	−58				
−26	−22	−26	−37	−49	−62				
−28	−24	−28	−39	−52	−65				
−30	−26	−30	−42	−55	−68				
−32	−27	−32	−44	−58					
−34	−29	−34	−47	−61					
−36	−31	−36	−49	−64					
−38	−33	−38	−51	−67					
−40	−35	−40	−54	−69					

From R. G. Steadman, 1971, "Indices of windchill of clothed persons," *Journal of applied meteorology*, 10: 678.

b. If the air temperature is 12 °F, what wind velocity is necessary to produce an equivalent temperature of 0 °F? _____

c. On a given day there is a 35-mph wind and a windchill of 0 °F. What is the ambient temperature? _____

Name: _____

Laboratory Section: _____

Exercise 10

SOIL WATER BALANCE

Drought has many different definitions, largely depending on the user. Drought is always a shortage of water in some form, and most often it is in terms of shortage of water for agriculture. This exercise involves calculating the soil moisture balance to determine if, and when, there isn't enough moisture in the soil to supply the needs of plants. All vegetation needs water, and in most cases gets the water it needs from the soil, not directly from precipitation. As long as there is water in the soil for plants to obtain there will be no stress on the plants, even if there is no rainfall. Precipitation is needed to restore the soil moisture available. The demand for moisture is highest in summer, when temperatures are high, and lowest in the winter when it is cooler. Drought occurs when the soil moisture drops to zero and there is no moisture available for the plants.

DEFINITIONS

P Mean monthly precipitation (rain, snow, or sleet) in inches.

PE Potential evaporation or water need. This is the amount of soil water needed if plant growth is to be maximized. This is directly related to mean monthly precipitation.

ST Soil moisture storage. The actual amount of moisture in the soil, in inches. The maximum amount of moisture the soil can hold varies a great deal from place to place with soil type.

AE Actual evaporation or water use. The amount of water actually used by the plants. It can be less than PE when there is insufficient soil moisture to meet the demand.

D Soil moisture deficit. A deficit exists when potential evaporation (PE) is greater than precipitation (P) and there is no water left in the soil ($ST = 0$). It is calculated as the difference between PE and AE.

S Surplus. A surplus is excess moisture which the soil cannot hold. It will run off the soil to become streamflow. A surplus occurs when precipitation is greater than potential evaporation and the soil is saturated with water.

PROBLEMS

Table 10.1 contains the data for precipitation and potential evaporation for Greensboro, North Carolina; Denver, Colorado; and Los Angeles, California. Calculate the soil moisture surplus or deficit for the remaining months for Greensboro, North Carolina, and for the other two cities. For each city assume that the soil moisture capacity is 4 in. Soil moisture capacity is the maximum amount of water that can be stored in the soil in the zone in which the plant roots are found. For Greensboro the soil moisture is assumed to be full at the beginning of January, at Denver the initial soil moisture is 1 in., and for Los Angeles the initial soil moisture is 1.2 in.

1. Calculate the value of $P - PE$ for each month. If $P - PE$ is positive, there was more precipitation during the month than was needed by the vegetation.

Table 10.1 Calculation of Soil Moisture Surplus and Deficit

	Jan.	Feb.	Mar.	Apr.	May	June	July	Aug.	Sept.	Oct.	Nov.	Dec.	Year
Greensboro, North Carolina													
PE	.2	.3	1.0	2.2	3.8	5.5	6.1	5.5	3.9	2.1	.8	.2	31.6
P	3.3	3.3	3.7	3.4	3.4	3.5	4.7	4.5	3.6	2.8	2.7	3.1	42.0
P – PE	3.1	3.0	2.7	1.2	-0.4	-2.0	-1.4	-1.0	-.03	0.7	1.9	2.9	11.6
ST	4.0	4.0	4.0	4.0	3.6								
AE	0.2	0.3	1.0	2.2	3.8								
D													
S	3.1	3.0	2.7	1.2									
Denver, Colorado													
PE	0.0	0.0	0.6	1.4	3.1	4.5	5.0	4.3	3.1	1.7	0.5	0.0	24.2
P	0.4	0.5	1.0	2.1	2.4	1.4	1.8	1.4	1.0	1.0	0.6	0.7	14.3
P – PE	.4	.5	.4	.7	-.7	-3.1				.7	.1	.7	
ST													
AE													
D													
S													
Los Angeles, California													
PE	1.3	1.4	1.9	2.3	3.0	3.7	4.6	4.5	3.8	2.9	2.0	1.5	32.9
P	3.1	3.1	2.6	1.1	0.3	0.1	0.0	0.0	0.2	0.5	1.1	2.7	14.8
P – PE													
ST													
AE													
D													
S													

2. For the remaining calculations it is best to work through the process all the way for each month and then go on to the next month. Calculate ST. The datum obtained represents the soil moisture status at the end of the month. Any surplus of precipitation over potential evaporation will first go to replenish soil moisture. If soil moisture is at capacity, all of the excess will be surplus. If the soil moisture capacity is not full, the amount needed to reach capacity goes into soil moisture storage, and any remaining will be surplus. For January, in Greensboro, the soil moisture is at capacity at the beginning of the month, and so the excess of precipitation becomes surplus (S) and will provide water to fill lakes and streams.

3. Calculate actual evaporation (AE). It will be equal to PE if there is that much water available from precipitation or groundwater storage at the end of the previous month. Note that for Greensboro in January $AE = PE$. When the combined amount of water in groundwater storage and precipitation is less than PE, AE will equal $ST + P$.

4. Calculate the surplus or deficit. There can be a surplus only when soil moisture is full. There can be a deficit only when soil moisture storage is zero. When soil moisture storage is at capacity at the end of the previous month, $S = P - PE$. When $ST = 0$ at the end of the previous month, $D = PE - P$.

5. Utilizing the precipitation total and potential evaporation total for the year, which city has the driest climate? _____

6. For how many months each year does Denver normally have a soil moisture deficit? _____

7. For which of the summer months (April to September) does the demand for moisture exceed precipitation in Los Angeles? _____

8. Which of the three cities has the most months during the year in which demand for moisture exceeds precipitation? _____

9. Which of the three cities has the greatest disparity between moisture demand and precipitation in a single month? _____ In which month does this occur? _____ What is the amount of the deficit? _____ in.

10. In which city does the actual amount of soil moisture vary the most through the year? _____

11. The city of Greensboro has an average annual surplus of precipitation over potential evaporation of 9.4 in. Even though there is a surplus for the year, there is a time during the year when there is a soil moisture deficit. When does the shortage occur? _____

12. Which of the three cities does not have a soil moisture surplus at any time of the year? _____

13. Which city has the most months with a soil moisture deficit? _____

14. Which city has the most months with a soil moisture surplus? _____

Exercise 11

THE EFFECTS OF CONTINENTAL POSITION ON CLIMATE

The relative position of a city or other geographical feature on a land mass often has a considerable bearing on the climate of that place. The world ocean is the major reservoir of heat on the surface of the Earth, and the relationship of a place to this heat source has a significant bearing on temperatures. Places that are far removed from the influence of the ocean are said to have a continental aspect to the climate. Table 11.1 contains the data for Port Hardy, British Columbia, and Winnipeg, Manitoba. Port Hardy is located on Vancouver Island, and Winnipeg is in a central prairie province. These two cities are within 100 km of being at the same latitude, so the annual receipt of solar energy is very similar.

PROBLEMS

1. From the data in Table 11.1, determine the following temperature relationships for the two stations.

	Port Hardy	**Winnipeg**
Mean July temperature	13.6	19.9
Mean January temperature	2.4	−18.1
Mean annual temperature	8.0	2.7

Does Port Hardy or Winnipeg have the higher mean July temperature? _____ Which of the two stations has the lower mean January temperature? _____ Which of these two cities has the greater difference in temperature through the year? _____

2. Why does Winnipeg have a greater temperature range than Port Hardy?

TOPOGRAPHIC BARRIERS

A second facet of continental location is related to topographic barriers. Masses of hills or mountains greatly affect precipitation. Precipitation is heavier on the windward coasts of the topographic barrier and less on the leeward flanks. Table 11.1 gives the temperature and precipitation data for Kamloops, which is in the Fraser River Valley, British Columbia.

Table 11.1. Effects of Continental Position on Climate

	Elevation	Latitude	Longitude
Port Hardy, British Columbia	23 m	50°41'N	127°22'W
Winnipeg	240 m	49°41'N	97°14'W
Kamloops, British Columbia	345 m	50°43'N	120°25'W
Antofagasta, Chile	122 m	23°28'S	70°26'W
La Quiaca, Argentina	3459 m	22°06'S	65°36'W
São Paulo, Brazil	759 m	23°33'S	46°37'W

Temperature (°C)

	Jan.	Feb.	Mar.	Apr.	May	June	July	Aug.	Sept.	Oct.	Nov.	Dec.	Mean Annual
Port Hardy	2.4	3.5	3.8	6.5	9.7	11.9	13.6	13.9	11.9	8.9	5.3	4.0	8.0
Winnipeg	-18.1	-14.1	-8.2	3.7	11.4	16.6	19.9	18.9	12.4	6.3	-4.3	-12.4	2.7
Kamloops	-6.1	-2.4	2.5	8.8	14.4	17.4	20.9	19.2	15.0	8.2	1.2	-2.3	8.1
Antofagasta	20.0	20.3	18.9	16.5	15.1	13.6	13.4	13.5	14.4	15.3	17.0	18.2	16.4
La Quiaca	12.5	12.1	11.8	9.8	6.3	3.0	3.8	6.1	9.1	10.9	11.7	12.3	9.2
São Paulo	21.7	21.5	20.7	18.6	16.2	15.3	14.9	16.2	17.7	18.8	19.2	20.4	18.4

Precipitation (mm)

	Jan.	Feb.	Mar.	Apr.	May	June	July	Aug.	Sept.	Oct.	Nov.	Dec.	Mean Annual
Port Hardy	180.9	159.3	132.7	95.1	60.4	74.7	40.7	66.8	122.3	204.9	229.0	270.4	1637
Winnipeg	25.4	20.8	23.2	31.2	51.5	97.2	75.5	69.9	50.4	41.2	33.7	18.6	539
Kamloops	35.5	21.5	9.1	6.3	15.3	39.4	20.4	22.0	18.1	15.3	18.6	24.4	246
Antofagasta	0.0	0.0	0.0	0.0	0.0	0.0	0.3	0.1	0.0	0.0	0.0	0.0	0.4
La Quiaca	74.1	65.9	48.1	5.4	1.5	1.7	1.1	0.7	3.5	8.5	42.0	67.1	320
São Paulo	243.3	220.3	140.9	86.4	71.9	52.0	30.6	49.0	61.8	131.3	125.1	152.2	1365

PROBLEMS

3. Complete the following, using the data (in millimeters) contained in Table 11.1.

	Port Hardy	Kamloops
Average precipitation during the driest month	_40.7_	_6.3_
Average precipitation during the wettest month	_210.4_	_39.4_
Mean annual precipitation	_1637_	_246_

Note that during the driest month at Port Hardy there is usually more rainfall than there is during the wettest month at Kamloops. Since Kamloops is inland from the Pacific Ocean, it also has a greater variation in temperature than does Port Hardy, but not as extreme as that of Winnipeg, which is still farther inland.

4. Why does Kamloops have lower amounts of precipitation than Port Hardy does?

5. a. Does Kamloops or Port Hardy show the effects of continentality more clearly? Why?

   b. Why is this continental effect less obvious at Kamloops than at Winnipeg?

OCEAN CURRENTS

In midlatitudes there are ocean currents flowing along the coastlines of the continents. These currents can have a marked effect on the climate, depending on the temperature characteristics of the current. Often cities at the same latitude but on the opposite sides of the continent will have quite different climates. Antofagasta, Chile, and São Paulo, Brazil, serve as illustrations.

PROBLEMS

6. The effects of the different currents can be determined by comparing the temperatures at São Paulo and Antofagasta. First it is necessary to adjust the temperatures to the same elevation since São Paulo is 637 m higher in elevation than Antofagasta. The actual impact of the current is greater than indicated by the data in the table. São Paulo temperatures can be corrected for elevation by increasing the monthly means by a rate of 0.64 °C for each 100 m of elevation.

Insert in the blanks below the data for Antofagasta taken from Table 11.1 and the adjusted data for São Paulo. From this information it can be noted that the effects of the warm current on temperatures at São Paulo are detectable throughout the year.

	January	July	Annual
São Paulo	_____	_____	_____
Antofagasta	_____	_____	_____

7. Describe the impacts of the cold and warm currents on the temperature and precipitation at São Paulo and Antofagasta.

ELEVATION

Elevation also has a direct effect on climate. The rate of change of mean temperature with elevation is about 1000 times as great as with latitude. The data for La Quiaca, Argentina, illustrate well the effects of elevation on temperature. La Quiaca is located in the Andes Mountains north and east of Antofagasta at an elevation of 3459 m, and it is actually nearer the equator than Antofagasta or São Paulo.

PROBLEMS

8. Insert the requested temperatures in the following table:

	January	July	Annual
São Paulo	21.7	14.9	18.4
Antofagasta	20.00	13.4	16.4
La Quiaca	12.5	3.7	9.2

Explain the temperature differences between these three stations situated along the same parallel of latitude.

Exercise 12

KÖPPEN SYSTEM OF CLIMATIC CLASSIFICATION

After early attempts by the Greeks, no major effort was made to classify climates until the twentieth century. During this interval, however, scattered efforts were made to collect data pertaining to the atmosphere. Perhaps the best-known system of climatic classification at the present time is that by Vladimir Köppen of Austria (1846–1940). His classification is based essentially on the distribution of vegetation. His assumption was that the type of vegetation found in an area is closely related to temperature and moisture. General relationships were already known when Köppen's classification was produced, but Köppen attempted to translate the boundaries of selected plant types into climatic equivalents. The Köppen system is based on monthly mean temperatures, monthly mean precipitation, average annual precipitation, and mean annual temperature.

Köppen recognized four major temperature regimes: one tropical, two midlatitude, and one polar. After identifying the four regimes he assigned numerical values to their boundaries (see Table 12.1). The tropical climate was delimited by a cool-month temperature average of at least 18 °C. This temperature was selected because it approximates the poleward limit of certain tropical plants. The two midlatitude climates are distinguished on the basis of the mean temperature of the coolest month. If the mean temperature of the coolest month is below –3 °C the climate is microthermal, and if the temperature is above –3 °C it is mesothermal. The fourth major temperature category is the polar climate. The boundary between the microthermal and polar climates was set at 10 °C for the average of the warmest month, which roughly corresponds to the northern limit of tree growth.

The system has been subjected to criticism from two aspects. There is no complete agreement between the distribution of natural vegetation and climate. This is to be expected since factors other than average climatic conditions affect the distribution of vegetation. The system is also criticized on the basis of the rigidity with which the boundaries are fixed. Temperatures at any site differ from year to year, as does rainfall, and the boundary based on a given value of temperature will change location from year to year. In spite of the criticisms and the empirical basis of the classification, it has proven usable as a general system.

PROBLEMS

Table 12.2 contains climatic data for a number of cities in North America. The problem is to classify these cities by climatic type. After you have classified the North American cities, go to Table 12.4 and classify these climatic data sets. Table 12.4 also contains two blank data sets. Your instructor may wish to provide these two sets of data for you to classify.

Table 12.1. Major Climatic Types of the Köppen System

Type	Code Letter	Boundary Element
Tropical humid	A	Mean temperature of the coolest month $\geq 18\,°C$
Dry	B	Evaporation > precipitation
Humid mesothermal	C	Mean temperature of the coolest month between $-3\,°C$ and $18\,°C$, and warmest month $>10\,°C$
Humid microthermal	D	Mean temperature of the coolest month $<-3\,°C$
Polar	E	Warmest month mean temperature $<10\,°C$

Subdivisions of the major classes

Major Type	Subclass 1	Subclass 2	Boundary Element
A	Af		Precipitation in the driest month ≥ 60 mm
	Aw		Precipitation in the driest month <60 mm and $<(100 - r/25)$. r = precipitation in mm
	Am		Precipitation in the driest month <60 mm but $>(100 - r/25)$. r = precipitation in mm
B	BS		1. $r < 20t$, 70% of precipitation in winter
			2. $r < 20(t + 7)$, even precipitation distribution
			3. $r < 20(t + 14)$, 70% of precipitation in summer
	BW		4. $r < 10t$, 70% of precipitation in winter
			5. $r < 10(t + 7)$, even precipitation distribution
			6. $r < 10(t + 7)$, 70% of precipitation in summer
	BWh, BSh		7. Mean temperature of the coolest month $\geq 18\,°C$
	BWk, BSk		8. Mean temperature of the coolest month $<18\,°C$
C	Cs		Summer dry; 1 mo with less than 30 mm of precipitation One winter month with at least three times the precipitation of driest summer month
		Csa	Warmest month mean temperature $>22\,°C$
		Csb	Warmest month mean temperature $<22\,°C$; at least 4 mo $>10\,°C$
		Csc	1–3 mo $>10\,°C$ but $<22\,°C$
	Cw		Winter dry; one summer month with at least 10 times the precipitation of the driest winter month
		Cwa, Cwb, Cwc	The criteria are the same as for Cs climates
	Cf		At least 30 mm of precipitation in the driest month, or does not meet the criteria for Cw or Cs
		Cfa, Cfb, Cfc	The criteria are the same as for Cs climates
D	Df, Ds, Dw		Criteria for f, s, and w are the same as for C climates
		a, b, c	Criteria for a, b, and c are the same as for C climates
		d	Mean temperature of the coldest month below $-38\,°C$
E	ET		Mean temperature of the warmest month between $0\,°C$ and $10\,°C$
	EF		Mean temperature of the warmest month $<0\,°C$

Table 12.2. Climactic Data for Several North American Cities

	Jan.	Feb.	Mar.	Apr.	May	June	July	Aug.	Sept.	Oct.	Nov.	Dec.	Year
Eureka, Northwest Territories (80°00′N 80°56′W)													
	−36[a]	−37	−38	−27	−10	3	6	4	−7	−22	−31	−35	−19
	3	2	1	2	3	3	16	14	11	9	2	2	69
Climatic type													
Tanana, Alaska (65°10′N 152°06′W)													
	−25	−22	−16	−4	8	14	15	12	5	−6	−17	−24	−5
	16	16	13	3	19	31	50	71	45	19	15	16	314
Climatic type													
Edmonton, Alberta (53°34′N 113°31′W)													
	−14	−10	−6	4	11	14	17	16	11	5	−3	−8	3
	24	20	21	28	47	80	85	65	34	23	22	25	474
Climatic type													
Vancouver, British Columbia (49°11′N 123°10′W)													
	3	4	6	9	13	15	18	17	14	10	6	4	10
	139	121	96	60	48	51	26	36	56	117	142	156	1048
Climatic type													
Montreal, Quebec (45°30′N 73°35′W)													
	−9	−6	−2	7	14	19	22	21	16	10	3	−5	7
	87	76	86	83	81	91	102	87	95	83	88	89	1048
Climatic type													
Urbana, Illinois (40°06′N 88°14′W)													
Cel.	−2	−1	4	11	17	22	25	24	20	14	5	0	12
Precip.	55	53	81	90	107	115	89	77	77	76	67	53	940
Climatic type													
Albuquerque, New Mexico (35°03′N 106°37′W)													
	2	5	8	14	19	25	26	25	22	15	7	3	15
	8	7	13	9	11	12	30	34	14	26	9	13	185
Climatic type													
New Orleans, Louisiana (30°57′N 90°04′W)													
	13	15	17	21	25	28	29	29	27	22	16	14	21
	98	101	136	116	111	113	171	136	128	72	85	104	1369
Climatic type													
Key West, Florida (24°31′N 81°47′W)													
	21	22	23	25	27	28	29	29	28	26	24	22	25
	38	51	44	64	70	102	106	108	166	149	71	43	1012
Climatic type													

[a]The upper figure in each pair of figures represents mean temperature in degrees Celsius, and the lower figure represents precipitation in millimeters.

Procedure

1. First, determine if the station has a polar climate (E). Note in Table 12.1 that in an E climate the warmest month has a mean temperature of less than 10 °C. Although four of the major climatic types are based on temperature, only one—the polar climate—is based on temperature alone. Thus one can quickly determine whether a station represents a polar environment just by examining the temperature of the warmest month. For example, according to the data for Key West, Florida, the mean temperature of each month is above 10 °C, and so Key West does not have an E climate. If the temperature of the warmest month is below 10 °C, determine whether the climate is tundra (ET) or icecap (EF).

2. If the station does not have an E climate, determine whether it has an arid climate (B) or a humid climate (C, D). What determines if an area has an arid climate or not is the relationship between the precipitation and evaporation. Evaporation depends upon the temperature of the region and available moisture. If the major precipitation season comes in winter when temperatures are low, there is less evaporation and the precipitation is more efficient. If precipitation takes place primarily in the summer months, it is less effective because more water is lost to evaporation. For purposes of classification, winter is defined as October through March and summer as April through September in the Northern Hemisphere. For the Southern Hemisphere these are reversed, winter being the six months from April through September.

    The dry climates are broken down into four categories depending on the degree of dryness and the temperature regime. They are BSh, BSk, BWh, and BWk. There are two major types of arid climates, the steppe (S) and desert (W).

    a. First note the total annual precipitation. If it exceeds 300 mm, in all likelihood the climate is not dry.

    b. Determine the seasonal distribution of precipitation by finding if 70% of the precipitation occurs in the summer or winter six months. For example, for Albuquerque, the precipitation is not concentrated in one season. Seventy percent of the precipitation does not occur in either summer or winter; hence Albuquerque essentially has an even distribution of precipitation through the year.

    c. Next determine if there is less precipitation available than is needed to be a humid climate. The amount of precipitation needed (r) can be computed from the temperature, using criterion 2 in Table 12.1 for even distribution of rainfall. When the calculated r is greater than the mean annual precipitation, the climate is arid. If the calculated r is less than the mean annual precipitation, then the climate is not dry. The calculated value of r using criterion 2 for Albuquerque is 440 mm. Albuquerque has a dry climate since it needs 440 mm of precipitation to be a humid climate and receives only 185 mm.

    d. If the climate is dry, it is necessary to determine whether it is a steppe (S) or desert (W) climate. If the calculated value of $r/2$ is greater than the mean annual precipitation, then the climate is a desert (BW). For Albuquerque $r/2$ is 220, which is greater than the precipitation for Albuquerque, and hence this is a desert climate.

    e. There are two subcategories of each dry climate depending upon whether the temperature meets the requirements for an A climate. Determine if the station has a hot or cold desert climate using criterion 7 or 8 in Table 12.1.

3. Determine if the station has a tropical climate (A). The station has an A climate if it is not an arid climate and if the mean temperature of all months is 18 °C or above. If the mean temperature of any month is below 18 °C, the station has a midlatitude climate and you should go to step 4.

    a. There are three major categories of the A climate. These subcategories are distinguished on the basis of the seasonal regime of precipitation. There are three possibilities: Af, Aw, and Am. If the precipitation in every month exceeds 60 mm, it is a tropical wet climate

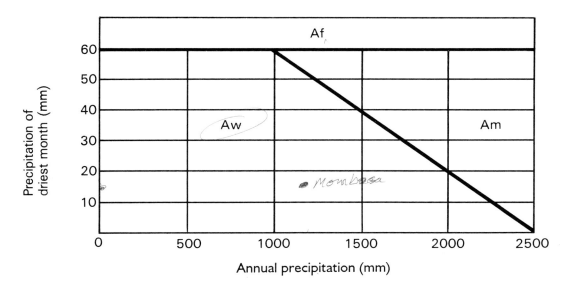

Figure 12.1. Division of tropical humid climates based on seasonal moisture patterns

(Af). The other two types of A climate each have at least a short dry season, and the difference between the tropical wet-and-dry climate (Aw) and the tropical monsoon climate (Am) depends on the extremes of the wet and dry seasons. If precipitation in millimeters in the driest month is less than $(100 - r/25)$ where r is the annual precipitation in millimeters, the climate is tropical wet and dry (Aw).

 b. If precipitation in the driest month is less than 60 mm but greater than $(100 - r/25)$, then it is a monsoon climate (Am).

 c. The classification of the A climates into subcategories can be simplified by using Figure 12.1. Find the place in the graph matching the precipitation in the driest month and the total annual precipitation. The climatic type can be read directly from the graph.

 d. There are other subcategories in Table 12.3 which may apply. Check to see if they can be added to form a third or fourth descriptive variable.

4. Determine if the station has a humid mesothermal (C) or humid microthermal climate (D). These are humid climates classified on the basis of the mean temperature of the coolest month.

 a. The station has a C climate if it is not arid, the temperature of the warmest month is above 10 °C, and the coolest month temperature is between –3 °C and 18 °C.

 b. The station has a D climate if it is not arid, the temperature of the warmest month is above 10 °C, and the coolest month is below –3 °C.

Table 12.3. Miscellaneous Classes of the A, C, and D Climates

Subclass 3	Criteria
x	Rainfall maximum in late spring or early summer; dry in late summer
h	High frequency of fog
i	Mean annual temperature range less than 5 °C
g	Warmest month precedes the solstice
t[1]	Hottest month delayed until autumn
s[1]	Maximum rainfall in autumn

Table 12.4. Data for Several Tropical Stations

Jan.	Feb.	Mar.	Apr.	May	June	July	Aug.	Sept.	Oct.	Nov.	Dec.	Year
Nairobi, Kenya (1°16′S 36°47′E)												
18[a]	18	19	19	18	16	15	16	17	19	18	18	18
46	51	102	206	160	46	18	25	25	53	109	81	922
						Climatic type						
Iquitos, Peru (3°19′S 78°18′W)												
26	26	24	25	24	23	23	24	24	25	26	26	25
259	249	310	165	254	188	168	117	221	183	213	292	2619
						Climatic type						
Mombasa, Kenya (4°01′S 39°43′E)												
28	28	28	28	26	25	24	24	25	26	27	28	26
30	14	59	192	319	100	72	69	71	86	74	76	1163
						Climatic type						
Kano, Nigeria (12°03′N 8°32′E)												
21	24	28	31	30	28	26	25	26	27	25	22	26
0	T	2	8	71	119	209	311	137	14	T	0	872
						Climatic type						
New Delhi, India (28°43′N 77°18′E)												
14	17	23	29	34	34	31	30	29	26	20	16	25
25	22	17	7	8	65	211	173	150	31	1	5	715
						Climatic type						
Al-Hofuf, Saudi Arabia (25°15′N 49°43′E)												
14	16	21	25	31	34	35	34	32	27	21	16	26
23	8	16	16	1	0	0	T	0	1	1	6	79
						Climatic type						

Station _____

__	__	__	__	__	__	__	__	__	__	__	__	__
__	__	__	__	__	__	__	__	__	__	__	__	__
						Climatic type						

Station _____

__	__	__	__	__	__	__	__	__	__	__	__	__
__	__	__	__	__	__	__	__	__	__	__	__	__
						Climatic type						

[a] The upper figure in each pair of figures represents mean temperature in degrees Celsius, and the lower figure represents precipitation in millimeters.

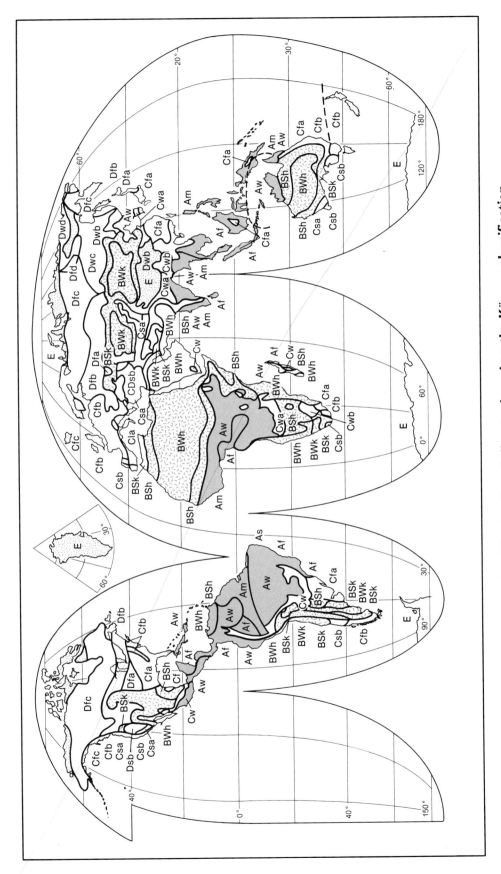

Figure 12.2. Distribution of climates based on the Köppen classification

c.	There is a wide variety of subcategories of the C and D climates depending on other temperature attributes and on the seasonal distribution of precipitation. The criteria for the subcategories are in sections C and D of Table 12.1. The second letter in the classification is based on the seasonal distribution of precipitation. One of the subcategories f, w, and s will describe the precipitation regime.

d.	The third level classification for these climates is also based on temperature, in this case the temperatures of the warm season. The third letter in the code will be a small letter a to d. Examine the warm month temperatures to see which of the criteria fit.

e.	It is possible that one of the other special subcategories will also apply to the classification. If so, it would be added to the classification as the fourth letter.

Name: _____

Laboratory Section: _____

Exercise 13

INTRODUCTION TO WEATHER MAPS

A weather map, or *synoptic chart,* shows the status of the atmosphere at a particular time. Weather maps thus give a historical record of atmospheric conditions. These maps also can be used to predict weather for different points on the surface of the Earth. The National Weather Service is continually updating these synoptic charts of the atmosphere. They are stored in computers and can be obtained from the National Weather Service at any time of day or night. Charts for 7 A.M. eastern standard time are printed for later distribution.

Weather maps provide actual data reported from selected stations. The data from these stations, as well as other data, are used to provide the information to produce the map. The graphic system of summarizing the data on the chart is the station model (Figure 13.1 is a sample station model with a complete set of data). Most weather stations do not report all of this information. This way of presenting weather data saves space on the map and avoids a clutter of information. (See also Appendix B: Key to Weather Maps.)

PROBLEMS

1. Figure 13.2 shows the weather data for Des Moines, Iowa, at 7 A.M. eastern standard time 7 May 1983. Interpret the symbols and indicate the weather conditions that existed when the observations were made.

    In a paragraph describe the weather in Des Moines at the time of observation.

2. Determine the following weather conditions for Miami using the data on the daily weather map for 7 May 1983 (Figure 13.3):
    Current temperature
    Dew point

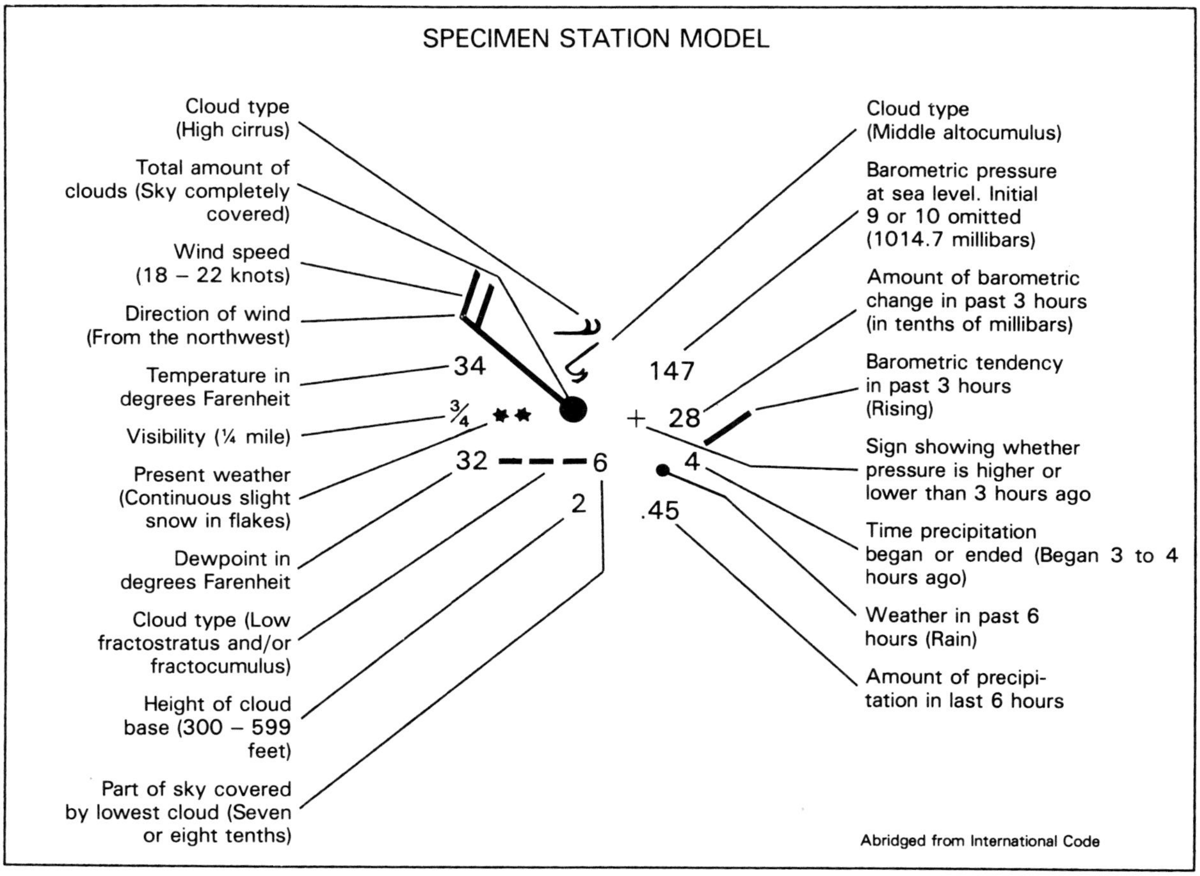
SPECIMEN STATION MODEL
Cloud type (High cirrus)
Total amount of clouds (Sky completely covered)
Wind speed (18 – 22 knots)
Direction of wind (From the northwest)
Temperature in degrees Farenheit
Visibility (¼ mile)
Present weather (Continuous slight snow in flakes)
Dewpoint in degrees Farenheit
Cloud type (Low fractostratus and/or fractocumulus)
Height of cloud base (300 – 599 feet)
Part of sky covered by lowest cloud (Seven or eight tenths)
Cloud type (Middle altocumulus)
Barometric pressure at sea level. Initial 9 or 10 omitted (1014.7 millibars)
Amount of barometric change in past 3 hours (in tenths of millibars)
Barometric tendency in past 3 hours (Rising)
Sign showing whether pressure is higher or lower than 3 hours ago
Time precipitation began or ended (Began 3 to 4 hours ago)
Weather in past 6 hours (Rain)
Amount of precipitation in last 6 hours
34
¾
32
6
2
147
+
28
4
.45
Abridged from International Code

Figure 13.1. Sample station model (National Weather Service)

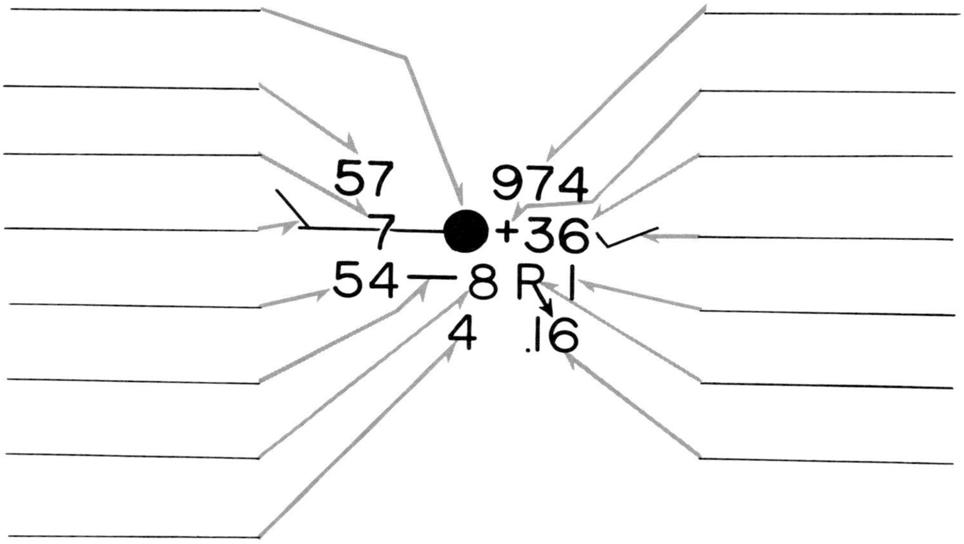
57
974
7
+36
54
8
R
I
4
.16

Figure 13.2 Weather data for Des Moines, Iowa (National Weather Service)

Barometric pressure in millibars
Amount of change in barometric pressure in the past 3 hr
Pressure tendency
Wind velocity in miles per hour
Wind direction
Total amount of clouds
Cloud type
Percentage of sky covered by lowest cloud form
Height of cloud base

3. In a paragraph, describe the current weather and the weather for the past several hours (if it is available) in the station data for the following cities:

Great Whale, Quebec

Waco, Texas

Phoenix, Arizona

4. Using the station data presented on the map for 7 May 1983 (Figure 13.3), find the station reporting each of the following atmospheric conditions (give the station and data):

	Station	Data
Highest current temperature	_____	_____
Lowest current temperature	_____	_____
Highest dew point	_____	_____
Lowest dew point	_____	_____
Highest barometric pressure	_____	_____
Lowest barometric pressure	_____	_____

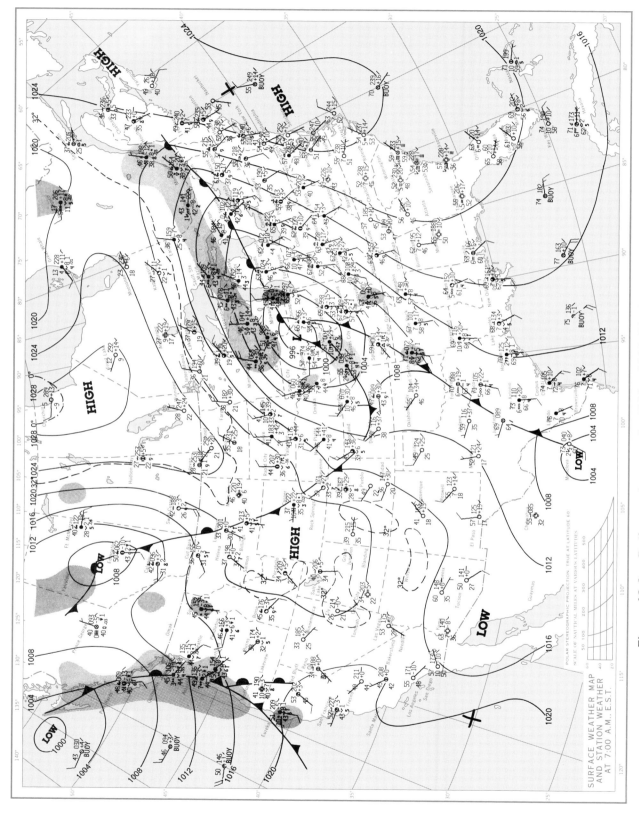

Figure 13.3. Daily weather map for 7 May 1983 (National Weather Service)

SURFACE WEATHER MAP
AND STATION WEATHER
AT 7:00 A.M., E.S.T.

POLAR STEREOGRAPHIC PROJECTION TRUE AT LATITUDE 60

SCALE IN NAUTICAL MILES AT VARIOUS LATITUDES

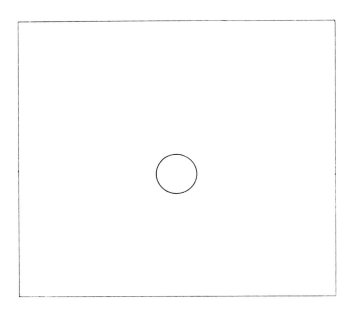

Figure 13.4. Station model exercise

5. A station reports the weather information given below. Construct a station model on Figure 13.4 showing the information.

Current temperature is 59 °F.

Dew point is 43 °F.

Barometric pressure is 1018.4 mb.

Barometric pressure up 1.6 mb in the last 3 hr.

Barometric pressure dropped and then rose in the last 3 hr.

The sky is clear.

Wind is calm.

6. Several supplemental maps are shown with each daily weather map (Figure 13.5). One shows the highest and lowest temperatures for the past 24 hr, and another shows precipitation areas and amounts. Using the map of temperature extremes determine the following:

The highest temperature recorded for the day

The lowest temperature recorded for the day

The lowest range in temperature for the 24-hr period

The highest range in temperature for the 24-hr period

The map of precipitation areas and amounts shows the areas that had precipitation during the 24 hr ending at 7:00 A.M. eastern standard time, with amounts of precipitation to the nearest 0.01 in. Incomplete totals are underlined. *T* indicates a trace of precipitation. In the snowfall season, dashed lines show the depth of snow on the ground in inches at 7:00 A.M. eastern standard time.

On the map for 7 May 1983, the area that had received precipitation in the previous 24 hr was extensive, though the amounts were generally small. What was the maximum amount of precipitation and in which city did it occur?

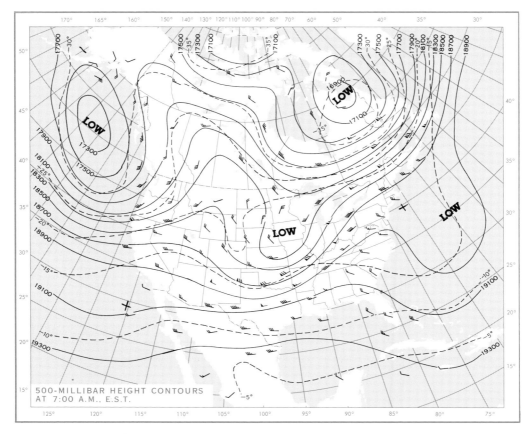

500-MILLIBAR HEIGHT CONTOURS
AT 7:00 A.M., E.S.T.

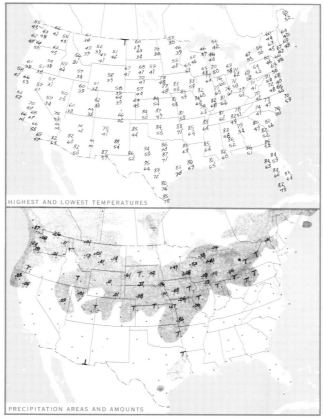

HIGHEST AND LOWEST TEMPERATURES

PRECIPITATION AREAS AND AMOUNTS

Figure 13.5.   Supplementary weather maps for 7 May 1983

Name: _____

Laboratory Section: _____

Exercise 14

WEATHER MAPS—STORMS AND FRONTAL SYSTEMS

From the data supplied by each weather station, the distribution of temperature, pressure, wind, humidity, and precipitation can be determined. The distribution of atmospheric pressure is shown by isobars constructed with the normal interval being 4 mb. When the pressure gradient is extremely weak, 2- or 3-mb intervals are used. Refer to Exercise 13 and Appendix B for the key to symbols used on the weather map.

PROBLEMS

1. Using the map of 25 May 1971 (Figure 14.1), find the isobars with the highest and lowest values and record them below.

   Highest _____
   Lowest _____

   Centers of high and low pressures are normally marked on the maps either with the words *high* and *low* or the capital letters *H* and *L* overprinted on the map. It must be remembered that low and high pressure are relative terms only. A well-developed cyclone or anticyclone will have a spatial distribution of pressure associated with it such that the isobars form closed circular lines. Such a low-pressure system exists on the map of 25 May 1971. What is the lowest station pressure indicated on the map? _____ At what station is this reported? _____

2. Surface fronts are indicated on the map in their approximate position at the time of observation. In the space below indicate how each of the different fronts is shown.

   Cold front
   Warm front
   Occluded front
   Stationary front

3. The circulation around a low-pressure center is normally counterclockwise and inward toward the low-pressure center. List the wind directions at the following cities:

   Kapuskasing, Ontario _____
   La Crosse, Wisconsin _____
   Grand Rapids, Michigan _____
   Wiarton, Ontario _____

   Do the wind vectors verify the counterclockwise circulation around the cyclone? _____

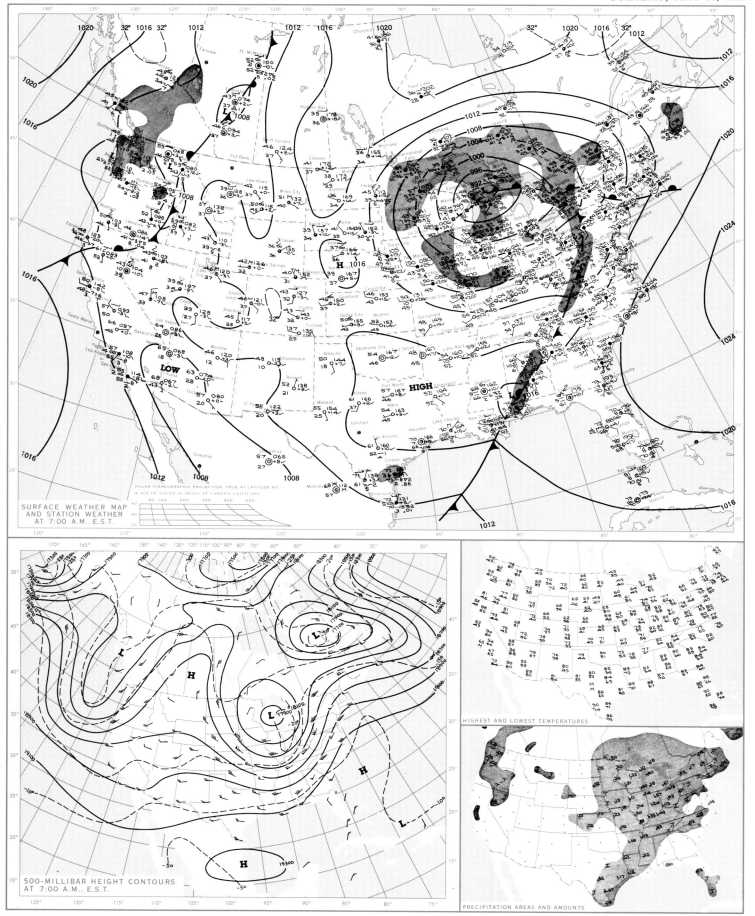

Figure 14.1. Daily weather map for 25 May 1971 (National Weather Service)

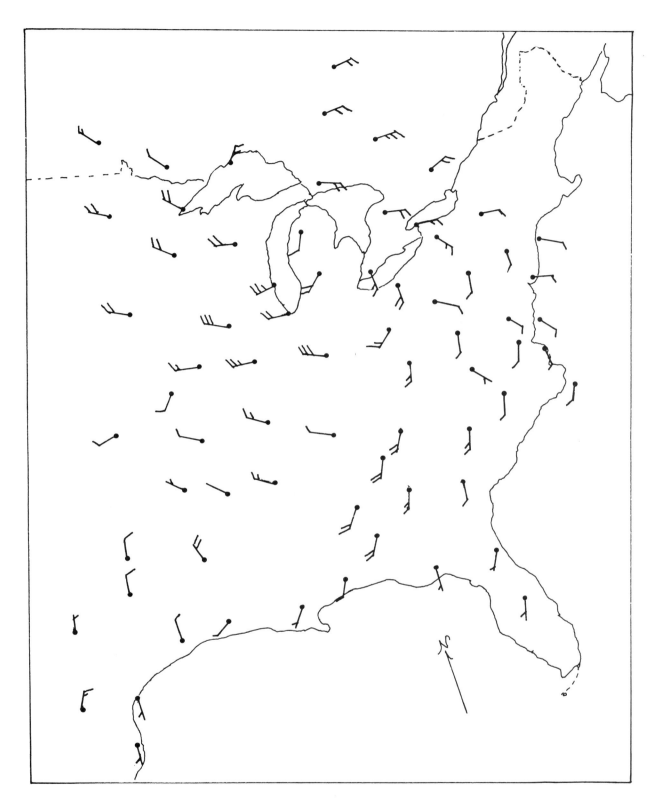

Figure 14.2.   Wind associated with low-pressure center, 27 November 1965

4. The direction and rate of movement of the low-pressure center are often shown on the map. This is the case for the map of 25 May 1971. In what general direction is the storm moving? _____ How many miles has it traveled in the past 18 hr? _____

5. The precipitation pattern around the low-pressure center is both typical and well defined. Note the narrow band of precipitation along the cold front and the widespread activity around the center of the storm.

    What form of precipitation is occurring along the cold front at Atlanta, Georgia; Birmingham, Alabama; and Elkins, West Virginia? _____ What form of precipitation is occurring north of the storm center at Sault Ste. Marie, Ontario; Lake Head, Ontario; and Duluth, Minnesota? _____

6. Note the temperature differentials along the cold and warm fronts. Complete the table below.

West of the Cold Front	°F	East of the Cold Front	°F
Memphis, Tennessee	_____	Charlotte, North Carolina	_____
Evansville, Indiana	_____	Augusta, Georgia	_____
Columbus, Ohio	_____	Raleigh, North Carolina	_____
Detroit, Michigan	_____	Philadelphia, Pennsylvania	_____

    What is the average temperature in the *warm sector* (use the four stations from the warm sector listed above)? _____

7. As a low-pressure center moves across the continent and the cold and warm fronts rotate around the low, there is often a pronounced shift in wind direction accompanying the passage of a front. This is particularly the case with cold fronts. A clockwise shift of 90 degrees or more may take place in a period of minutes. Figure 14.2 shows wind direction and velocity associated with a well-developed midlatitude low on 27 November 1965. Locate the low-pressure center and mark it with a large *L*. Then draw in the cold front and warm front as you think they were on that day.

Exercise 15

THE WEATHER OF 15–21 MARCH 1971

The month of March is normally a period of considerable weather activity over North America. At this time of year extreme contrasts in the airstreams result in varied atmospheric elements. The series of seven weather maps (Figures 15.1–15.7) covering the period from 15 March to 21 March 1971 illustrate some of the elements of this variable spring weather. The map of 15 March shows a deep low-pressure center located over the Great Lakes; it had originated over the Great Plains and moved rapidly northeastward. Associated with the low-pressure center were well-defined cold and warm fronts. The map in Figure 15.1 entitled *Highest and Lowest Temperatures* contains the highest and lowest temperatures recorded in the previous 24 hr. Since the time for which these maps are drawn is 7 A.M., the high temperatures are normally those that were recorded on the previous afternoon, in this case on 14 March. The lowest temperatures shown are those for the early morning of 15 March. On 14 March the low-pressure center was drawing warm, moist Gulf air northward over the Great Plains and eastern United States. As a result, temperatures were unseasonably warm. Some Florida cities recorded temperatures in the 90s, as did Texas. Temperatures ranged upward into the 80s as far north as Missouri, Tennessee, and North Carolina. Stations in New Jersey, Pennsylvania, and Virginia recorded temperatures in the 70s, and New England in the 60s. The highest temperature recorded on 14 March was 105 °F at Zapata, Texas. Determine the daily high temperatures for the following cities for 14 March:

Kansas City, Missouri _____

St. Louis, Missouri _____

Laredo, Texas _____

Corpus Christi, Texas _____

Farther west the cold air was being drawn southward over the mountain states. Note the low temperatures for 14 March at the following:

Winslow, Arizona _____

Albuquerque, New Mexico _____

The counterclockwise circulation around the low-pressure center is characteristic of northern-hemisphere cyclones. The north and south temperature contrasts can be considerable at this time of year, as was suggested earlier. While the data are not exactly comparable, determine the 7:00 A.M. 15 March temperatures at Edmonton, Alberta; Hudson Bay, Saskatchewan; and Armstrong, Ontario.

Edmonton, Alberta _____

Hudson Bay, Saskatchewan _____

Armstrong, Ontario _____

This storm (low-pressure) system moved rapidly northeastward, and heavy snowfall occurred in many places. As the associated cold front moved eastward, it triggered violent storms and high winds. Some tornadoes were spawned through the Ohio River Valley.

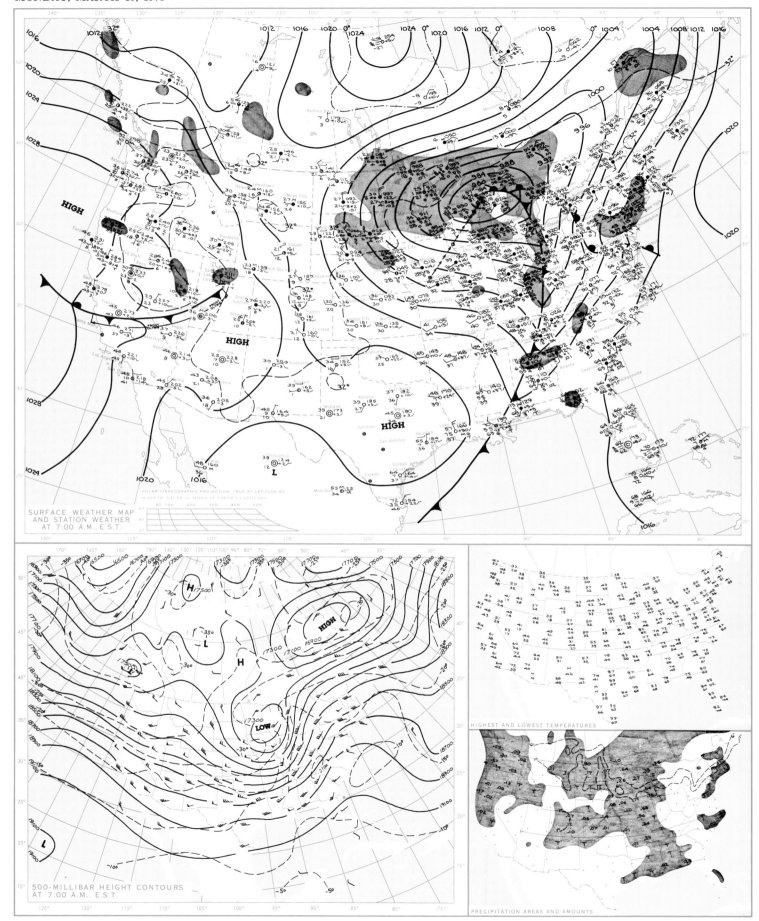

Figure 15.1. Daily weather map for 15 March 1971 (National Weather Service)

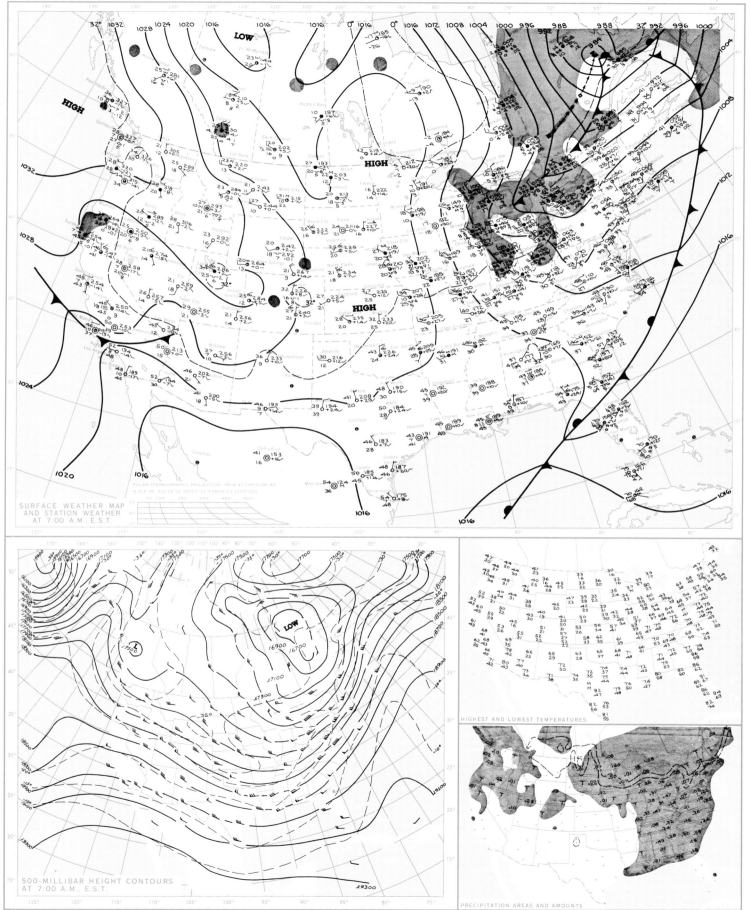

Figure 15.2.   Daily weather map for 16 March 1971 (National Weather Service)

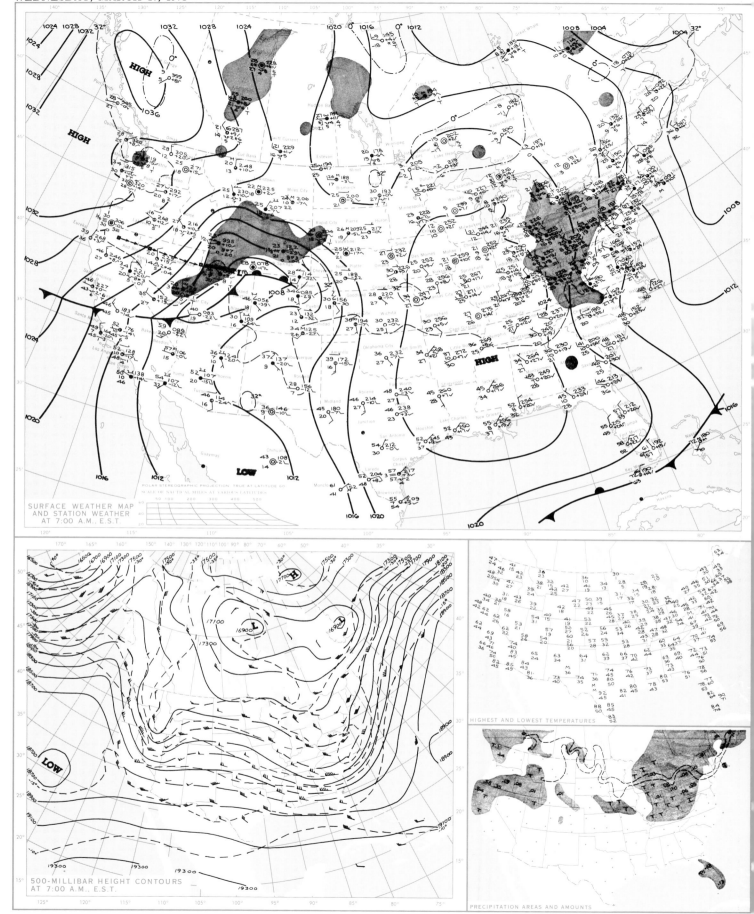

Figure 15.3. Daily weather map for 17 March 1971 (National Weather Service)

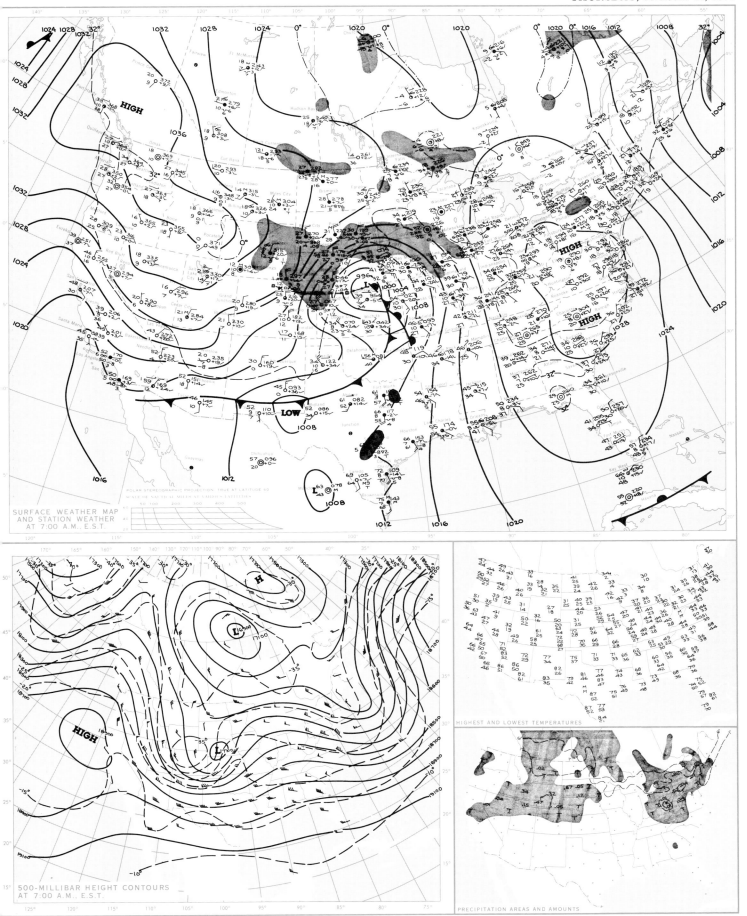

Figure 15.4.   Daily weather map for 18 March 1971 (National Weather Service)

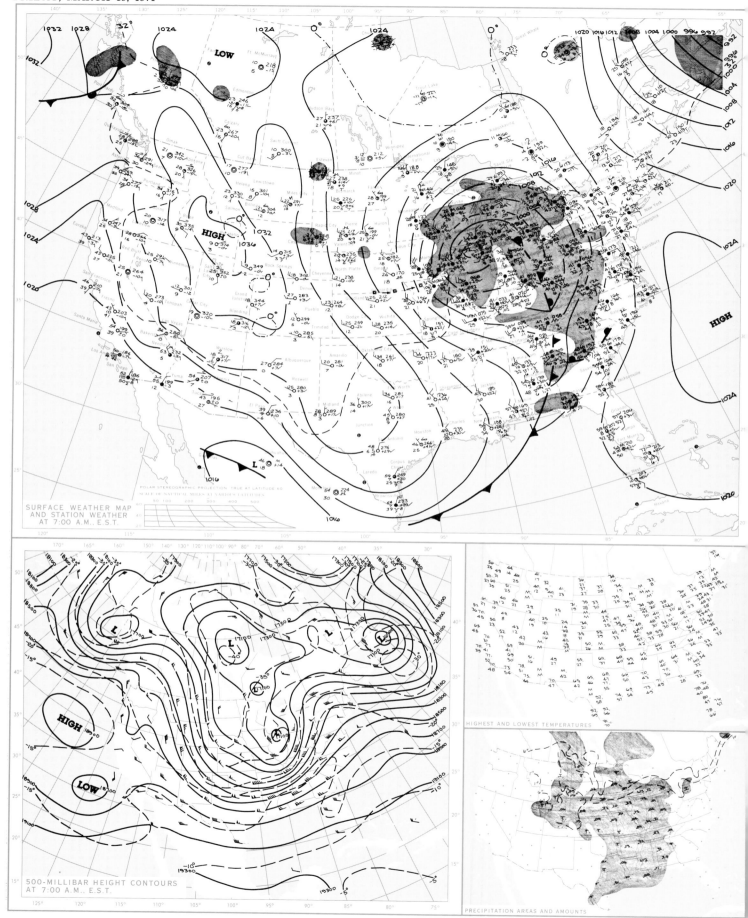

Figure 15.5. Daily weather map for 19 March 1971 (National Weather Service)

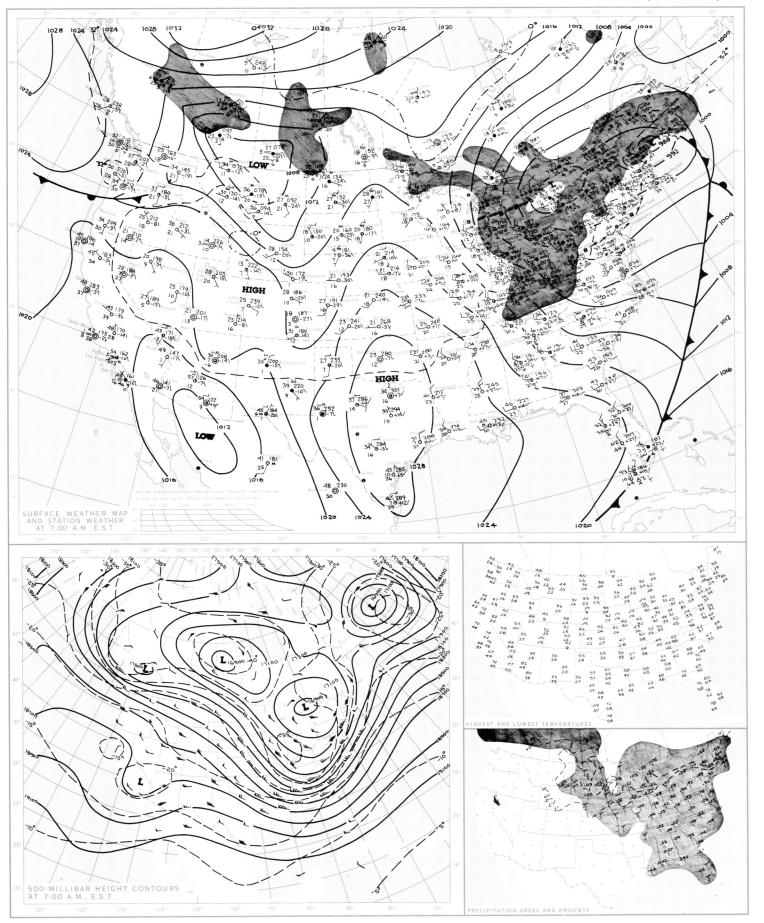

Figure 15.6. Daily weather map for 20 March 1971 (National Weather Service)

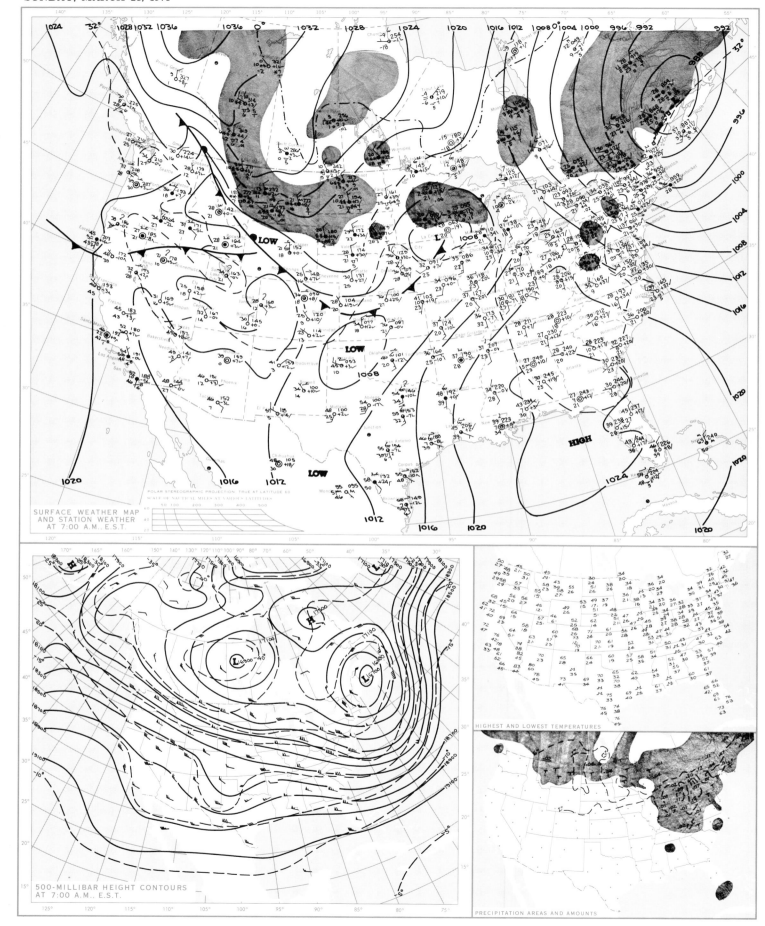

Figure 15.7.   Daily weather map for 21 March 1971 (National Weather Service)

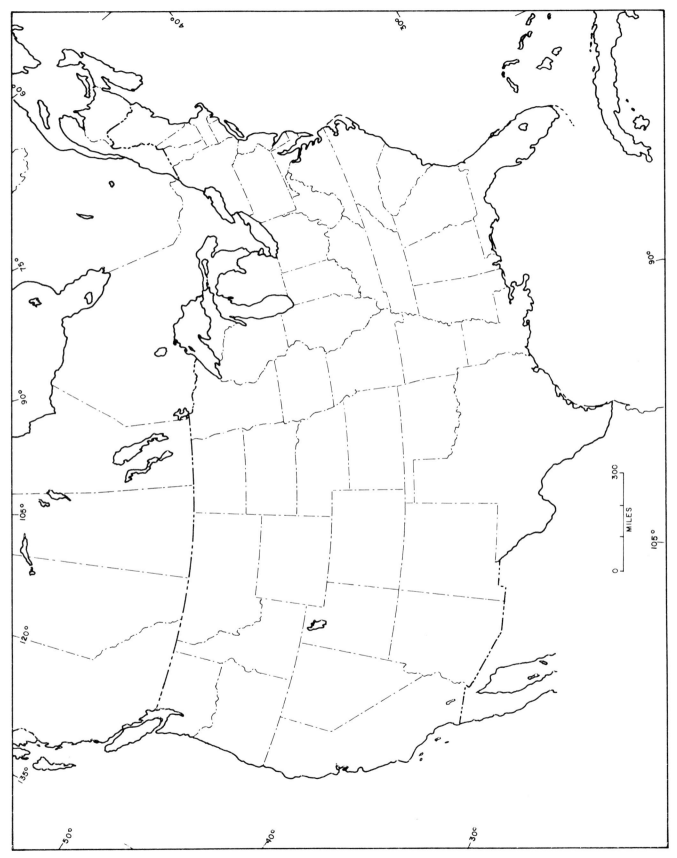

Figure 15.8. Map for plot of passage of midlatitude cyclone 17–20 March 1971

On 17 March, a new low-pressure system developed over Utah and started moving eastward. As it crossed the Great Plains, heavy snow and high winds developed again. Dust storms were severe in Colorado, Texas, and Oklahoma. In Grand Junction, Colorado, visibility was reduced to less than 0.5 mi by dust. Rapid City, South Dakota, received 3 in. of snow accompanied by winds gusting to 50 mph. Blizzard conditions occurred over northern Kansas and southern Nebraska. Hays, Kansas, reported 115-mph winds and a period of over 3 hr when wind velocities did not drop below 65 mph. Snowfall ranged upward to 15 in. as the system moved eastward toward the Atlantic.

A cold airstream from Canada was drawn southward behind the low-pressure center, bringing below-freezing temperatures over the Southeast. This stream can be seen as the high-pressure ridge extending from Canada to the Gulf on the maps of 19 and 20 March. Note the low temperatures recorded at the following two cities for the 24 hr period ending at 1:00 A.M. 19 March.

Tallahassee, Florida _____
Jacksonville, Florida _____

Temperatures in the lake states were even much colder. Subzero temperatures were recorded in parts of northern Michigan and Wisconsin. Eagle River and Land O'Lakes, Wisconsin, recorded −11 °F on 17 March, and −12 °F was recorded at Marquette County Airport in Michigan on 18 March. Cold temperatures prevailed in the South until after 21 March. On 21 March temperatures went down to the freezing mark again in the Gulf states, with Tallahassee recording a low of 26 °F, Jacksonville 30 °F, and Tampa 35 °F.

PROBLEMS

1. On the outline map of North America (Figure 15.8), insert the fronts of the low-pressure system centered over northeastern Utah on 17 March 1971. Then insert the fronts for the system as it moved eastward on 18, 19, and 20 March, putting the appropriate date beside the location of the system on each date. Is this a typical path for depressions across North America? _____ Why or why not?

2. On the map of 15 March 1971 a cold front is shown over California, Nevada, and Utah. The temperature contrast across this cold front is not very great. What factor or factors are most important in producing the relative warmth of the air to the north of the cold front?

3. On 18 March 1971 there was a band of precipitation extending from Wyoming to Illinois.
   a. What was the form of this precipitation? _____
   b. At La Crosse, Wisconsin, it was snowing at the time of the observation. How long had precipitation been taking place? _____ How much precipitation had occurred in this time? _____

Exercise 16

THE URBAN HEAT ISLAND

[handwritten annotations: overnight cooling; Incr. cloud cover → less heat escaping; more heat escaping; surface for; heat absorption; more dust; more convection]

We are slowly becoming aware that the landscape is not a neutral surface on which we can build without environmental cost. Urbanization is bringing about lower groundwater levels, increased flooding, and a changing climate. The lesson we must learn from these changes is that future urban growth must be planned to involve not only socioeconomic factors but also the natural environment.

This exercise is an examination of just one impact of urbanization—that of temperature changes.

One way that many of us become aware of a difference between the climate in rural and suburban areas and that of the center of the city is by a radio weather forecast such as this: "The high today in downtown Indianapolis will be 2 °C, while in the suburbs it will be −1 °C."

The 3 °C difference in the above example is a result of the *heat-island effect,* which is one of the distinctive properties of many urban climates. The characteristics of an urban climate are determined by heat production, the discharge of pollutants, and the topography of the city.

The sources of heat in a city are extensive, ranging from automobiles to residential heating sources to factories. The impact of the heat from these sources results in the city becoming an island of higher temperatures surrounded by a sea of lower temperatures in the rural areas (hence the term *heat island*). When annual temperature means are compared, cities are approximately 0.5–0.75 °C warmer than the surrounding areas. The maximum difference between downtown and the suburbs will fluctuate according to the time of day, day of the week, or the season.

One of the greatest impacts of urbanization on climate is the injection of pollutants into the atmosphere. English diarist John Evelyn wrote in 1661 about the atmosphere of London in the following terms:

> For when in all other places the Aer is most Serene and Pure, it is here Ecclipsed with such a Cloud of Sulphure, as the Sun itself, which gives day to all the World besides, is hardly able to penetrate and impart it here; and the weary Traveller at many Miles distance, sooner smells, than sees the City to which he repairs.

Smoke (particulate matter), sulfur dioxide, and oxides of nitrogen are among the common constituents of air pollution. In times of severe air pollution, a city will have a gray to yellowish gray cover over it called a *dust dome.* The pollutants increase air temperature by trapping heat in the lower atmosphere.

The distinctiveness of a given city's climate is a function also of its natural and man-made topography. The construction of buildings has the effect of increasing the roughness (and relief) of the Earth's surface with the climatic outcome of reducing wind speed. Air pollution is at its most severe on calm days when there is no venting of the pollutants by a wind. Within a city there may be areas of more severe pollution wherever there are depressions or valleys. There is a tendency for the low areas to be collecting points for air pollution because of either downhill air drainage or the stilling of the wind.

PROBLEMS

1. A survey was undertaken to assess the heat-island effect in Bloomington, Indiana, on 4 November 1971 between 6 A.M. and 7 A.M. The data are to be found in Figure 16.1.

   Insert isotherms at 0.5 °C intervals. Use pencil at first. When you think the isotherms are correctly located, use a black felt-tip pen (or ink pen) to produce the finished map. Once the map is complete, answer the following questions.

2. What is your explanation for the area of lower temperatures near Fairview School and Rose Hill Cemetery on the west side of the city?

3. Why are the temperatures higher around the courthouse?

4. Would a soils map or a land-use map be more useful for interpreting the isotherm pattern? _____ Why?

5. The heat island affects the vegetation of the city; trees and flowers blossom sooner in the city than in the suburbs. Why is this?

6. What nighttime conditions (temperature and wind) will lead to the most distinctive urban heat island?

7. Draw a graph of the temperature along Walnut Street. Begin at Hillside Drive and go north to the edge of the map. Join the points with a continuous line. Describe your results in a short paragraph on the next page.

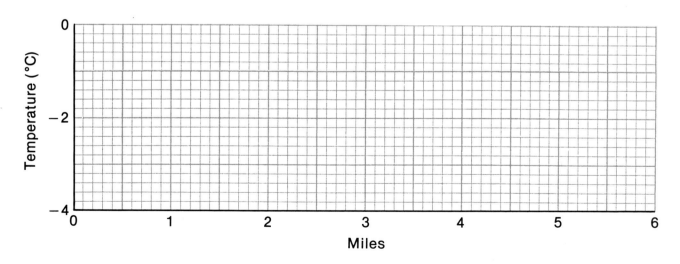

Graph on which to plot profile of Walnut Street temperature

Exercise 17

DISTRIBUTION OF TEMPERATURE

Temperature varies a great deal from place to place, and at any place varies through time. Over North America, there is a pattern that prevails much of the time but that can be greatly distorted for short periods. This exercise deals with the seasonal patterns of mean temperatures over the continent.

PROBLEMS

Table 17.1 contains the mean January and July temperatures for a number of cities in the United States and Canada. The January data are plotted on Figure 17.1.

1. Construct an isothermal map for January on Figure 17.1. Use isotherms with an interval of 5 °F. Begin with the 15 °F isotherm. Once the map is completed, answer the following questions, using the map and Table 17.1.

    a. In which month is there the greatest difference in temperature between Montreal and Key West? _____

    b. In which month is the temperature gradient from Montreal to Key West the steepest?
    _____

    c. In January the 20 °F isotherm bends northward around Toronto and Lansing. How can you explain this poleward bend in the isotherm?

    d. In January most of the isotherms bend equatorward over the continent. In other words, it is colder over the central United States than on either coast. What factors are associated with this pattern?

    e. In July the difference in mean temperature from south to north is very small and quite uniform over the eastern states. In the western part of the country the case is somewhat different. From the data in Table 17.1, determine the difference between the mean July temperatures of Yuma, Arizona, and Cody, Wyoming.

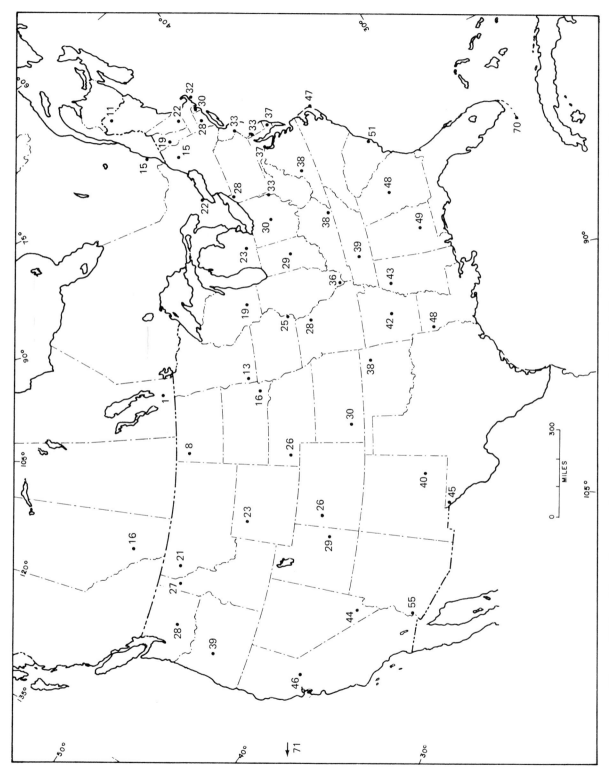

Figure 17.1. Mean January temperatures over the United States and southern Canada (Data derived from H. L. Nelson, 1968, *Climatic data for representative stations of the world*. Lincoln: University of Nebraska Press)

Table 17.1. Mean January and July Temperatures in °F for Selected Cities in the United States and Canada

	Jan.	July		Jan.	July
Montgomery, Alabama	49	82	Las Vegas, Nevada	44	89
Yuma, Arizona	55	92	Concord, New Hampshire	22	70
Little Rock, Arkansas	42	81	Trenton, New Jersey	33	76
Sacramento, California	46	74	Roswell, New Mexico	40	79
Grand Junction, Colorado	26	78	Lake Placid, New York	15	63
Hartford, Connecticut	28	73	Cape Hatteras, N. Carolina	47	78
Wilmington, Delaware	33	76	Williston, North Dakota	8	70
Washington, D.C.	37	78	Columbus, Ohio	30	75
Key West, Florida	70	84	Tulsa, Oklahoma	38	83
Macon, Georgia	48	81	Salem, Oregon	39	67
Hilo, Hawaii	71	75	Erie, Pennsylvania	28	72
Coeur d'Alene, Idaho	27	69	Providence, Rhode Island	30	73
Cairo, Illinois	36	80	Charleston, S. Carolina	51	81
Indianapolis, Indiana	29	76	Sioux Falls, South Dakota	16	74
Burlington, Iowa	25	77	Nashville, Tennessee	39	80
Dodge City, Kansas	30	79	El Paso, Texas	45	82
Middlesboro, Kentucky	38	75	Moab, Utah	29	78
Shreveport, Louisiana	48	83	Montpelier, Vermont	19	67
Caribou, Maine	11	65	Roanoke, Virginia	38	77
Salisbury, Maryland	37	77	Yakima, Washington	28	73
Nantucket, Massachusetts	32	68	Wheeling, West Virginia	33	75
Lansing, Michigan	23	71	Madison, Wisconsin	19	72
Pipestone, Minnesota	13	71	Cody, Wyoming	23	69
Batesville, Mississippi	43	80	Calgary, Alberta	16	62
Hannibal, Missouri	28	77	Winnipeg, Manitoba	1	68
Kalispell, Montana	21	66	Toronto, Ontario	22	69
Scottsbluff, Nebraska	26	73	Montreal, Quebec	15	70

Extracted from H. L. Nelson, 1968, *Climatic data for representative stations of the world* by permission of the University of Nebraska Press. Copyright 1968 by the University of Nebraska Press, Lincoln.

f.   What conditions give rise to the high temperatures around Yuma, Arizona?

g.   Why are the temperatures in Yuma, Arizona, higher than those in the area east of the Mississippi River?

h.   What factors give rise to the lower temperatures at Cody, Wyoming?

Exercise 18

TOPOGRAPHIC MAPS AND THEIR INTERPRETATION

A fundamental part of the geographer's craft is a thorough knowledge of maps. Maps can be used for storing information, for analysis, and for description, but to appreciate these different functions, a student must acquire a thorough grounding in map interpretation.

Once a student has learned the basic techniques of reading topographic maps, he has literally a world of landscapes available to him; the skills learned in studying North American maps can be applied to foreign maps. The ability to read topographic maps with ease and understanding has many useful applications in the fields of landscape architecture, engineering, geology, city planning, and related disciplines.

This section is devoted to building up your cartographic background so that when you come to the exercises devoted to map interpretation you are not hindered by an inability to comprehend the mass of information a map provides.

SCALE

It is possible to construct maps the same size as the real world (such a map would have a scale of 1:1—see later in this section for an explanation), but such maps would not be very useful and maps are usually drawn so that the area of the map is less, much less, than the portion of the Earth's surface that is being mapped. Scale is expressed as a ratio such as 1:1 or 1:63,360 or 1:1,000,000 with the convention being that the left-hand side of the ratio expresses the distance on the map and the right-hand side the distance in the real world. There are three basic ways of showing scale on a map.

Statement of Scale. This method gives the map reader the scale in linear terms, with which most people are familiar; it is expressed in the following ways:

> 1 in. equals 1 mi
> 1 in. equals approximately 8 mi

Representative Fraction. This is shown as follows:

> 1:1,000,000 or $\dfrac{1}{1,000,000}$
>
> 1:24,000 or $\dfrac{1}{24,000}$

The ratio form is preferred over the fraction, which is still to be found on older maps.

Linear (Graphic) Scale (Figure 18.1). This indication of scale has the purpose of helping the map interpreter to measure distances, using dividers or some substitute, directly on the map.

When a scale is being translated into a representative fraction, it must be remembered that the units on either side of the ratio are kept in the same dimension. For example, 1:24,000 can be read as

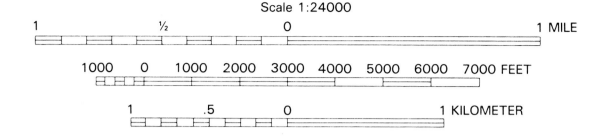

Figure 18.1. Linear (graphic) scale of a map

meaning 1 in. on the map represents 24,000 in. on the actual land surface. It can also mean that 1 cm on the map represents 24,000 cm on the actual land surface.

If linear scales need to be converted, it is worth remembering that there are 63,360 in. in a mile. So, if given the statement of scale 1 in. is equal to 5 mi, to convert that to a representative fraction multiply 63,360 × 5 = 316,800. The representative fraction is 1:316,800.

The terms *small scale* and *large scale* are frequently used to describe different map series.

Large scale   Small scale
1:1,000 ————————————————→ 1:1,000,000

There is no standard practice in using these terms, though the U.S. Army Map Services uses the following:

Large scale ⋮ Medium scale ⋮ Small scale
←——— 1:75,000   1:600,000 ———→

LOCATION

Where are we located? Where is the site of the cirque with the moraine in it? Where is the sinkhole that is the entrance to major cave systems? All these questions raise the concept of location, and the response can be made with varying degrees of locational exactness.

Nominal Locations. For many purposes it is sufficient to say:

"The area south of Toronto."
"French Lick."
"Burbank."
"The southern half of the Willamette Valley."

Township and Range. Most states west of the Appalachians have their land subdivided on the basis of a grid system called *township and range*. It is comprehensive enough in its coverage of the country to make examining its construction worthwhile, for it provides a straightforward location schema.

The starting place for the establishment of a township-and-range system is a selected *meridian* (north–south line) and a chosen parallel of latitude (east–west line) called a *baseline*. From these locational lines, 6-mi² townships are measured out; each township, in turn, is divided into 1-mi² sections.

The areas indicated in Figure 18.2 are described as follows. One is SE¼ of the NE¼ of Sec. 4, T2N, R3W. Written out, the other parcel is the southwest quarter of the southwest quarter of section 4, tier 2 north, and row 3 west.

Latitude and Longitude. On a sphere there is no logical place that can be used as a reference point (or a starting point) for the establishment of a coordinate system. Nevertheless, the Earth, although an almost perfect sphere, can have a coordinate system with a reference point because it rotates and the poles can "anchor" the coordinates (Figure 18.3).

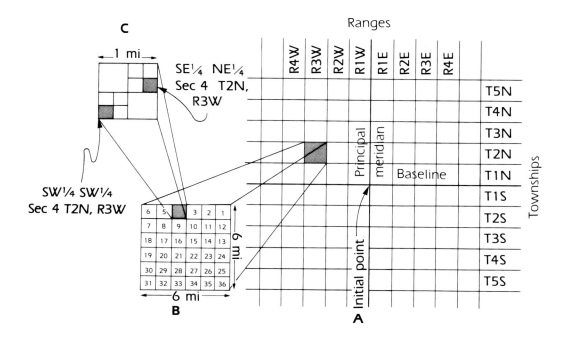

Figure 18.2.   Diagram showing subdivisions of the land-office grid system (From W. K. Hamblin and J. D. Howard, 1989, *Exercises in physical geology*, 7th ed. New York: Macmillan Publishing Company)

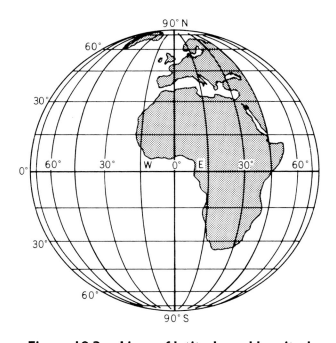

Figure 18.3.   Lines of latitude and longitude

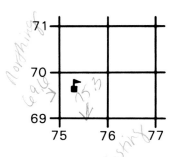

Figure 18.4. **Reference for the school in the Canadian Military Grid System is 753696**

The Canadian Military Grid System. Canadian maps of a scale of 1:50,000 and larger have a grid of horizontal and vertical lines superimposed on them for a rapid way of locating and referencing a point (Figure 18.4). On Figure 18.5, the grid and its identifying numbers are printed in blue.

MEASURES OF RELIEF

Relief is a term used in several ways: in one meaning, it implies the general topography or shape of an area (that is, it is a hilly relief). Another meaning is that it refers to the difference between the highest and lowest elevations for a given area. Topographic maps are our response to the need to express relief in precise and meaningful cartographic form. The variety of methods used to carry out this mission is wide; only a few will be discussed here.

Contours. The use of contour lines is the geographer's most precise method of representing the shape of a landform. Contour lines can be defined as lines joining places of equal elevation (Figure 18.8). Theoretically, there are an infinite number of contours that can be placed on a map, but a selection is made and the frequency of contours is indicated by the *contour interval* (the height between the contour lines). It is standard practice to make every fifth contour darker and heavier to aid the interpreter. Contour intervals can vary from 1 to 100 feet, and the interpreter must check this on each map.

The cartographer adopts standard procedures when constructing contours, and recognition of these facts can be of great help to map interpretation:

1. Contour lines do not cross one another, though they may merge to represent a cliff.
2. Contours enclose progressively higher ground. If a contour encloses a depression, the contour line is marked by ticks perpendicular to the contour line and pointing downslope.
3. A contour line will be continuous and form a closed loop.
4. Where a contour line crosses a stream, there is a "V" pointing upstream.
5. It is common for every fourth or fifth contour to be accented with a heavier line.

Spot Elevations. These are elevations at particular points. Many of these points can be found in the countryside because they are marked by brass tablets. The variety of spot elevations is revealed by examination of the U.S. Geological Survey *Topographic Map Symbols* (see inside the back cover of this manual). In map interpretation, these elevations are supplementary to contours, and their function is primarily in adding extra information to the depiction of relief.

Shaded Relief. A most effective pictorial method is a contour map with shading added to it creating the illusion of a three-dimensional landscape. The U.S. Geological Survey produces a set of

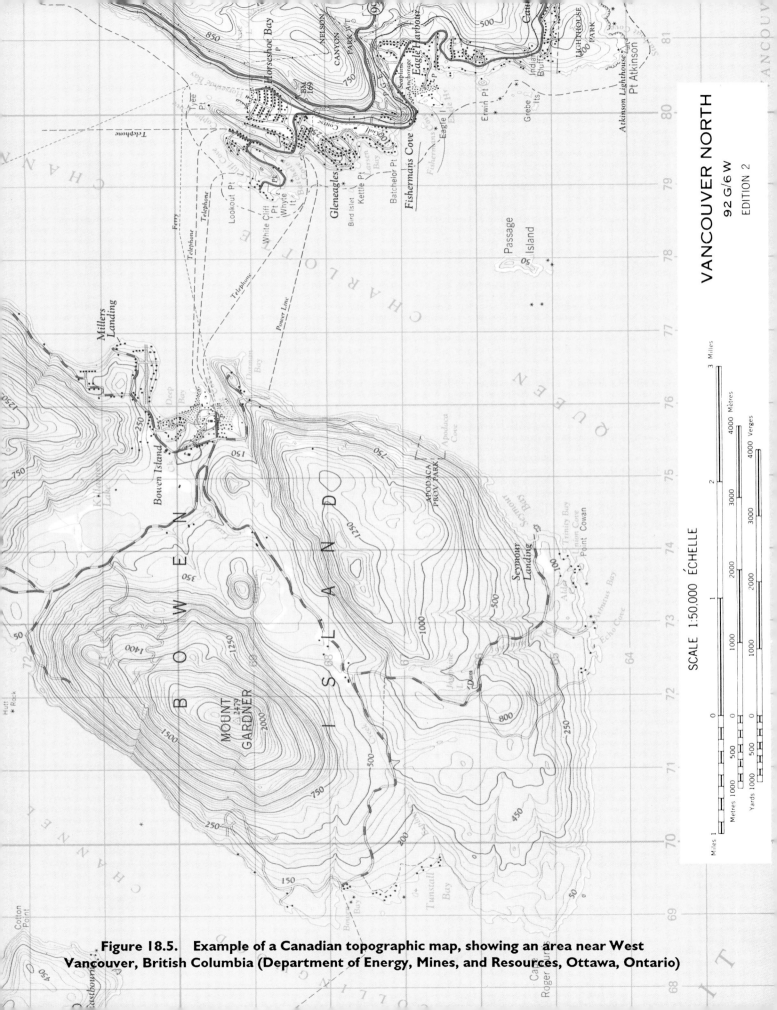

Figure 18.5. Example of a Canadian topographic map, showing an area near West Vancouver, British Columbia (Department of Energy, Mines, and Resources, Ottawa, Ontario)

maps that have shaded relief. An example is shown in Figure 18.6, where the east sides of the hills and mountains have been shaded using an air brush (a technique of paint spraying).

Layer Shading.   To accentuate the effect of a contour map, the area between contours is colored so that an immediate distinction can be made between lowland and highland regions. For this technique to reach any real level of effectiveness, the color must be carefully selected.

Hatchuring.   This system of representing relief uses a set of lines drawn down the maximum slope, with the width of the line proportional to the slope. Some of the most effective hatchured maps are those produced by the Swiss map makers.

Physiographic Symbols and Landform Representation.   The cartographer uses a wide variety of methods to depict the landforms of an area in a way that makes them immediately recognizable. Furthermore, these methods allow the cartographer to emphasize particular points of the landscape that have special geographic significance. It is assumed that the landscape is lit by sunlight from the west-northwest. The eastern side of the high ground (hills, mountains, etc.) is highlighted by the use of continuous brown color or the closer spacing of hatchure lines. The map of a portion of British Columbia (Figure 18.7) demonstrates the effectiveness of physiographic symbols. The lowland area around Campbell River and the mountains northeast of Powell River are all clearly distinguished.

A GUIDE TO SELECTED CHARACTERISTICS OF A TOPOGRAPHIC MAP

Study Figure 18.9 with care. The circled numbers on the map correspond to the enumerated list below. The scale of this map is 1:24,000.

1.   Note that every fifth contour is thickened and the contour interval is 10 feet.
2.   The contour spacing here clearly shows the distinction between gentle and steep slopes. It is of interest to observe that the steepest slopes have been left forested.
3.   Careful checking of this landscape will reveal that it is dotted with small depressions, which are indicative of limestone terrain. Each depression contour delimits the extent of a given depression.
4.   The 10-ft contour interval is effective on the rolling land where the presence of additional contour would give a very "crowded" look to the map. However, in the floodplain this interval is too wide, because the land is not flat but very gently sloping. A 5-ft contour interval would have been more revealing.
5.   River valleys are indicated by the V shape of the contours. The contours form Vs pointing upstream on Stout Creek and in the tributary valleys, which have flowing water for only part of the year.
6.   This small scar across the floodplain is evidence that Bean Blossom Creek did not always follow its present channel.
7.   The spacing of contours not only shows the interpreter the steepness of a slope; it also gives an indication of the profile of the slope. The slope indicated by line ⑦ has the following form.

8.   Scattered on the map are four ⑧ s, all illustrating different varieties of spot elevations. The symbols associated with the spot elevations should be checked against those listed on the USGS *Topographic Map Symbols* (see inside back cover).
9.   This number is located adjacent to distinctive cultural features. Learn to recognize the symbols used for these features.

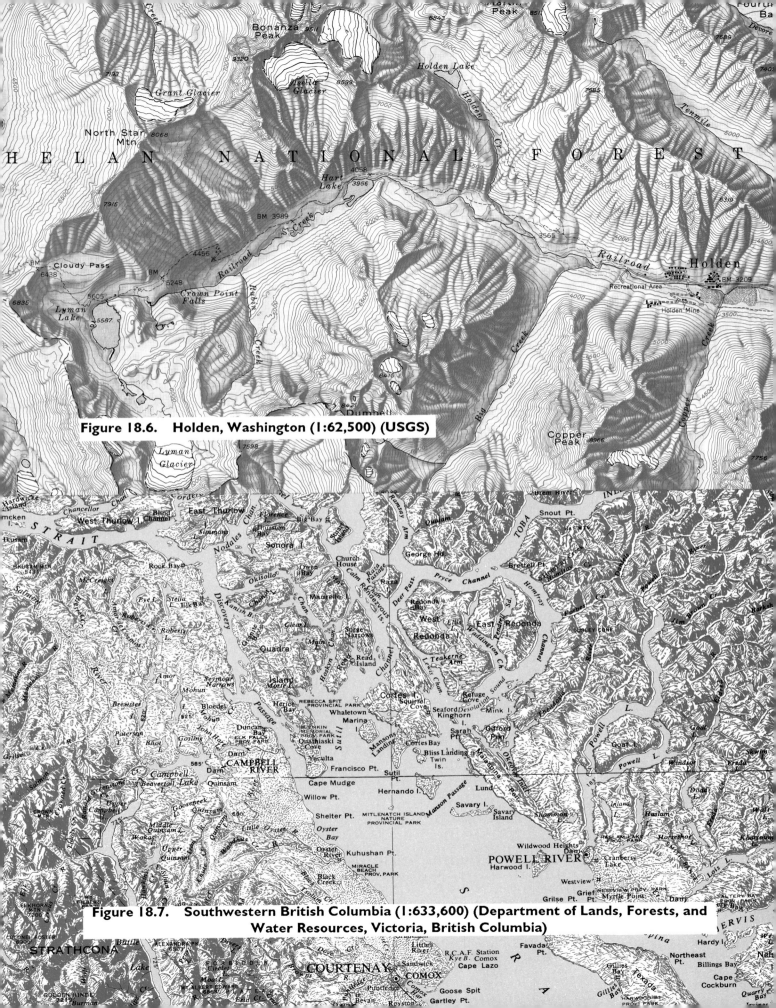

Figure 18.6. Holden, Washington (1:62,500) (USGS)

Figure 18.7. Southwestern British Columbia (1:633,600) (Department of Lands, Forests, and Water Resources, Victoria, British Columbia)

PROBLEMS

1. What is the representative fraction of a map that has a scale of 1 cm to 500 m?

2. You are a county planner and you have the task of calculating the areas of certain farms. Which of the following map scales is most suitable for this task? (Circle the correct answer.)

    1:250,000   1:100,000   1:24,000

    Why?

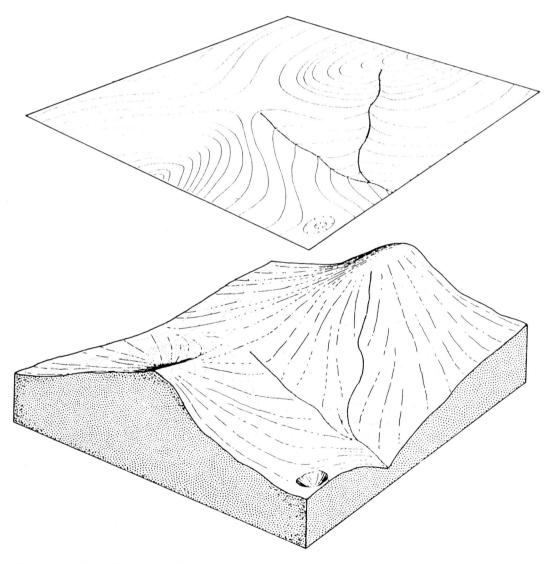

Figure 18.8. Diagram of the relationship between topographic features and contour lines

Figure 18.9. Topographic map of an area near Bloomington, Indiana (1:24,000) (USGS)

3. The map in Figure 18.9 is drawn to a scale of 1:24,000. What information is on the map that permits you to develop with relative ease a graphic scale (aside from converting the representative fraction)?

4. What is the approximate distance to the nearest 0.1 mi from the pumping station to the filtration plant?

5. How many miles are represented by 1 in. on the map (Figure 18.7) of a section of British Columbia (1:633,600)? _____
    What is the airline distance from Powell River to Courtenay? _____

6. How many symbols are used to show roads in Figure 18.9? _____
    What do these symbols represent in terms of road type?

— — — can equal property line

7. Examine the shapes of the lakes in the southwest quadrant of section 9 (Figure 18.9). What evidence is there that these lakes are artificial?

8. In the southwest corner of the map (Figure 18.9) there are several quarries. What is unusual about the contours in the area of these quarries?

9. Compare and contrast the methods of showing relief in Figures 18.6 and 18.7. shaded relief — no contour — artist's drawing — physiographic

10. The ridge between Stout Creek and Griffy Creek (Figure 18.9) has a very interesting pattern of forest on it. What is your explanation for this pattern?

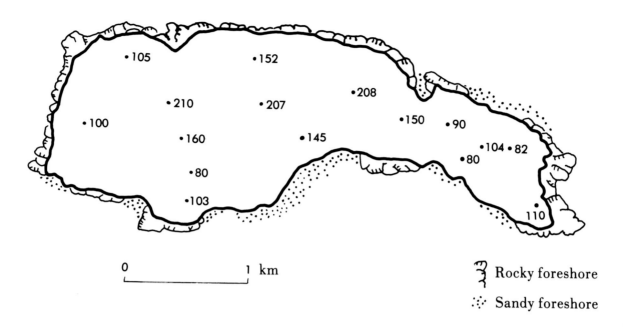

Figure 18.10.   Reid Island

11. What are the Canadian military grid coordinates for the top of Mount Gardner (Figure 18.5)?

12. What does the symbol * represent in Figure 18.5?

13. In Figure 18.5, Fishermans Cove is printed in black and in blue. What is the purpose of this duplication?

14. Is there a school on Bowen Island (Figure 18.5)? _____ If so, what is the symbol used for a school?

15. Show the topography of Reid Island (Figure 18.10) by inserting contour lines for elevations of 100 and 200 m. Do the preliminary work in pencil. Refer to Exercise 1 for guidance on drawing isolines.

Exercise 19

INTERPRETATION OF AERIAL PHOTOGRAPHS

One of the most effective tools that the physical geographer uses for the interpretation of landforms is the aerial photograph.[1] The benefits of using aerial photographs are many.

When a scene is viewed through the medium of an aerial photograph, there is an immediate feeling of "naturalness," for the images can be intuitively understood by the observer. This advantage of an air photograph contrasts with the abstract view of the world from a topographic map.

The topographic map is the result of a selective process with symbols representing selected real-world features. Many facts of the landscape have to be omitted; otherwise, the map would be too crowded with information. This selectivity is achieved at the expense of complex reality, which is the forte of the aerial photograph. The complexity of the photograph is balanced by the insights it provides into the real world. Each and every feature observed by the camera is recorded.

Aerial photographs do not suffer from problems of human error in the way that maps do, with misplaced symbols, wrongly located roads, and the like.

Aerial photographs for any given part of the United States can be obtained by writing to

National Cartographic Information Center
U.S. Geological Survey
GSA Building
Washington, DC 20242

and for Canada by writing to

National Air Photographic Library
Department of Energy, Mines and Resources
615 Booth Street
Ottawa, Ontario K1A 0E9

THEORY OF STEREOVISION

Aerial photographs are taken with cameras designed for this specific purpose. The aircraft taking the photographs fly along designated *flight lines,* which are parallel but so spaced that photographs from adjacent lines overlap (see Figure 19.1). The overlap between photographs is needed so that stereovision can be attained.

In normal vision, the observer sees objects in three dimensions, namely length, width, and depth. The ability to see depth depends on sight with two eyes, each at an equal distance from

---

[1] The student wishing to pursue this topic in more depth is referred to T. E. Avery, *Interpretation of Aerial Photographs,* 4th ed. (Macmillian Publishing Company, New York, 1985).

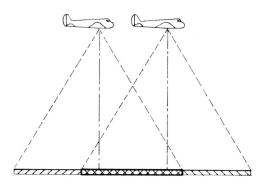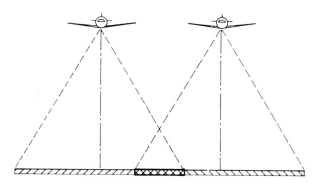

Figure 19.1. Overlap and sidelap in aerial photographs

the object but viewing it from a different position, or angle. Each eye registers a slightly different image. These images are fused or combined by the optic nerves and brain to give depth perception or a third-dimensional view of the object. The distance between the eyes is so short that the angle and difference become so small at great distances that it is difficult to register depth perception.

When viewing two sidelapping aerial photographs under the stereoscope, one sees the same ground area from widely separated positions. The right eye is viewing the area in one photograph, the left eye the same area in another photograph. The effect is the same as if a person were viewing the area with one eye located at one camera position and the other eye at the next camera position. The brain so fuses the images that one sees the relief in the photograph, or the third dimension. (USDA, 1951, *Soil survey manual,* Agricultural Handbook No. 18, p. 77.)

AERIAL-PHOTOGRAPH IDENTIFICATION NUMBERS

Not only is the information on the aerial photograph useful for procuring photographs (because the identification numbers are given), but the date and time (when provided) are most valuable for identifying crops and ground cover, for this information can be linked to the season (Figure 19.2).

THE SCALE OF PHOTOGRAPHS

The scale of an aerial photograph depends on the flying altitude of the aircraft and the focal length of the camera lens (Figure 19.3). The scale of the photograph is therefore

$$S = \frac{f}{H}$$

If the camera has a focal length of 6 in. and the lens is 6000 ft above the ground, then

$$S = \frac{f}{H} = \frac{0.5 \text{ ft}}{6000 \text{ ft}} = \frac{1}{12,000} \quad \text{representative fraction}$$

or, as it is usually written, 1:12,000.

When the photo interpreter faces a situation in which he has no knowledge of the scale of the photograph he is using, it is necessary to compare the length of a known object on the photograph with the length of the object in reality. The scale of the photograph can then be calculated from the ratio

$$\frac{\text{Length of the object on the photograph}}{\text{Length of the real object}}$$

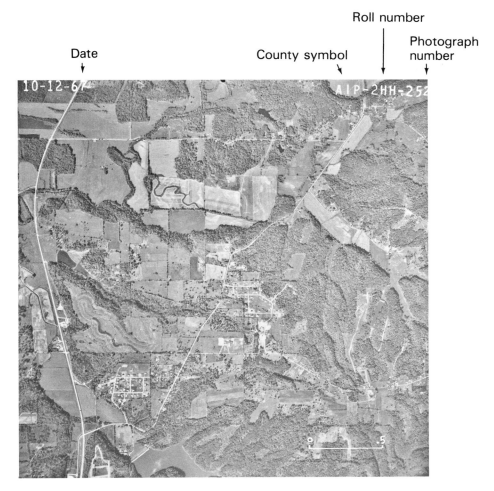

Date → 10-12-6?   County symbol →   Roll number   Photograph number
                                    AIP-2HH-252

Figure 19.2.   Identification numbers on an aerial photograph (USDA, Agricultural Stabilization and Conservation Service)

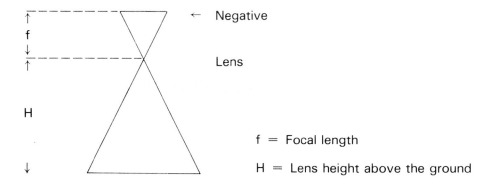

← Negative

Lens

f = Focal length

H = Lens height above the ground

Figure 19.3.   Factors determining scale in aerial photography

Unfortunately, this is a difficult technique to apply to photographs that do not have the imprint of human beings on them. Although we have very good ideas about the size of objects made by humans, the size of natural objects is often very difficult to estimate.

The effect of scale on the amount of detail that can be perceived is illustrated by Figure 19.4.

OBLIQUE AND VERTICAL AIR PHOTOGRAPHS

There are two types of photographs in general use for interpretation purposes (Figure 19.5).

Oblique. Oblique photos can be regarded as the normal view of the Earth's surface. In viewing one of these photographs there is immediate recognition of the scene that is photographed.

Vertical. A vertical angle is more difficult to comprehend because it is only very rarely that a person views an object in the plan view. For this reason maps have been dealt with first in the manual so that a feeling for the vertical photograph is gained from the "vertical" topographic map. The map is nothing but a stylized vertical view of the world. Figure 19.12 includes an oblique and a vertical photograph of the same area.

USEFUL PROPERTIES OF AERIAL PHOTOGRAPHS

Whereas maps have symbols with an established meaning, aerial photographs have different tones and patterns that must be distinguished and given a meaning by the interpreter.

Size. In using this property of an object, the photo interpreter must use an object or shape that is recognizable and from this absolute size he or she can place the other objects into their relative size brackets. For example, most commercial buildings can be distinguished easily from single-family residences by size alone (Figure 19.6).

Shape. Of all the properties in this list, shape is frequently the factor that provides the key evidence for the interpreter. This is especially the case with respect to landform interpretation, where

Figure 19.4.   Air photographs of a partly cutover area of ponderosa pine in Arizona. The scales of the photographs are 1:15,840, 1:6000, and 1:3000 (U.S. Forest Service)

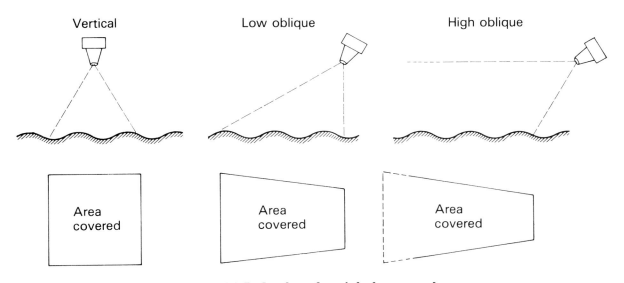

Vertical   Low oblique   High oblique

Area covered   Area covered   Area covered

Figure 19.5. Angles of aerial photography

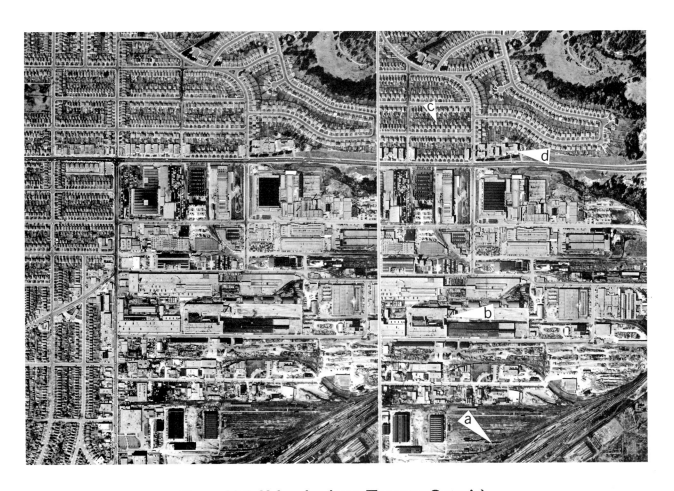

Figure 19.6. Urban land use (Toronto, Ontario)

the external form of a feature is its identifying mark. With features formed by humans, shape can be puzzling as frequently as it can be illuminating, because we are so used to viewing objects from a side view rather than a plan view.

Tone. This property of a photograph is a result of the different light reflectivities of the surfaces that compose the Earth's crust. With black and white photography, tone is expressed by differing degrees of grayness (white and black colors occur, though not very frequently). No feature has a constant tone, for this will vary with the reflectivity of the object, the weather, the angle of light on an object, and moisture content of the surface. For example, water can be either black or white, depending upon the angle of the sun's rays and the camera's view.

The sensitivity of the response of tone to all the aforementioned variables makes it a very discriminating factor. Slight changes in the natural landscape are more easily comprehended because of tonal variations. The forest comes across as a complicated but rich source of information; the differing tones illustrate the species, canopy types, and age of vegetation.

Pattern. The spatial distribution of man-made or natural objects is frequently a vital clue to their identity. Excellent aids are those systematic and orderly patterns such as orchards, housing subdivisions, or waves on a lake. The arrangement or pattern of glacial features like drumlins, moraines, and outwash plains also can be a critical factor in deciphering the landforms of a region.

Texture. This is a difficult property to describe, but it is essentially a way of characterizing the smoothness or coarseness of the image on the photograph. Texture involves the total sum of tone, shape, pattern, and size, which together give the interpreter an intuitive feeling for the landscape he is analyzing. This property is not one that can be defined accurately but is nevertheless vital to the understanding of aerial photographs.

EXAMPLES OF AERIAL PHOTOGRAPHY

Figures 19.7–19.15 illustrate a variety of natural and artificial landscapes. Examine each photograph with an awareness of the properties described in the previous section.

PROBLEMS

1. Discuss two situations (with your reasons) where aerial photographs are less useful than maps.
   a.

   b.

2. You are given the following information about an aerial photograph

   Focal length of the camera = 10 in.
   Flight altitude   = 15,000 ft

   What is the scale of this photograph (expressed as a representative fraction)? _____

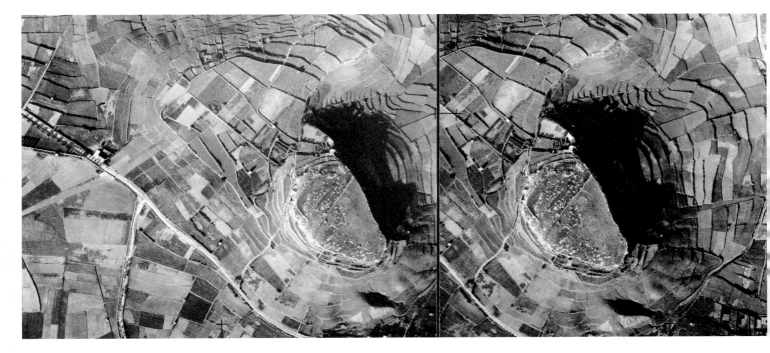

Figure 19.7.   Terraced farming in a dry climate (Malta)

Figure 19.8.   Football stadium and surrounding parking lots in Bloomington, Indiana (USGS)

Figure 19.9.   Forested slopes around a reservoir (USGS)

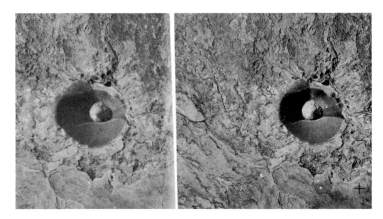

Figure 19.10.   Cinder cone (Stikine Plateau, British Columbia) (Department of Energy, Mines and Resources, Ottawa, Ontario)

Figure 19.11.   Roads, viaducts, and field patterns—island of Malta

Figure 19.12.   Oblique and vertical views of a hilltop village on Malta

Figure 19.13.   Residential land use (USGS)

Figure 19.14.   Rural land use along the St. Lawrence River in Quebec (1:34,684) (Geological Survey of Canada, A11660—290 and 291)

Figure 19.15.   Okanagan Valley near Penticton, British Columbia (Department of Lands, Forests, and Water Resources, Victoria, British Columbia)

3. Identify the features at the very tips of the arrows in Figure 19.6.

   a.

   b.

   c.

   d.

4. The people who settled the area in Figure 19.14 were French. Where in the United States would you expect to find such a pattern of long lots and long linear fields?

5. The linear village in the lower part of Figure 19.14 is located on an advantageous physical site. Explain.

6. The Okanagan Valley scene (Figure 19.15) is a complex rural and low-density residential landscape. After studying the photograph, answer the following questions:

   a. What are the three major types of transportation in this area?

   b. What kind of agriculture is carried on here?

   c. How has the river been modified?

7. Illustrated in Figure 19.13 are different types of residential development. You can predict from the photograph which housing will be more expensive to buy. What evidence can you obtain from the photograph to support this assertion?

8. The left-hand side of Figure 19.11 has a fine example of the benefits of shadow in photo interpretation. Find the example and describe what you are probably looking at.

9. In Figure 19.12 carefully examine the extent and shape of the shadow cast by the hill village in both photographs. One photograph is more detailed than the other. Which one is it? _____ What evidence did you use to arrive at your answer?

Name: _____

Laboratory Section: _____

Exercise 20

LANDFORMS REFLECTING GEOLOGIC STRUCTURE

Although most of the landform exercises in this manual deal with the impact of different external processes (glaciers and water, for example) on the landscape, it must always be kept in mind that many landforms have a component that is in no way related to surface processes but rather is the effect of structure.

In a strict geologic sense, the term *structure* applies to the breaks in, and geometric shapes of, rock bodies such as

Anticlines and synclines
Normal, reversed, and strike-slip faults
Monoclines

In physiography, however, structure is used in a way that includes not only folds and breaks in rocks but also the resistance of given rock bodies to erosion and the dip and strike of rock joints. Hence, *structure* is a term with both specific and general meanings. By reference to the structure of the geologic units, it is possible to interpret the apparently puzzling surface configuration of the landscape (Figure 20.1).

PROBLEMS

Little Dome, Wyoming (Figure 20.2). The interaction of lithology (type of rock), structure, and landforms is often most elegantly expressed in areas where the crust has been folded in a dome, as it has to form Little Dome in Wyoming. The Weald of southeastern England and the Black Hills of South Dakota are other examples of large partially eroded domes.

1. Is this a symmetrical or asymmetrical dome? _____ What is the reason for your answer?

2. Identify two "flatirons" on the photograph. Use a colored arrow to locate them.
3. Draw a diagrammatic topographic section across Little Dome along the *x-y* line.
4. Use a set of ten dip arrows spaced around the dome to show the dip of the rocks. An enlarged version is illustrated:

This runs parallel to the strike ⟶ ╱╲ This points down the dip.

107

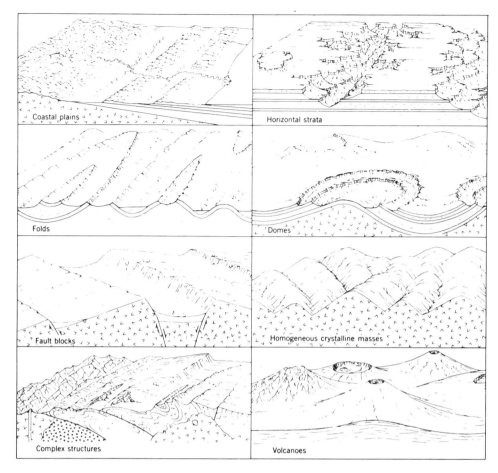

Figure 20.1. Landforms in differing structural situations (From A. N. Strahler, 1969, *Physical Geography*, 3rd ed., copyright 1969 by John Wiley and Sons, New York)

Harrisburg, Pennsylvania (Figures 20.3 and 20.4)
5. Using Figure 20.3 as the guide, identify on the map (Figure 20.4):
    a. Anticline
    b. Synclinal mountain or ridge
    c. Pitching syncline
    Write these terms on the map beside the actual feature.

6. Explain how the Harrisburg map has been used to support the theory of superimposed drainage.

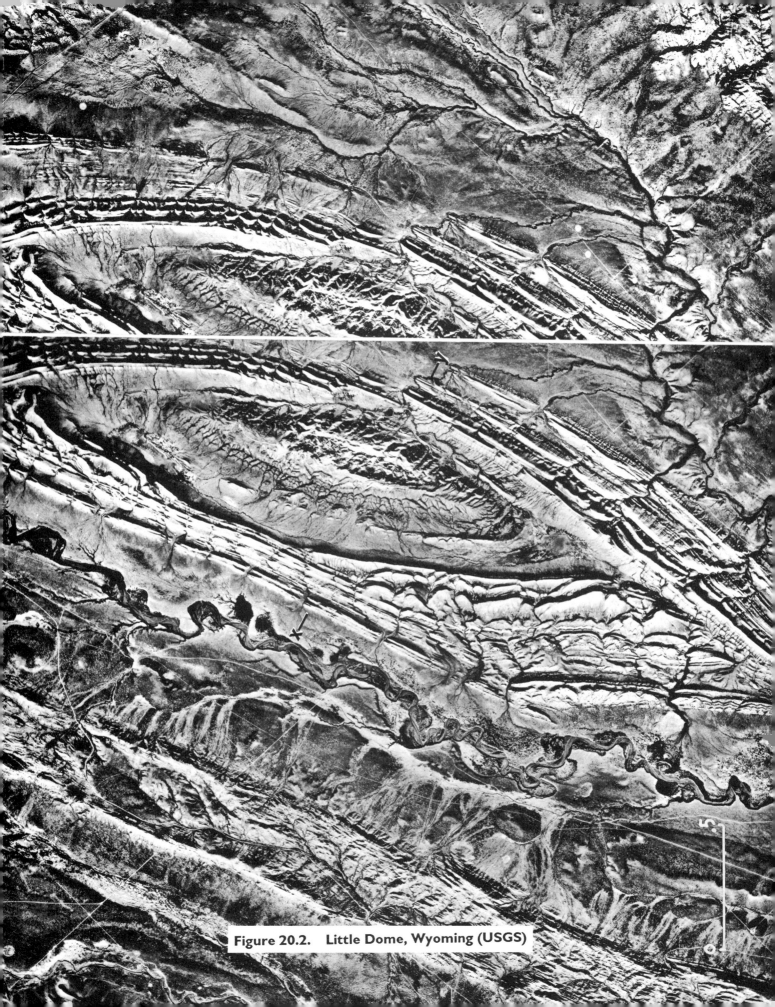

Figure 20.2.   Little Dome, Wyoming (USGS)

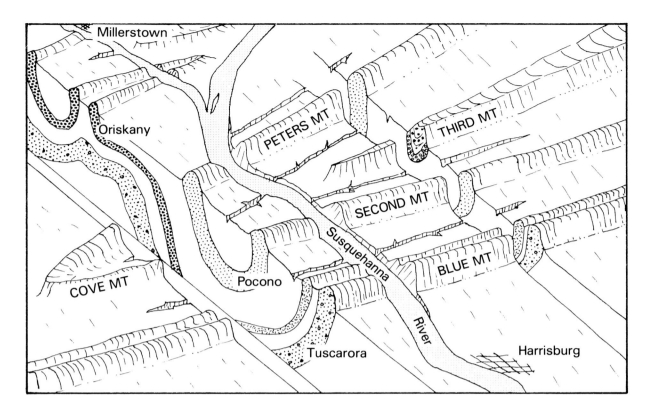

Figure 20.3. Diagrammatic view of the folded Appalachians near Harrisburg, Pennsylvania. Three of the ridge-forming rock bodies are identified: the Pocono, Oriskany, and Tuscarora groups. (After A. K. Lobeck, 1924, *Block diagrams*. New York: John Wiley and Sons)

7. Make a sketch map of the area covered by the topographic map to include:
    a. All the major rivers
    b. Crest lines of all the ridges
    With this sketch map in front of you, how would you divide the drainage pattern into drainage types? What would be the reason for your division?

8. Differential erosion of the weak and strong beds shows the tight-fold structure of the Appalachian Mountains very clearly. Using Figure 20.3, color the outcrop of the Pocono and Tuscarora formations on Figure 20.4.

9. What is the relief of Blue Mountain in the area just north of Harrisburg?

Guelb er Richât, Mauritania (Figure 20.5)

10. The symmetry of the landforms forming the dome is very nearly perfect. (You will observe that the French use very detailed symbols to denote cliffs [scarps] and ridge crests.) Why do you think it is probable that the very center of the dome is composed of igneous rock?

11. What type of drainage pattern is present? _____

12. Identify the following landforms on the map (use an arrow with a letter):
    a. Flat-topped ridge   b. Sharp-crested ridge   c. Butte

    d. Wadi (arroyo): a steep-sided valley typical of arid areas.

13. One indication of the aridity of this area is the care taken to show the occurrence of wells (Fr., *puits*). Mark the locations of five wells with colored dots.

14. If you were to stand on the outer rim of the dome, would the central area of Guelb er Richât be at approximately the same elevation as you are, or much lower? _____

Appalachian Mountains (Figure 20.6)

15. Figure 20.6 has indirect evidence of structure, which in this case refers to the dip of the beds.
    a. What are the white crenulated lines that follow the valleys?

    b. Do these lines closely follow the contours? _____
    c. What is the dip of the beds? (Give a qualitative, not quantitative, answer.)

    d. Is there evidence of more than one coal seam? _____

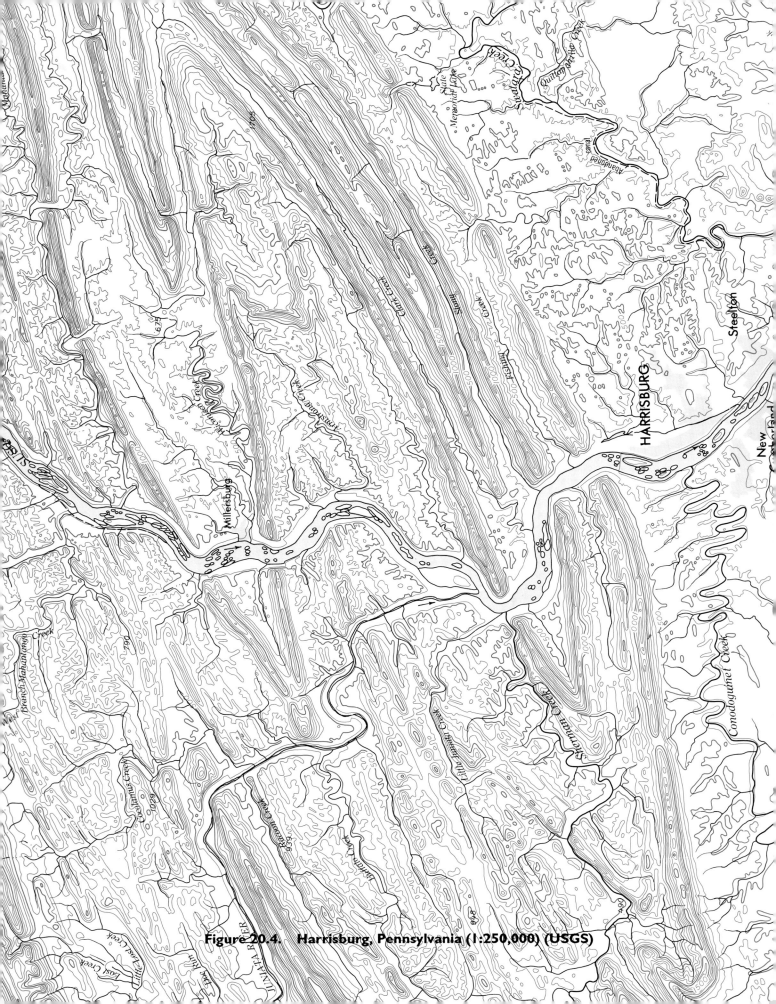

Figure 20.4. Harrisburg, Pennsylvania (1:250,000) (USGS)

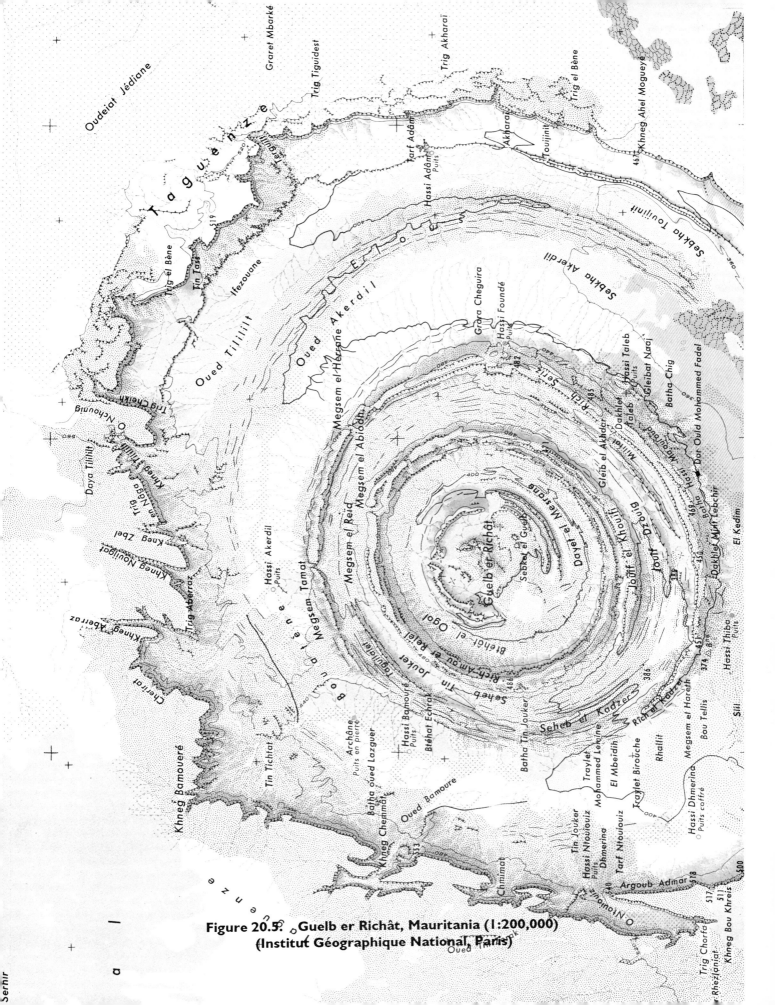

Figure 20.5. Guelb er Richât, Mauritania (1:200,000)
(Institut Géographique National, Paris)

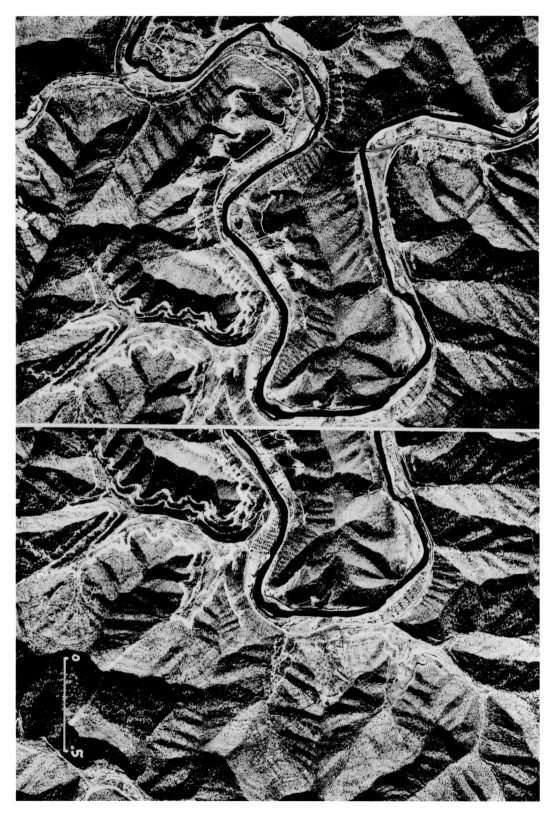

Figure 20.6. Coal mining in the Appalachians (USGS)

Exercise 21

VOLCANIC LANDFORMS

Clear proof that the Earth is an active, living planet is provided by the numerous zones of volcanic activity over its surface. Areas of crustal weakness, associated with mountainous areas like the Rockies and the Himalayas, are the places where volcanic activity is largely concentrated.

A convenient method of classifying volcanic landforms is that based on whether the *magma* (melted rock) cooled within the crust or on the Earth's surface:

Intrusive volcanic forms	Extrusive volcanic forms
Dikes	Central-vent volcanoes
Sills	Cinder cones
Batholiths	Calderas
Laccoliths	Volcanic plugs

Before working on this exercise, review in your textbook the section on volcanic activity.

PROBLEMS

Menan Buttes, Idaho (Figure 21.1)

1. Suddenly rising out of the Snake River floodplain in Idaho are twin cones, the Menan Buttes. The following questions help to define the dimensions of the features:
   a. What is the relief of the buttes? (To define the base of the cones, use the 4850-ft contour line; for the top of the cone use the highest elevation on the rim.)

      South cone: _____ft

      North cone: _____ft
   b. What is the depth of depression at the top of the south cone? (To define the top of the depression, use the highest elevation on the rim.) _____ft.

2. What does the jumbled, chaotic topography in the northwest corner of the map represent?

3. Why do you think these cones are relatively recent (in terms of geological age)?

Figure 21.1.   Menan Buttes, Idaho (1:24,000) (USGS)

Des Chutes River, Oregon (Figure 21.2).   Some of the most extensive volcanic regions on the Earth's surface have been formed, not by central-vent volcanoes, but by the outpourings of huge volumes of basaltic lava from fractures in the Earth's crust. These fractures are referred to as linear-vent volcanoes.

4. The outpouring of lava in the Columbia River Plateau was such that we can observe today several lava beds superimposed one upon another. What evidence is there from Figure 21.2 to support the preceding statement?

5. What has happened to the surface features that existed before the lava flows (Figure 21.2)?

Figure 21.2.   Basaltic lava flows exposed by the downward cutting of the Des Chutes River, Oregon (Oregon State Highway Department)

6. There is evidence of landslides in Figure 21.2. Indicate landsliding on the photograph by outlining with a colored pencil the area involved.

Country adjacent to Spanish Peaks, Colorado (Figure 21.3)

7. What volcanic features formed the ridges near Spanish Peaks?

8. Are these features *more* or *less* resistant than the rock into which they are injected? What reason would you give for your answer?

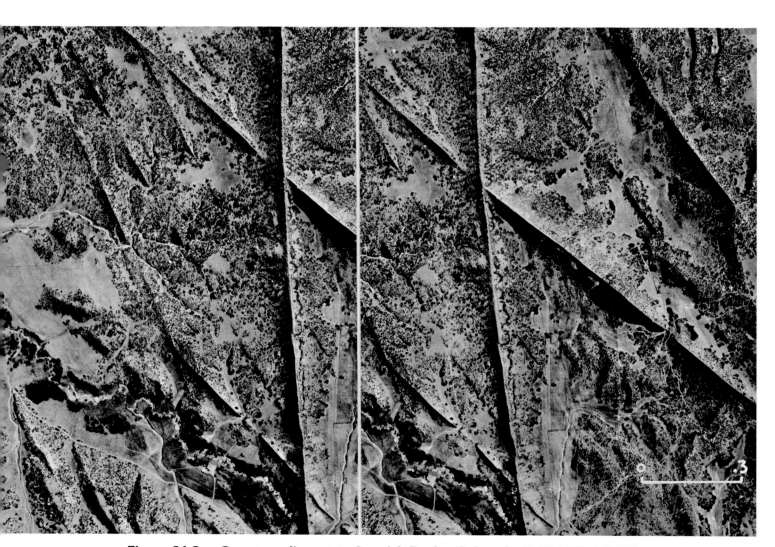

Figure 21.3.   Country adjacent to Spanish Peaks, Colorado (1:20,000) (USGS)

9. Study the features in Figure 21.3 carefully and decide which system of ridges is *younger* (you can identify a particular system by its trend).

Mount Capulin, New Mexico (Figure 21.4)

10. Mount Capulin is a *scoria* cone (scoria is a relatively fine volcanic ash—4 mm to 32 mm in diameter) that has suffered very little erosion. Given that scoria is very permeable and this is an area of semiarid climate, how would you explain the lack of erosion?

11. Aside from the well-preserved cone, there is another clear volcanic feature on Figure 21.4 (the arrow points to it).
    a. What is it, and what evidence is there that it was once flowing?

    b. Put an arrow on the photograph to show the direction of flow.
12. What type of drainage pattern is evident on the cone? (Examine Figure 22.3 before answering this question.) _____
13. What is the diameter of the cone at its base (to the nearest 0.1 mi)? _____

Mount Pagan (Figure 21.5)

14. The dominant feature of Figure 21.5 is Mount Pagan, a basaltic lava cone located within the remnants of a caldera. Identify and discuss what the arrows are pointing toward.
    a.

    b.

    c.

    d.

    e.

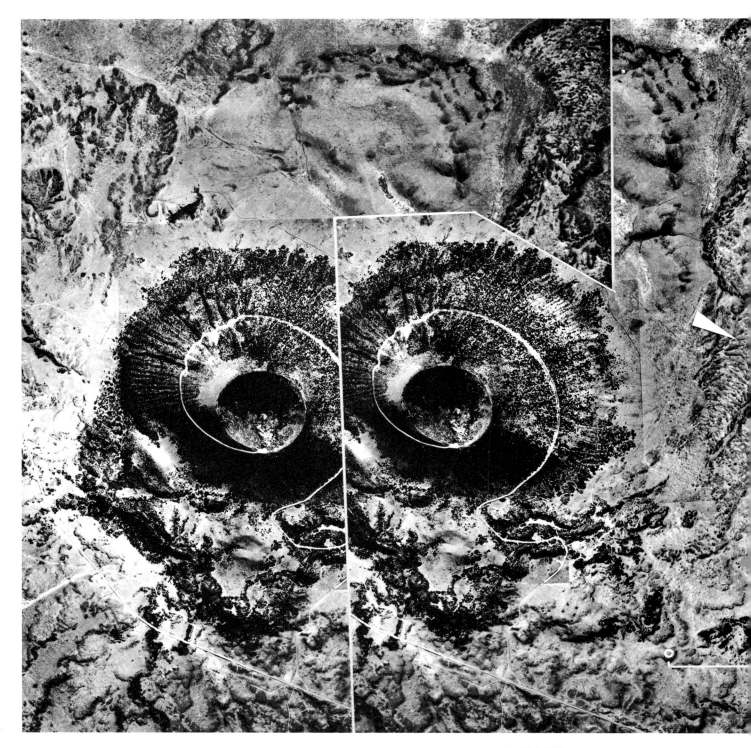

Figure 21.4.   Mount Capulin, New Mexico (1:20,000) (USGS)

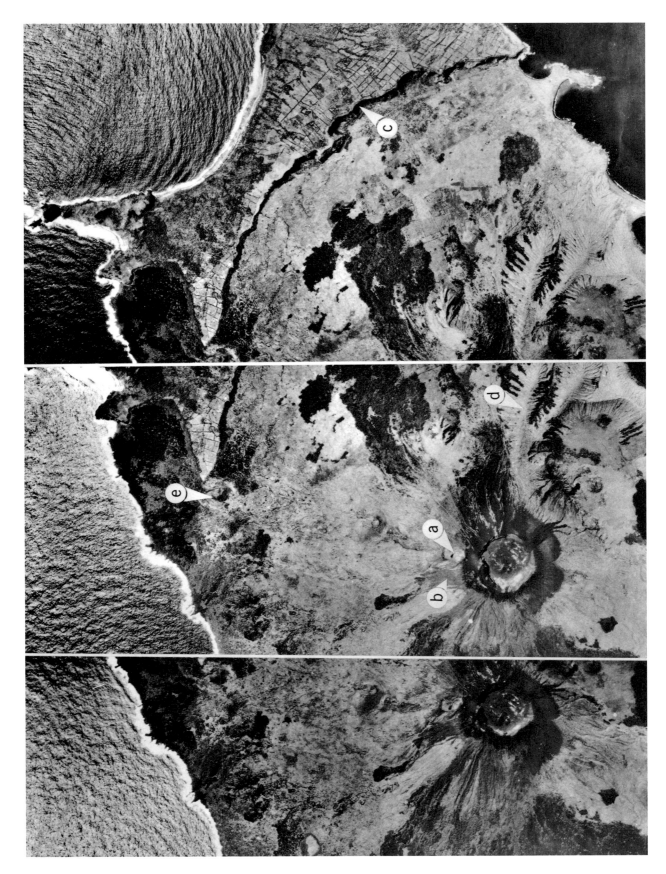

Figure 21.5. The volcanic cone of Mount Pagan, Mariana Islands (1:30,000) (USGS)

Name: _____

Laboratory Section: _____

Exercise 22

THE DRAINAGE BASIN

The *drainage basin* (watershed, catchment) is an area of the Earth's surface within which there is an ordered movement of water. In each basin there is a set of stream channels called the *drainage net*. All precipitation falling on the watershed (that is not removed by evapotranspiration) is carried away by the streams or by underground drainage (see Exercise 27). In a physical sense the basin can be thought of as a system with a series of interacting parts (see Figure 22.1).

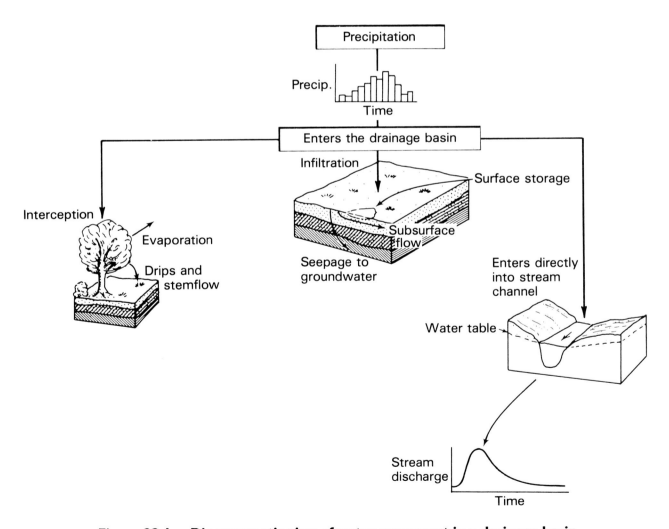

Figure 22.1. Diagrammatic view of water movement in a drainage basin

It should be recognized that an understanding of the physical nature of drainage basins is a necessary prerequisite to an understanding of human use and management of them. As an organizing device, the drainage basin plays an important role in urban and regional planning because it is now recognized that human actions in one part of a basin will affect, often radically, another part. An example of the use of a drainage basin as an administrative area for planning and development is provided by the Tennessee Valley Authority, which operates in the basin of the Tennessee River.

DEFINITION OF THE BASIN'S BOUNDARY

Preliminary to any kind of analysis of a drainage basin is the placement of the boundary or *stream divide* around the basin. The watershed boundary is the divide around a stream system marking the point where water on the surface has a choice—it flows into one river system or into another. The groundwater divide is usually, but not always, coincident with the surface boundary of the basin.

STREAM ORDER

At first glance, many river systems seem to be chaotic in their spatial patterns. However, the chaotic aspect of stream nets can be partly resolved if a stream classification system is adopted (Figure 22.2). A hierarchy of streams and river basins can be developed on the basis of ordering streams within a given basin. In the ordering system illustrated by Figure 22.2, every unbranched tributary is designated as a first-order stream; where two first-order streams join, the stream becomes second order; where two second-order streams join, the result is a third-order stream, and so on. The stream basin in Figure 22.2 is fourth order.

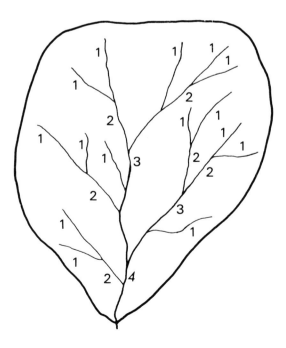

Figure 22.2.   Ordering (classification) of stream channels

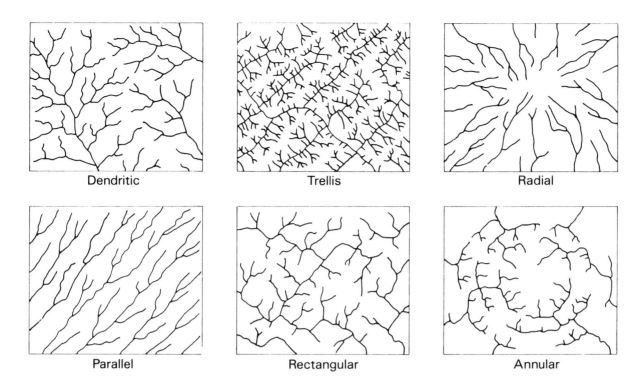

Dendritic

Trellis

Radial

Parallel

Rectangular

Annular

Figure 22.3. Drainage patterns

STREAM-NET PATTERNS

In the previous section the stream net was regarded simply in terms of a quantitative classification scheme. An alternate way to classify drainage nets is by the geometric patterns they exhibit. That is, the net is described as if the observer were in an aircraft flying over the basin. The particular pattern of a stream net is a reflection of the structure, lithology, and landforms of a region. Therefore, in map and air-photo interpretation the drainage pattern is frequently the most sensitive piece of evidence the analyst can use (Figure 22.3).

Dendritic stream patterns.   This is the most common of all stream patterns. It is found in regions where there are no clear-cut structural or lithologic controls—that is, areas of geologic uniformity. The term *dendritic* is used to describe the "treelike" branching of the stream channels.

Parallel stream patterns.   This pattern will develop as a response to a pronounced regional slope such as an exposed dip slope of some formation. Often the controls at work giving rise to this pattern are not obvious.

Trellis stream patterns.   The streams in this pattern join one another at approximate right angles. Trellis patterns develop in those areas where there are differentially eroded rock bodies and the streams flow along the strike of the rocks; in some places the streams follow intersecting faults. The Ridge and Valley physiographic province of the Appalachian region has excellent examples of trellis patterns.

Rectangular stream patterns.   This pattern is developed where joints in the bedrock cross at right angles and provide areas of weakness.

Radial stream patterns.   Where streams diverge from a central point (symmetrical hills, volcanoes) a radial pattern forms. The pattern is also formed for the reverse reason, in that it can reflect streams converging in a basin.

Annular stream patterns.   These are typically developed where streams are formed on a partially eroded dome (see Figure 20.5).

125

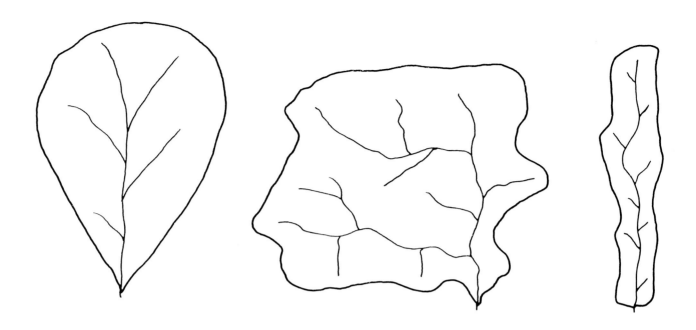

Figure 22.4.   Examples of drainage-basin shapes

DRAINAGE-BASIN SHAPE

As illustrated in Figure 22.4, a drainage basin can take almost any shape. Shape plays a major role in controlling the time sequence by which water enters a main tributary of a basin. The shape of a basin reflects the geologic history, structure, lithology, and climate of the region.

The elongate basins will usually have smaller flood peaks than the tear-shaped drainage basins, because the runoff resulting from a rain will arrive at the main channel at about the same time whether the tributary is near the mouth or the headwaters.

RELIEF

Relief is defined as the difference in elevation between the highest and lowest elevations in the basin. The latter is found at the point where the stream leaves the map.

DRAINAGE DENSITY

Drainage density (D_d) can be defined as

$$D_d = \frac{\Sigma l}{A}$$

where D_d = drainage density (miles per square mile)
Σl = sum of all the stream lengths in the basin (miles)
A = area of the drainage basin (square miles)

Drainage density is a measure of the texture of the landforms in a drainage basin because the higher the drainage density, the more intricate the dissection of the landscape. High drainage densities tend to occur in areas of impermeable rocks, high relief, and sparse vegetation cover, whereas low drainage densities occur in areas of permeable rocks and low relief.

PROBLEMS

1. Insert the drainage-basin divide for the creek east of St. Michael Chapel (Figure 22.5). Use the bridge 0.10 mi southeast of the chapel as the mouth of the basin. For the sake of convenience, we shall identify this stream as Chapel Creek even though there is no name for it on the topographic map.

2. a. The relief of the Chapel Creek basin is _____ ft.
   b. Why is this relief an important measure in any attempt to evaluate the potential erosion rate of a basin?

3. a. What is the area of the Chapel Creek basin in square miles? _____
   b. Calculate the drainage density of the basin using all streams colored black.

   $$D_d = \frac{\Sigma l}{A} = \underline{\hspace{4cm}} \text{mi/mi}^2$$

   c. If all the seasonal stream channels were inserted on the map (use contour indentations as guides), what would be the impact on drainage density?

4. a. What is the stream order of Chapel Creek? _____
   b. What type of stream net pattern is shown by Chapel Creek? _____
   c. How many first-order streams are shown on the map (use black streams)? _____

5. What is the dominant drainage pattern in Figure 22.5? _____

6. Figure 22.6 is a plot of peak discharges against basin area for nearby drainage basins.
   a. Insert a best-fit straight line through the points on the graph.
   b. Using the area of Chapel Creek (previously calculated in Problem 3), find its peak discharge in cubic feet per second from Figure 22.6. _____ cfs.

7. At the bridge on Chapel Creek, the following measurements were made:
   Width of channel at water surface (w) = 10 ft
   Mean depth $(\bar{d})$ = 1.5 ft
   Mean velocity $(\bar{v})$ = 1.5 ft/sec
   What is the discharge of the stream? _____ cfs. Discharge $(Q) = w\bar{d}\bar{v}$

8. On a separate piece of graph paper, plot the long profile of Chapel Creek. The profile should extend from the bridge upstream to the origin of the first-order stream closest to Independence School. See Figure 22.7 for the method of drawing a profile.

Figure 22.5. Elsah, Illinois-Missouri (1:24,000) (USGS)

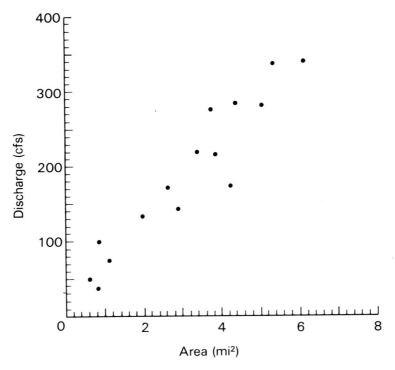

Figure 22.6. Plot of peak discharges

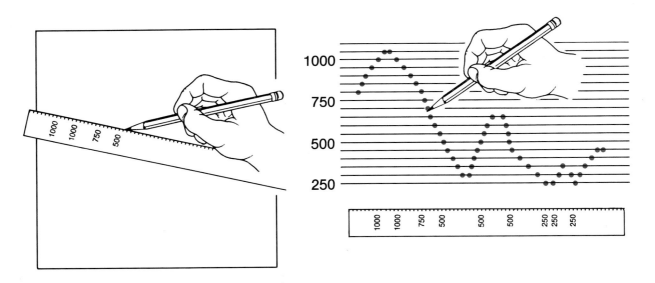

Figure 22.7. Constructing a topographic profile

Exercise 23

FLUVIAL LANDSCAPES *product of running water*

To achieve any level of real understanding about the evolution of the Earth's landscapes and human settlement thereon, one must have an appreciation of the effects of water as an agent of environmental change. Historically, human dependence on water has been shown clearly by the emergence of the so-called hydraulic civilizations on floodplains such as those of the Nile, Tigris-Euphrates, and Ganges. In North America, the flat slopes and rich soils of floodplains are areas of productive agriculture.

One of the most comprehensive attempts to order and explain fluvial landforms was made by American geographer William Morris Davis. His theory of landform development was based on evolutionary principles: he called it the "geographical cycle." Depending on the degree of stream erosion, a landscape can be classified using this theory into youthful, mature, and old-age stages of the cycle.

Review the following in your textbook:

Meanders and meander belts
Point bar deposits
River terraces
Levees
Yazoo-type streams
River rejuvenation

Selected features of a river landscape are illustrated by Figure 23.1:

a   Meandering stream
b   River terrace scarp
c   Point bar deposits
d   Oxbow lake
e   Deposition on the inside of a meander

PROBLEMS

Beatton River, British Columbia (Figure 23.2)

1. Is the Beatton River at a high- or low-water level? Support your answer with evidence from the figure.

2. There is clear evidence in the stereo pair in Figure 23.2 to show the stages in the abandonment of an oxbow. Marking the photograph where appropriate, explain this statement.

Figure 23.1. Stewart River, Yukon Territory. See the text for an explanation of items a–e. (Geological Survey of Canada, 99666)

3. What is the name of the feature that marks the progressive migration of a meander? _____ With a colored pencil, indicate by an arrow an area on the photograph with such features.

4. There is some indication that part of the area covered by the stereo pair is *outside* of the meander belt. Indicate where it is on the photograph.

Saint Mary River, Alberta (Figure 23.3)

5. What evidence is there that the Saint Mary River has been rejuvenated?

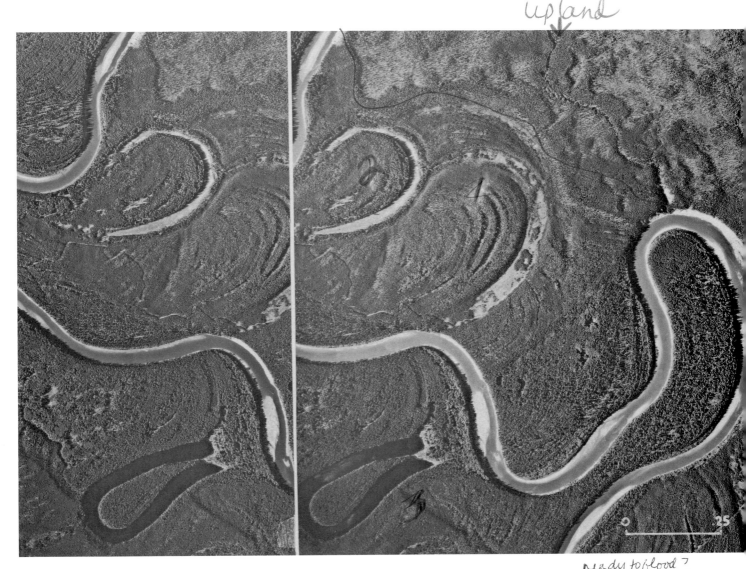

upland

ready to flood?

Figure 23.2. Beatton River, British Columbia (Department of Lands, Forests, and Water Resources, Victoria, British Columbia)

6. Using a colored arrow, point to an abandoned meander (use the right-hand photograph).
7. Does a, on the photograph, point to a natural mound of rock or one created by humans? Explain your choice.

8. Climatically, does Figure 23.3 depict an area with high or low precipitation? _____ Cite the evidence for your answer.

5 Alluvial Terrace

a

0 —— .25

Figure 23.3.   The floodplain of the Saint Mary River, Alberta (1:22,909) (Geological Survey of Canada, A6722—52 and 53)

Philipp, Mississippi (Figure 23.4)
9.   What is the Matthews Bayou?

10.   How would you classify the Tippo Bayou (that is, what kind of stream is it)?

Meandering

11. What evidence is there that humans have attempted to control the course of the Tallahatchie River?

12. Which way has the meander of the Tallahatchie River, immediately north of Philipp, been moving? _____ Why is the 5-ft contour interval, rather than a 10- or 20-ft interval, especially valuable for topographic map interpretation in this area of the map?

Sheep Mountain Table, South Dakota (Figures 23.5 and 23.6). The most intricate, deeply gullied landscapes to be found in North America are "badlands," of which the area east of Rapid City, South Dakota, is the best known. Badlands (Figures 23.5 and 23.6) were produced by a combination of the following:

Impermeable clays and shales
Semiarid climate
Intense thunderstorms
Incision of a major stream

13. The mesa (Sheep Mountain Table) that is apparent both on the map and in the air photograph is a tableland that is being gradually _____. What will be the result of the evolution of this landform in the distant future (that is, what will it look like in the geologic future)?

14. What is the total relief (highest elevation minus lowest elevation) of this map extract (Figure 23.6)? _____ ft.

15. Is this a region of high or low drainage density (exclude the mesa from your answer)? Compare the drainage density in Figure 22.5 before answering this question. _____

16. What parts of the mesa will be most rapidly consumed by erosion in the near geologic future? Use two or three arrows on the map to illustrate your answer.

Figure 23.4. Philipp, Mississippi (1:62,500) (USGS)

Figure 23.5. Badlands National Monument, South Dakota (1:17,000) (USGS)

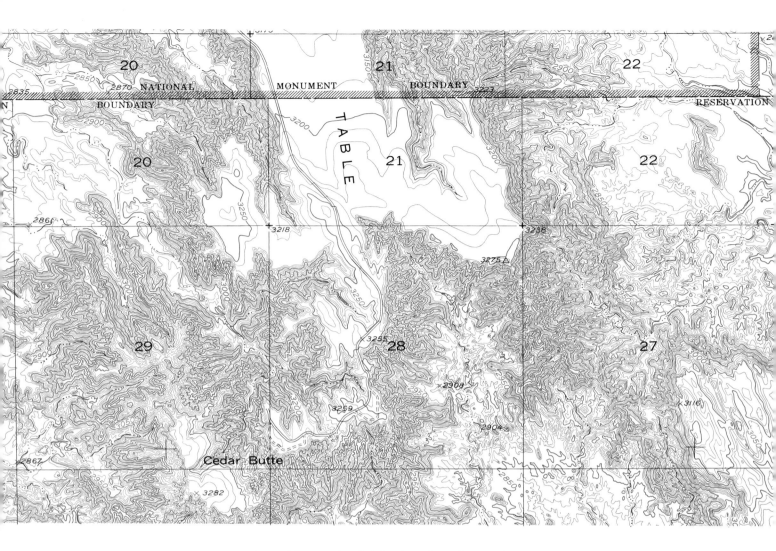

Figure 23.6.   Sheep Mountain Table, South Dakota (1:24,000) (USGS)

Name: _____

Laboratory Section: _____

Exercise 24

ALPINE GLACIATION

Figures 24.1 and 24.2 illustrate the modification of the landscape by valley glaciers. The area of British Columbia shown in Figure 24.1 is a typical example of alpine glaciation. The numbered arrows on Figure 24.1 refer to the following:

1. This is an *arête,* which is a sharply defined ridge often produced by the backward migration of two or more cirques.
2. *Lateral moraine.*
3. *Medial moraine.* The joining together of lateral moraines to form a medial is clearly shown in this photograph.
4. A *cirque glacier* leaving its area of accumulation. The supply of ice is sufficient for this glacier to contribute ice to the main glacier in the foreground.
5. The *ice fall* is a result of the glacier moving down a steepened section of the valley beneath the ice.
6. The *terminal moraine* of a cirque glacier that has largely disappeared except for a remnant on the headwalls of the cirque.
7. The *terminal moraine* of a small glacier located in a "hanging" valley to the right of the main glacier.
8. *Talus* slopes.

The Chief Mountain quadrangle of Montana (Figure 24.2) represents a landscape similar to that illustrated by Figure 24.1, except that the glaciers have largely disappeared.

PROBLEMS

1. Once you recognize that the intricate landscape in Figure 24.2 has been modified by glaciers, then most of the individual landforms will become apparent to you. Identify on Figure 24.2 the following features (write in the name of the landform in pencil directly on the map, and use an arrow if necessary):

    Three examples of a cirque
    Two examples of an arête
    One example of a horn
    One valley occupied by a major valley glacier in the past

2. What is the continental divide?

Figure 24.1. The centrally located peak in this oblique aerial photograph is Mount Waddington (13,104 ft), located in the Coast Mountains of British Columbia. Refer to the text for an explanation of the numbered arrows. (Department of Lands, Forests, and Water Resources, Victoria, British Columbia)

3. Examine the locations of the glaciers on this map (Figure 24.2). On which side of the mountain are most of the glaciers found? _____ What is your explanation for such an orientation?

4. The valley that originates at Longfellow Peak and extends in a curving fashion to the southwest has many examples of truncated spurs. How are truncated spurs formed?

Figure 24.2.   Chief Mountain, Montana (1:125,000) (USGS)

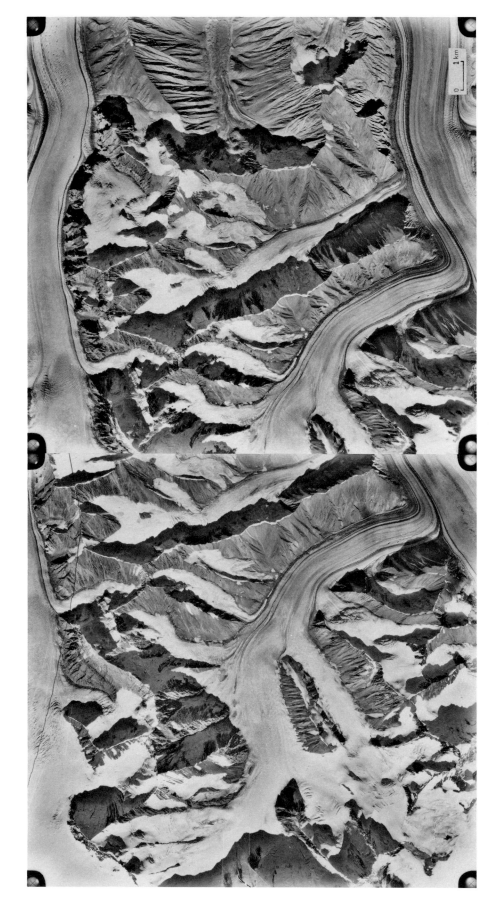

Figure 24.3. Kaskawulsh Glacier (1:70,000) (Geological Survey of Canada A15517—54)

Kaskawulsh Glacier (Figure 24.3)

5. Identify and label on the photographs the following features: lateral and medial moraines, cirque glaciers, icefalls, arêtes, truncated spurs, and a crevasse pattern.

6. Show with arrows the direction of flow of the main valley glaciers.

Mount Rainier, Washington (Figure 24.4)

7. How are moraines cartographically portrayed? Describe the symbols used.

8. a. In the central section of the Ingraham Glacier the contour lines are close together. What does this tell us about the valley beneath the glacier?

    b. If you were in a helicopter hovering over the glacier, how would you describe the area?

9. What evidence is there on this map of the presence of stratified (fluvial) sediment?

FIGURE 24.4. Mount Rainier, Washington (1:125,000). USGS.

Exercise 25

LANDFORMS OF CONTINENTAL GLACIATION–I

The only way to comprehend the landscape of the Midwest, the prairies, and the Canadian Shield is to recognize the influence of the extensive Pleistocene glaciers (continental glaciers or ice sheets) that shaped and molded the whole region.

FOUR GLACIATIONS

There were at least four glaciations during the Pleistocene in central North America. They are called

Wisconsin Glaciation	Youngest
Illinoian Glaciation	
Kansan Glaciation	
Nebraskan Glaciation	Oldest

The evidence for the four glaciations varies from place to place in both detail and form.

CONTINENTAL GLACIERS

Whereas the movement of ice in valley glaciers can be relatively rapid (many glaciers are recorded as moving at 3 ft per day with occasional accelerations to 200 ft per day), the movement of the great continental ice sheets was much slower (inches per month). The thickness of past ice sheets is extremely difficult to estimate but in some locations it is thought the ice could have been 2000–3000 ft thick.

DEPOSITIONAL FEATURES

A simple but effective way of classifying these forms is based on whether the sediment was moved mainly by ice or by water.

Unstratified. Broken rock material that has been transported by ice ranges in size from clay particles to boulders, all in the same deposit. This material is called *till.* Check in your textbook the following:

Drumlins
Terminal moraines
Till sheets
Recessional moraines

Stratified. During the summer, streams will frequently form on or in ice and these will move the morainic material as a fluvial sediment. Even more extensive fluvial action takes place on the outwash plains at the edge of the glacier. Whatever the environmental situation, the unstratified morainic material when moved by water is sorted and stratified. Check in your textbook the following:

Eskers
Outwash (outwash plains)
Lake sediments
Varves

EROSIONAL FEATURES

Although the more spectacular landforms of continental glaciation are depositional in origin, there is a whole suite of erosional forms. The ice as it moves over the bedrock will scrape, chisel, and erode it with the result that grooves and striations will be formed. Areas of weakness are selectively eroded, revealing joint and fault patterns.

THE RETREATING WOODWARD GLACIER, ALASKA

Figure 25.1 should be carefully examined because it shows, in rich detail, continental glaciation in operation (see also Figure 25.2). The figures show the following features:

1. Stagnant ice covered by morainic material. Close examination of the photograph will reveal occasional bare ice faces.

**Figure 25.1.   The terminus of the Woodward Glacier, Alaska
(Photograph by Bradford Washburn)**

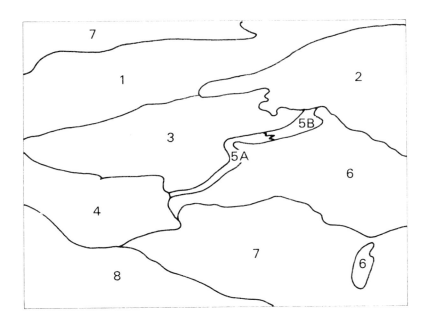

Figure 25.2.   This diagram of the photograph in Figure 25.1 locates the numbers used in the interpretation.

2. The Woodward Glacier with several stream channels incised into the ice.
3. This is a moraine-covered till plain. If the loose moraine were removed, the area would be very similar, in all probability, to the region designated 6.
4. This delta (it would be an outwash fan if the feature was developed on land rather than in water) grew at the time the ice extended over its exposed till plain.
5. Extending across the grooved till surface is an esker. This gravel ridge (5A) is braided into several branches. Closer to the glacier the ridge is less distinctive and the route of the esker is marked by erosional as well as depositional features.
6. The till plain that is emerging from beneath the Woodward Glacier has a grooved surface where the ice has moved over it. A remnant of the till plain can be observed in the outwash plain.
7. A braided meltwater stream is forming an extensive outwash plain that is overlapping the till plain. Islands in the braided channel that are a little higher are being colonized by vegetation.
8. An outwash area covered by vegetation.

PROBLEMS

Whitewater, Wisconsin (Figure 25.3)
1. Delimit the boundaries of the Kettle Moraine. Do this by drawing with a pencil directly on the map two lines marking the extent of this terminal moraine. What does this terminal moraine represent in terms of glacier movement?

2. Scattered over the map are many small kettle lakes. What is the origin of these lakes?

3. a. What is the clearest geomorphic evidence of ice movement on this map? (Hint: check the northwest corner of the map.)

   b. What was the trend of this ice movement (for example, north-south or east-west)?

4. From your theoretical knowledge of the type of deposits expected in front of and behind a terminal moraine, what would you predict the material to be in the southeast corner of the map? _____

Emerado, North Dakota (Figure 25.4)
5. The rivers on this map are all part of the Red River system, which drains eastern North Dakota and western Minnesota. During the Pleistocene the valley of the Red River was a glacially dammed lake. As the first phase of your analysis of this map, construct a profile from School No. 50 (in the southwest corner of the map) to the elevation 940 at a road intersection 5.5 mi east and 4 mi north. Use the vertical scale of 0.2 in. to 10 ft given on the graph (Figure 25.5).
6. On the profile you have just constructed, you will observe one poorly defined and two well-defined benches. From the map (Figure 25.4) you will observe that these benches are parallel to one another and extensive. How did the benches and intervening slopes come into existence?

7. On the benches there are some well-defined ridges; what is their origin?

   What would be the most likely type of rock material composing these ridges?
   _____

148

Figure 25.3. Whitewater, Wisconsin (1:62,500) (USGS)

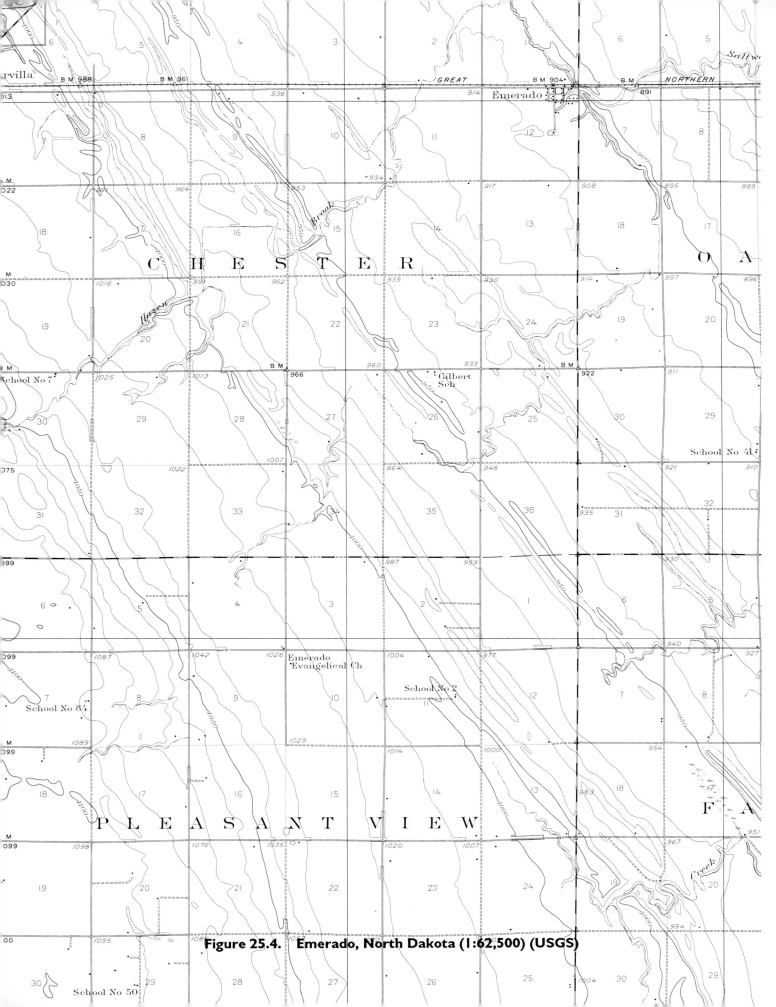

Figure 25.4.   Emerado, North Dakota (1:62,500) (USGS)

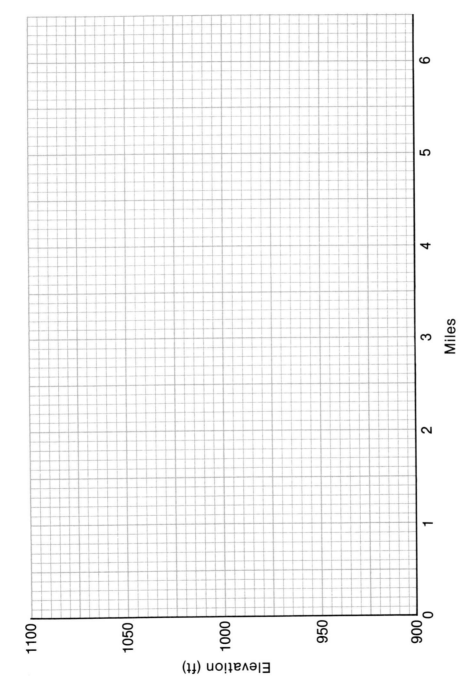

Figure 25.5.   Graph on which to plot profile of Red River Valley

Name: _____

Laboratory Section: _____

Exercise 26

LANDFORMS OF CONTINENTAL GLACIATION–II

The complexity of depositional landforms produced by the continental glaciers is clearly illustrated by the Jackson, Michigan, map (Figure 26.1). In the accompanying diagram (Figure 26.2), the direction of ice movement is shown, and it can be seen that the Jackson area is located between two ice lobes. Such an interlobate area is characterized by moraines and outwash materials in an almost bewildering pattern. In contrast, the landscapes in Figures 26.3 and 26.4 are much simpler.

PROBLEMS

Jackson, Michigan (Figures 26.1 and 26.2)

1. a. What is Blue Ridge?

    b. How was it formed?

    c. What is its average relief?

2. In the southwest corner of the map the landscape has a very disorganized appearance. Note the large number of lakes. How were these lakes formed and what is the name that is applied to them?

Palmyra, New York (Figure 26.3)

3. Describe, in general terms, the nature of the topography.

4. What is the dominant landform feature of the area?

Figure 26.1. Jackson, Michigan (1:24,000) (USGS)

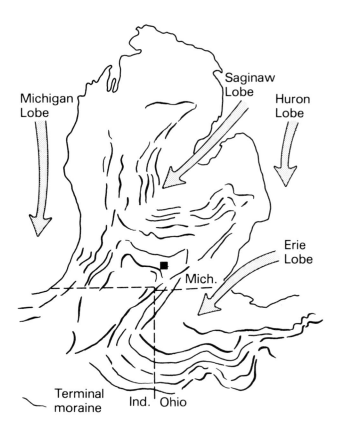

Figure 26.2. This schematic design shows the pattern made by the terminal moraines in relation to the ice lobes that formed the moraines. The location of the Jackson topographic map is indicated by the small black square. (After W. J. Wayne and J. H. Zumberge, 1965. *The quaternary of the United States.* Princeton: Princeton University Press, p. 70)

5. What is the composition of the feature you identified in problem 4?

6. What is the general trend of the ice that formed these features (assume that the top of the photograph is north)?

Figure 26.3.   The landscape of the region adjacent to Palmyra, New York (1:60,000) (USGS)

7. Using your textbook as a guide, give the location of another area in the United States or Canada where these features occur.

Passadumkeag, Maine (Figure 26.4)

8. What is the dominant feature of glacial origin on this map?

9. What clues are there to its lithologic nature?

10. On Figure 26.5, draw a profile along the line A-A'.

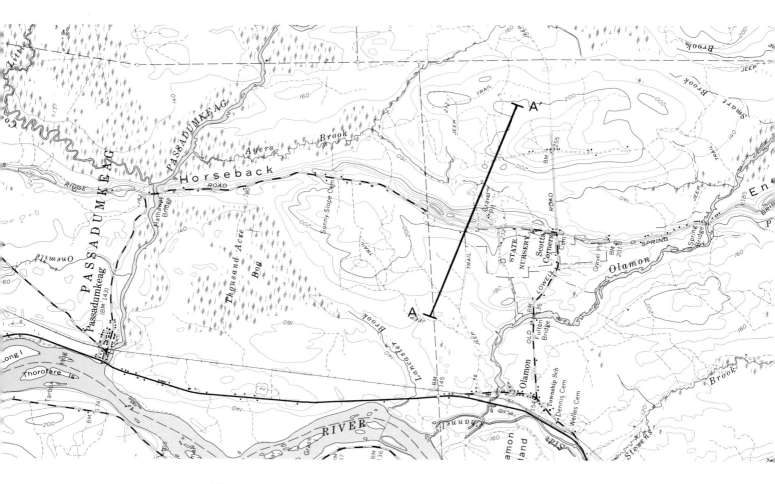

Figure 26.4.   Passadumkeag, Maine (1:62,500) (USGS)

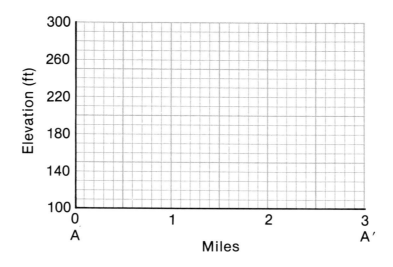

Figure 26.5.   Graph on which to plot profile A-A′

Exercise 27

LANDFORMS OF LIMESTONE TERRAIN

In areas where limestone is at or close to the surface, a set of landforms and underground features is formed that is distinctive enough to be given the name *karst topography*. Flanking the Adriatic Sea is a belt of limestone terrain, approximately 200 km wide, extending from Albania to the Italian border in western Yugoslavia. This is the region of the Dinaric karst—the classic example of such topography. Other areas of karst include sections of Indiana-Kentucky (Figure 27.1), southern Ontario, Puerto Rico, northern England, the Cévennes of France, and western Kwang Si Province, China.

ELEMENTS OF KARST TOPOGRAPHY

Solution. The process leading to the development of karst landforms is the solution of limestone. Carbon dioxide will enter into solution with rain and stream waters, increasing their acidity; this increased acidity results in faster limestone solution. When limestone terrains are examined in the field, those places where the limestone is in contact with running water are smooth, reflecting the removal of limestone by solution.

Underground water. In most areas of the world, karst landscapes are characterized by having very little surface water in the form of streams. Water is able to infiltrate very rapidly into the permeable limestone through surface depressions that will be identified in the next section as *sinkholes*. The water flows underground in caverns that can be very extensive; these underground streams may appear as springs or rises, which are characteristic of karst areas.

Landforms. The most common landform feature of karst areas is the *sinkhole* (some textbook authors favor the term *doline*), which is the most obvious expression of limestone solution. Sinkholes have dimensions that vary in diameter and in depth from a couple of feet to 100 ft. In general, the sinkhole is best described as a funnel-shaped depression. In places where the water table is high, the sinkholes may contain small lakes or ponds. However, the major function of the sinkhole in the karst landscape is to act as a conduit for surface water to enter the underground passageways and caverns in the limestone.

Where erosion has removed the soil cover over a limestone area, the revealed surface is usually very rugged, with deep grooves, pits, and flutings carved into it. Such a surface is called a *lapies* surface.

In the karst areas of Indiana and Kentucky, many streams have formed *blind valleys*. This condition arises when a surface stream goes underground by way of a doline and the stream valley is terminated by a bluff.

The karst found in tropical humid climates can be put into a separate category, for although sinkholes are present, the landscape has a very different appearance. Erosional remnants are found as individual hills with the intervening limestone largely removed; this is beautifully illustrated by the "tower" karst of Puerto Rico.

THE KARST REGION OF KENTUCKY AND INDIANA

Sections of central Kentucky and southern Indiana are underlain by extensive areas of Mississippian limestone. The spatial relationship of the physiographic regions is given by Figure 27.1.

The Crawford Upland and Mammoth Cave Plateau are equivalent physiographic units, though the Crawford Upland is not so karstified as its Kentucky equivalent.

The Mitchell Plain and Pennyroyal Plain are the most developed karst areas with sinkholes frequent and readily identifiable even on topographic maps.

The Kentucky karst regions are separated by the Dripping Springs Escarpment; there is no equivalent to this in Indiana. Park City, Kentucky, is located directly next to the escarpment.

PROBLEMS

Park City, Kentucky (Figures 27.2–27.4)

1.   After studying Figures 27.2 and 27.3, you will recognize that the two physiographic units shown in Figure 27.1 are represented in these figures (Mammoth Cave Plateau and the Pennyroyal Plain). On Figure 27.4, insert the Dripping Spring Escarpment, which is the boundary between the two regions, by way of a line like this:

Marking the top of the escarpment

After you have done this, write in the names of the physiographic units on the diagram.

2.   a.   Which physiographic unit has the largest number of sinkholes? _____
     b.   With the aid of a small arrow, point to an example of a blind valley on the Park City map in Figure 27.2 (use a colored pencil).

3.   Describe the differences in density (number per unit area) and morphology of sinks between the Mammoth Cave Plateau and the Pennyroyal Plain. To calculate density, count the number of sinks in the sample squares (quadrats) on the map (Figure 27.2).

4.   One of the most sensitive environmental aspects of karst regions is the ease and rapidity with which the groundwater can be polluted. Why should this be so? (Use your knowledge of underground conditions in karst.)

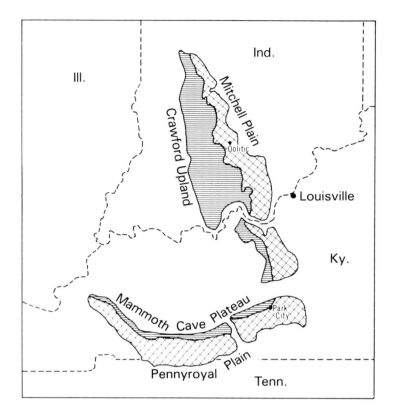

Figure 27.1   The karst areas of Indiana and Kentucky (After W. E. Davies and H. E. LeGrand, 1972, "Karst of the United States," in *Karst*, ed. M. Herak and V. T. Stringfield. Amsterdam: Elsevier Publishing Co., p. 496, Fig. 17)

5.   Between Chaumont and Park City there is a line of sinkholes. What kind of structural feature would you cite to explain this linear trend?

Manatí, Puerto Rico (Figure 27.5).   This stereo pair covers an area some 4 mi west of Manatí, near the northern coast of Puerto Rico.

6.   The solution of limestone is more rapid under warmer temperatures. Which area, Puerto Rico or Kentucky, is having its karst terrain more rapidly eroded? _____

7.   The Puerto Rican karst area has a very different appearance from those in temperate climates.

   a.   The bottom two thirds of the stereo pair is a complex mosaic of sinkholes and sharp ridges. As a sinkhole enlarges, what happens to the ridges?

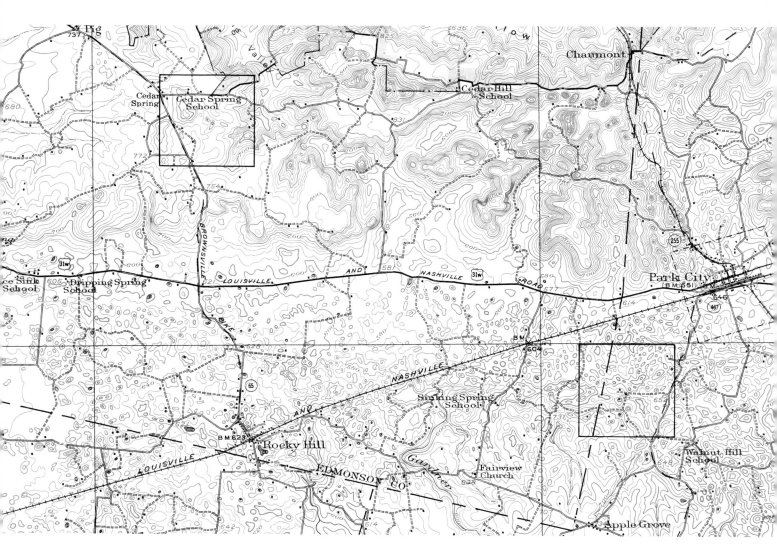

Figure 27.2. Mammoth Cave, Kentucky (1:62,500) (USGS)

b.   People's use of the sinkhole terrain is fairly intensive. What does the pattern of regularly spaced dots (objects) probably represent?

c.   Put an X on the stereo pair where you can find what might be a sinkhole opening.

8.   Compare and contrast the temperate area of karst (Figures 27.2 and 27.3) with the tropical karst (Figure 27.5).

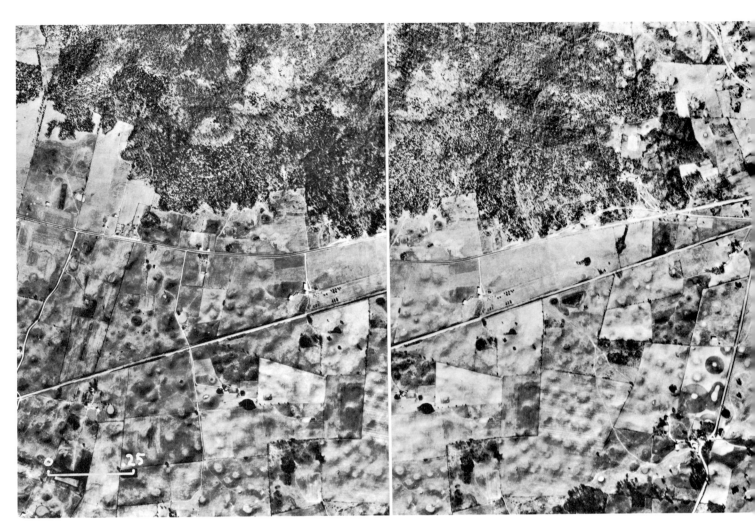

Figure 27.3.   Karst topography west of Park City, Kentucky (1:18,000) (USGS)

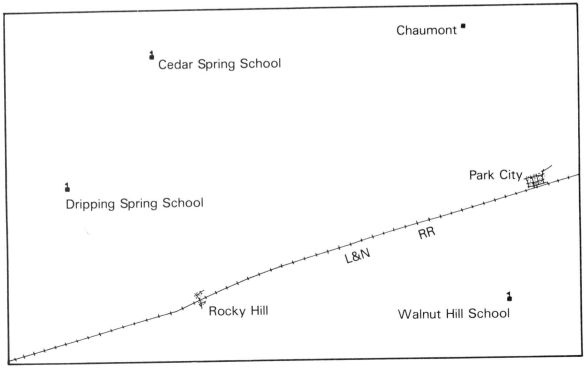

Figure 27.4.   Outline map of the Park City area

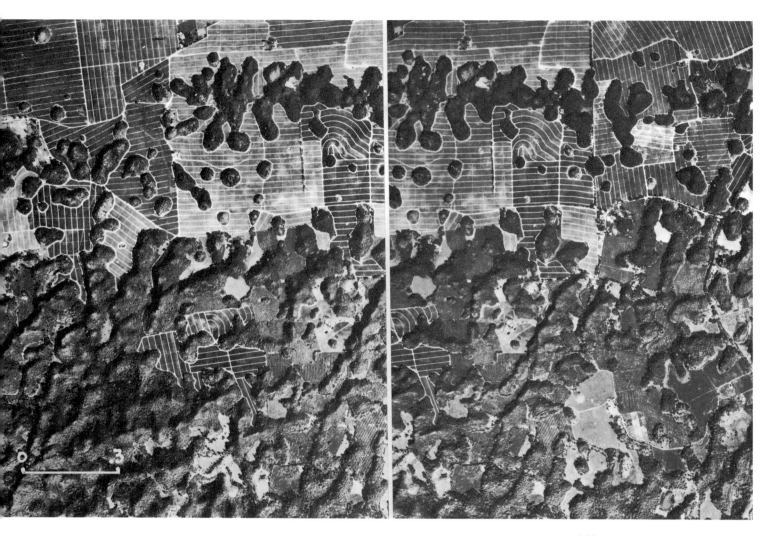

Figure 27.5.   Karst topography in northern Puerto Rico (USGS)

Exercise 28

LANDFORMS OF ARID REGIONS—INTRODUCTION AND ALLUVIAL FANS

Arid climates are prevalent over approximately one third of the Earth's land surface (Figure 28.1). Climatically, the world's desert regions are characterized by:

Low rainfalls (and low humidities)
Great rainfall variability—both in terms of time and spatial distribution.
High average wind speeds
Intense heating by day and cooling by night
Sparse vegetation (not a climatic factor but listed here for convenience)

This list represents the major *external* elements responsible for the nature of desert landforms; the structure and lithology of rocks in the desert areas are the *internal* elements involved.

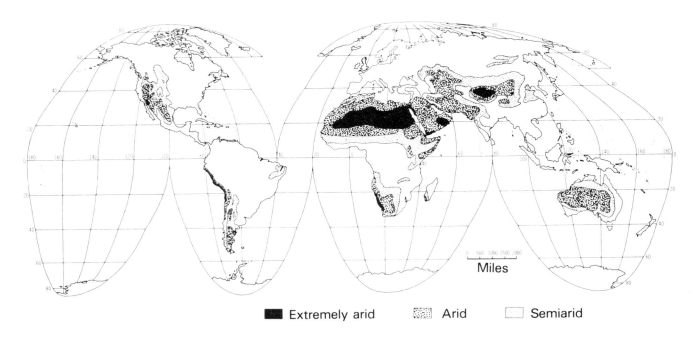

Extremely arid　　Arid　　Semiarid

Figure 28.1　The world's arid lands (After P. Meigs, 1953, Arid-zone research paper, UNESCO)

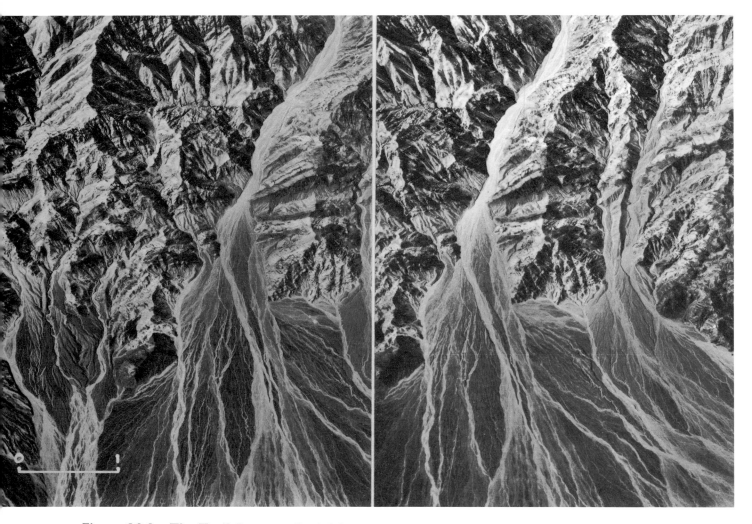

Figure 28.2 The Trail Canyon alluvial fan on the east flank of the Panamint Range, California (1:60,000) (USGS)

Hollywood has promoted the myth of extensive sand dunes typifying desert conditions and implying, at the same time, the efficacy of wind action. However, it is the action of water, strange as it may seem, and not the work of wind that is the prime agent of desert landscape evolution.

The key to the understanding of the action of water in the desert is its variability, because a place that might have been dry for 25 years can suddenly be inundated by a very intense thunderstorm. A dry *arroyo (wadi)* will be transformed into the channel of a raging torrent, and in the space of a few hours an amazing amount of erosion and sedimentation will have taken place.

In this and the succeeding exercises the following landforms will be examined: alluvial fans, dunes, and high mountain streams.

ALLUVIAL FANS

In arid areas alluvial fans are found on the flanks of mountain fronts. The traditional explanation for the formation of alluvial fans has been that they were formed by deposition caused by the drop in velocity of the stream as it left the mountains and flowed out over the plain. A different view of alluvial fan formation has been put forward, because the previous explanation is inadequate for locations where

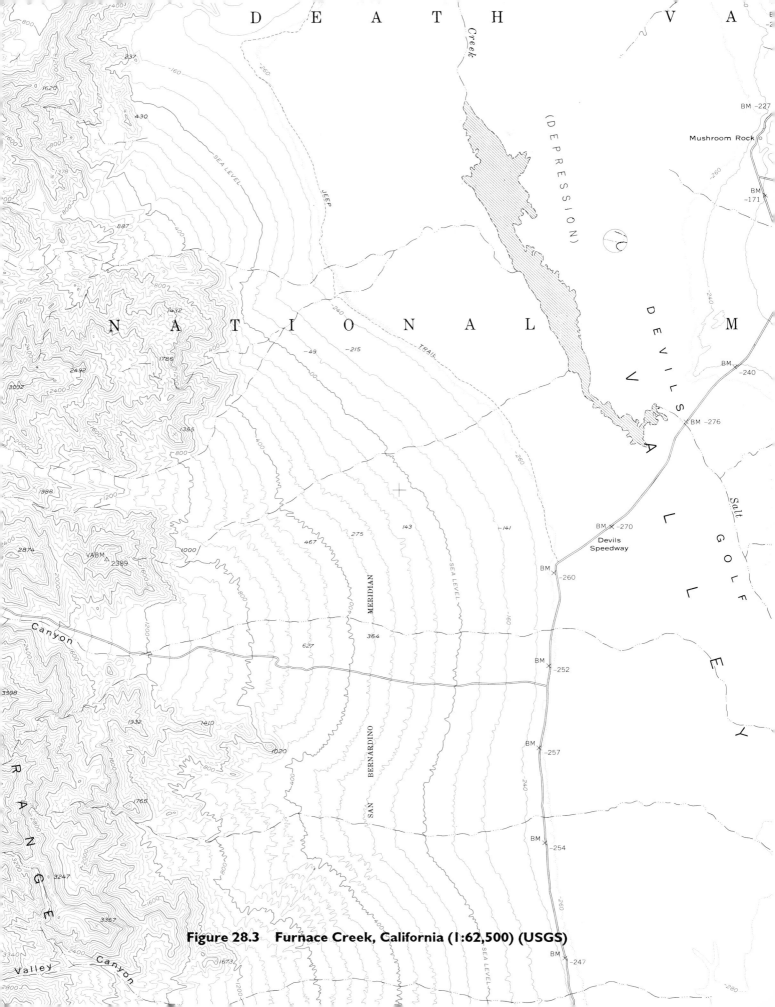

Figure 28.3   Furnace Creek, California (1:62,500) (USGS)

the stream profile is a smooth one, showing no interruption or break at the mountain front. When water in the stream reaches the mountain front, it has the tendency to spread out and not be confined to well-defined channels. This increase in width is accompanied by a drop in velocity and a decrease in depth; the outcome is that the sediment load is dropped.

PROBLEMS

1. In what ways is the stereo pair (Figure 28.2) more informative about the surface of the Trail Canyon alluvial fan than is the topographic map (Figure 28.3)?

2. The geologic map of Trail Canyon (Figure 28.4) indicates the changing positions of the stream channels (washes) crossing the fan. (Note: both desert varnish [a coating of iron and manganese oxide on bare rock surfaces] and weathered gravel indicate a lack of movement by water.)

   a. What is there about the pattern of the modern washes to indicate the fanlike spreading of alluvial material?

   b. Where does the alluvial material come from?

3. Does the material forming the Trail Canyon fan come from the watershed high in the Panamint Range or from side slopes or from both sources? Clearly indicate the evidence.

4. Using a colored pencil or black felt-tip pen, insert on Figure 28.3 the limits of alluvial fan sedimentation shown in the left photo of the stereo pair in Figure 28.2

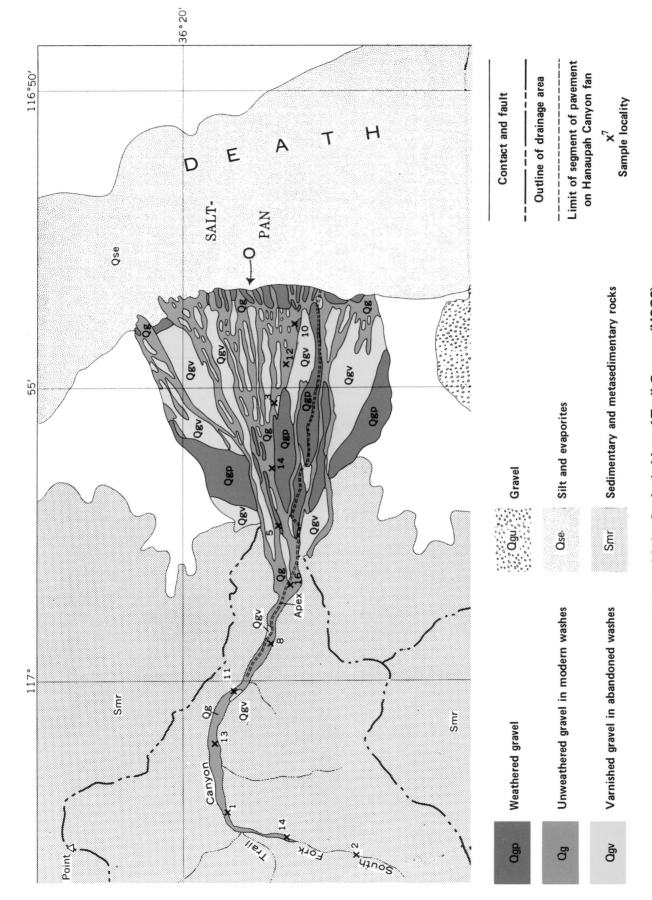

Figure 28.4 Geologic Map of Trail Canyon (USGS)

Contact and fault

Outline of drainage area

Limit of segment of pavement
on Hanaupah Canyon fan

x⁷
Sample locality

Qgu — Gravel

Qse — Silt and evaporites

Smr — Sedimentary and metasedimentary rocks

Qgp — Weathered gravel

Qg — Unweathered gravel in modern washes

Qgv — Varnished gravel in abandoned washes

169

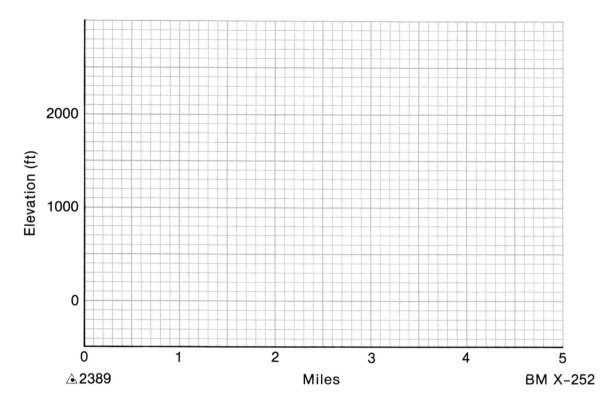

Figure 28.5. Graph on which to plot profile of Trail Canyon

5. Draw a profile across the Trail Canyon area (as shown on Figure 28.3) from the point △ 2389 to the bench mark (BM X-252) on the road that skirts the base of the fan.

6. What are the potential dangers to urban settlement on alluvial fans?

7. If the processes forming alluvial fans continue, what will happen to the low area of Death Valley?

8. Why should a permanent road avoid an alluvial fan?

Name: _____

Laboratory Section: _____

Exercise 29

LANDFORMS OF ARID REGIONS—DUNES

Dunes, those transient features of the desert landscape, are the result of a delicate adjustment between:

Wind strength and direction
Sand availability
The nature of the desert surface

From the interaction and balance between these variables there develops a variety of dune types.

Obstacle Dunes

Obstacle dunes form when sand collects in the lee of an obstacle (boulder, bush, or cliff) that interrupts the flow of the wind (Figure 29.1).

Barchan Dunes

Barchan, or *crescentic,* dunes are located perpendicular to the dominant wind direction wherever they are found (Figure 29.2). The tips of barchan dunes extend downwind. Whether these dunes are clustered in interacting groups or scattered individually is a function of sand supply. The greater the sand supply, the less clearly separated are the dunes.

Seif Dunes

Where sand is piled in long ridges, often extending over many kilometers, it is termed a *seif,* or *longitudinal,* dune (Figure 29.3). The seif dune is rarely a perfect, symmetrically shaped ridge but is

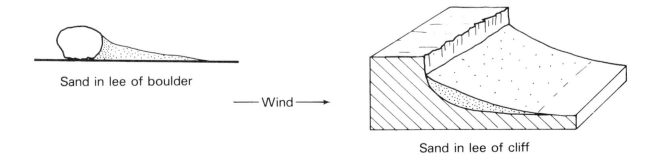

Sand in lee of boulder

— Wind ⟶

Sand in lee of cliff

Figure 29.1. Obstacle dunes

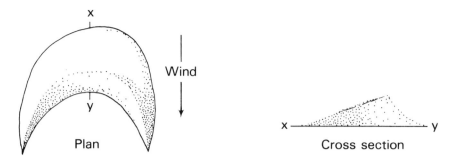

Figure 29.2.   A barchan dune

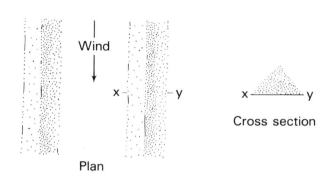

Figure 29.3.   Seif dunes

more often one with undulations in the crest line and frequent breaks in the ridge itself. Seif dunes run parallel with the dominant wind direction.

For both the barchan and seif dunes, the location of a given dune is an ever-changing response to sand supply and wind movements. However, as long as there is a steady supply of sand (and a steady wind) the dunes will remain in an area.

PROBLEMS

1. a.   Assume that the left-hand side of the air photo in Figure 29.4 is north. What is the direction of the dominant wind in this area? _____ What evidence indicates this wind direction?

    b.   Are there any dunes other than barchan dunes shown in this photograph? _____
    c.   Wind is clearly an important process in modifying this landscape. What other process is obviously at work? _____ What evidence is there of this process?

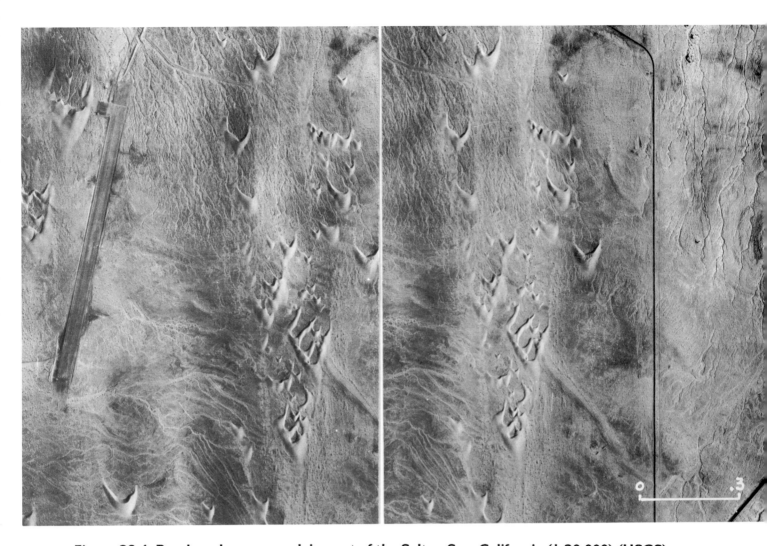

Figure 29.4. Barchan dunes on a plain west of the Salton Sea, California (1:20,000) (USGS)

2.   What is the major difference between the barchan dunes of the Peace River area (Figure 29.5) and the ones in California (Figure 29.4)? Describe the response of vegetation to these barchan dunes in Alberta. What factors would you suggest for this response? Note: Unless indicated otherwise, scales of photos are in miles.

3.   a. Figure 29.6 is a photograph of longitudinal dunes from the sand hills area of Nebraska. Why are these dunes similar, in one sense, to those of a very different shape in Alberta (Figure 29.5)?

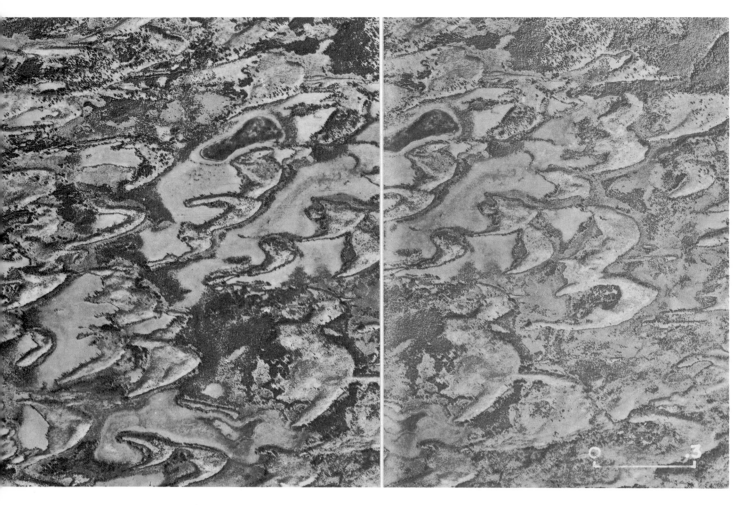

Figure 29.5.   Barchan dunes in the Peace River lowland of northern Alberta (1:20,265)
(Geological Survey of Canada, A14044 —144 and 145)

b. The major agricultural enterprise of this area (Figure 29.6) is cattle raising. With this information in mind, observe the areas of erosion (white colors denote erosion). Areas of erosion show a pattern (ignore the dunes in the upper portion of the photograph with systematic linear features on them). Describe the pattern and give an explanation.

c. Assuming the top edge of the photograph is north, what was the direction of dominant wind flow? _____

d. Do you think there is any justification for calling these dunes fossilized? _____

4. Some areas of dune development are characterized by a lack of definite pattern (Figure 29.7). Check a map of Colorado to determine the geographic setting of these dunes.

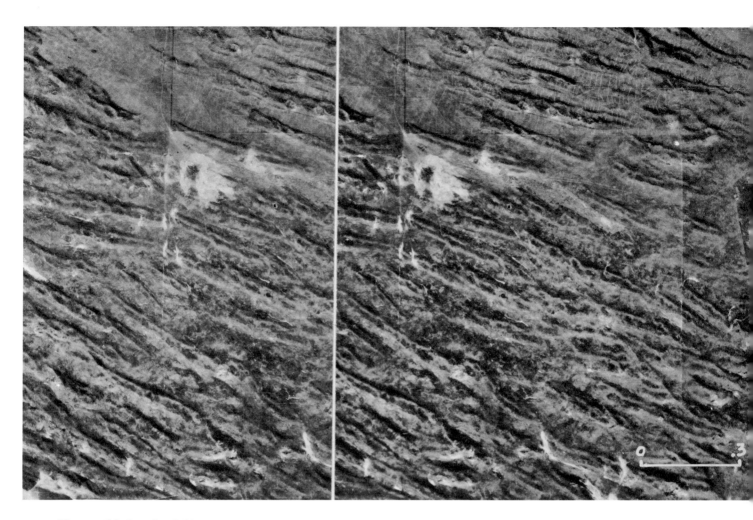

Figure 29.6.   Stabilized seif, or longitudinal, dunes near Lone Valley, Nebraska (1:20,000) (USGS)

a.   Given that the dominant wind is westerly (west is the bottom edge of the stereo pair) how would you explain the location of these dunes at the base of the Sangre de Cristo Mountains?

b.   What evidence is there for the assertion that water is helping to slow down the advance of the dunes into the area at the base of the mountains?

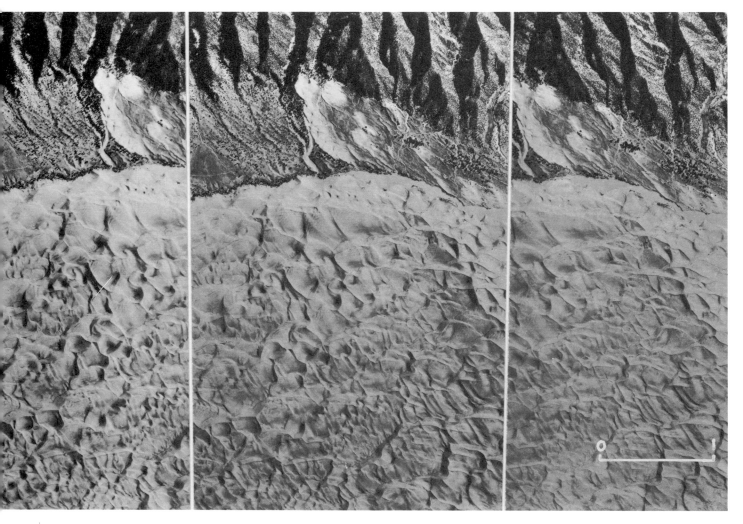

Figure 29.7. A portion of the Great Sand Dunes National Park flanking the Sangre de Cristo Mountains on the east side of the San Luis Valley in California (1:53,000) (USGS)

5. The availability of sand is a critical factor in the formation of dunes. List three different sources of sand for dune growth.

    a. _____

    b. _____

    c. _____

6. What evidence is there in Figure 29.4 that bushes, trees, or rocks are acting as obstructions to sand flow and forming obstacle dunes?

Name: _____

Laboratory Section: _____

Exercise 30

COASTAL LANDFORMS

The problems selected for study in this exercise show how coastlines are the result of the dynamic processes of marine erosion and deposition. Review in your textbook the following topics, which are essential background reading for these problems.

Wave erosion   Sand-spit formation
Longshore (beach) drifting   Cliff formation
Wave refraction

SHORELINE CLASSIFICATION

The variety of forms found in coastal areas is so large that classification of shoreline forms is a most useful aid to their understanding. The scheme outlined here is named after the man who developed it, F. P. Shepherd.

Shepherd's classification of coasts

1. Primary coasts
   a. Land-erosion coasts
      Ria coasts
      Drowned glacial-erosion coasts
      Drowned karst topography
   b. Subaerial deposition coasts
      River-deposition coasts
      Glacial-deposition coasts
      Wind-deposition coasts
      Landslide coasts
   c. Volcanic coasts
      Lava-flow coasts
      Tephra coasts (volcanic
         fragments)
      Volcanic-collapse or -explosion
         coasts
   d. Coasts shaped by diastrophic
      movement
      Faults coasts
      Fold coasts
      Sedimentary extrusions (salt
         domes, mud lumps)

2. Secondary coasts
   a. Wave-erosion coasts
      Wave-straightened coasts
      Coasts made irregular by wave
         erosion
   b. Marine-deposition coasts
      Barrier coasts
      Cuspate forelands
      Beach plains
      Mud flats or salt marshes
   c. Coasts built by organisms
      Coral-reef coasts
      Oyster-reef coasts
      Mangrove coasts
      Marsh-grass coasts

PROBLEMS

1. The intricate relationship between areas of erosion and sediment deposition in a marine environment is illustrated by Figure 30.1.

   a. What is the name given to this relatively flat-lying surface (see a on the photograph)? _____ How was it formed?

   b. There are several places where the feature identified in Problem 1a has been deeply eroded (see b on the photograph). What is your explanation for this differential erosion?

   c. What evidence is there to support the assertion that the dominant winds are westerly along this coast? (Hint: Check the vegetation.)

2. How would you classify the coastline in Figure 30.1 using Shepherd's coastal classification? Support your choice with evidence from the figure.

3. Bays and estuaries along this part of the Oregon coast (Figure 30.2) are partially closed by sand deposition. What do the spits and sand accumulation tell us about the availability of sediment along the coast?

4. a. What is responsible for the stabilization of the sand forming Netarts Spit (Figure 30.2)?

Figure 30.1.   The Oregon coast south of Waldport (Oregon State Highway Department)

b.   There are places on the spit where sand movement is active and the vegetation is being overwhelmed by the sand. Put an X on the photograph marking two places of sand advance.

c.   What prevents Netarts Spit from completely sealing off Netarts Bay?

d.   How can you locate the deep-water sections of the bay?

5.   In Figure 30.3 there is evidence of several marine terraces (ancient wave-cut platforms). Using a colored pencil, identify the terraces: 1 for the lowest terrace, 2 for the next highest, and so on.
6.   When the sea covered the wave-cut platforms, the steep slopes on the inland side of the platforms would have been called _____
7.   Mark an arrow (with WR printed beside it), to indicate an area on the stereo pair where wave refraction is evident.

Figure 30.2.   Netarts Spit, Oregon (Oregon State Highway Department)

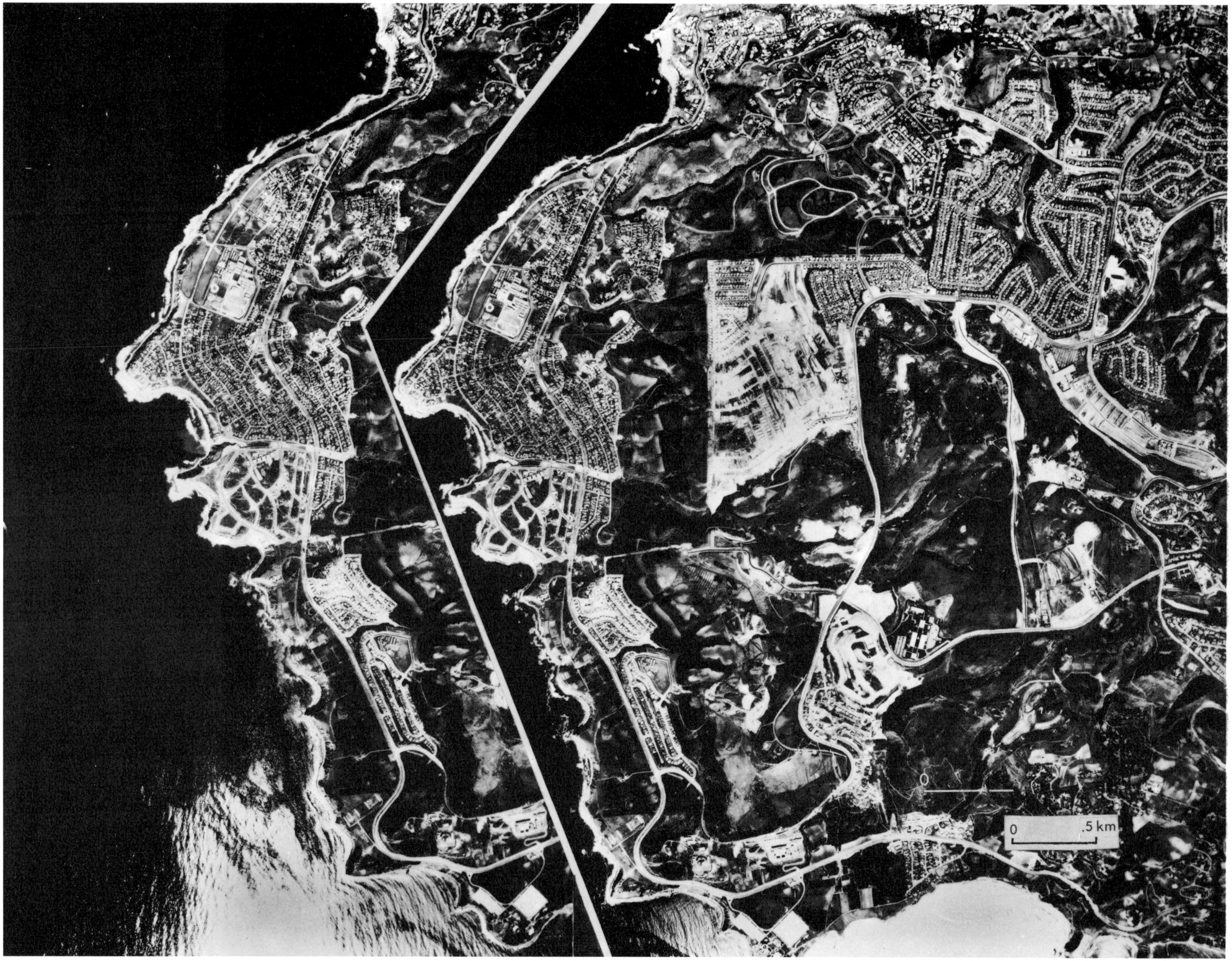

Figure 30.3. Palos Verdes Hills, Los Angeles, California (USGS)

Exercise 31

LAND-USE CHANGES AND ENVIRONMENTAL RESPONSES

This exercise is designed to illustrate the seemingly simple principle that a change in the environment in one place will have repercussions elsewhere. The environment is a single interrelated system, so changes do not occur in isolation.

Two contrasting landscapes—rural and urban—will be examined to illustrate the principle of interrelatedness.

URBAN LANDSCAPE: THE EFFECT OF URBANIZATION ON STREAMFLOW

A clear-cut trend of North American life is the growth and expansion of urban areas. The cities are spreading into the surrounding rural areas. The changes brought about by an increasingly urban population have environmental as well as socioeconomic impacts.

River basins are being covered by impermeable surfaces such as houses, roads, and parking lots. The effect on urban water resources has been dramatic as shown by the changes in

Streamflow—higher flood peaks, lower low flows - *greater difference*

Groundwater—falling water levels - *pumping for use*

Stream channels—increased erosion *gr. frequen higher flood peaks*

PROBLEMS

The watersheds in Figure 31.1 illustrate the impact of urbanization on a rural landscape. The hypothetical data in Table 31.1 represent the hydrographs resulting from two identical storms. Plot these data in on Figure 31.2, and identify the rural and urban hydrographs. Once the graph is completed, answer the following questions.

1. Which land-use condition gives rise to the greater peak flow?

2. a. *(earlier)* Why does one of the hydrographs peak more rapidly than the other? (Spell out the reasons.)

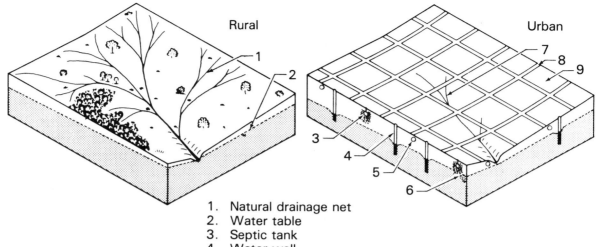

1. Natural drainage net
2. Water table
3. Septic tank
4. Water well
5. Storm sewer
6. Pollution of groundwater by septic tank
7. Reduction of the length of natural streams
8. Roads form an artificial drainage net
9. Increase in impermeability

Figure 31.1. **The urbanization of a rural watershed (From M. C. Roberts, 1972, "Watersheds in the rural-urban fringe,"** *National symposium on watersheds in transition.* **Fort Collins, Colorado: American Water Resources Association, pp. 388-393.)**

Table 31.1. **Streamflow Data for Two Storms of Identical Size**

Rural Watershed		Urban Watershed	
Time (hr) 1–2 August 1930	Discharge (cfs)	Time (hr) 15 July 1955	Discharge (cfs)
17.00	.25	13.00	.00
18.00	.50	13.42	.01
19.00	1.30	14.00	.33
20.00	2.60	14.33	2.00
21.00	2.93	15.00	3.30
22.00	2.62	15.18	4.20
23.00	2.10	15.36	4.70
24.00	1.65	16.00	4.33
		17.00	2.55
1.00	1.27	18.00	1.75
2.00	.95	19.00	1.17
3.00	.72	20.00	.75
4.00	.50	21.00	.50
5.00	.32	22.00	.25
6.00	.21	23.00	.10
7.00	.17	24.00	.00

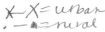

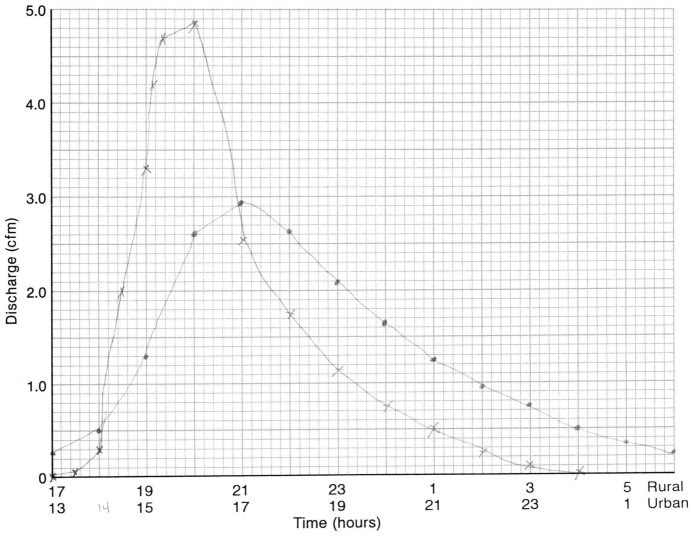

Figure 31.2. Graph on which to plot rural and urban discharge

b. What is the lag time between the two peaks?

3. What are the implications of this change in the flood peak (the highest point on the hydrograph) for the land directly adjacent to a major stream?

185

4. What is the ratio of the peak urban discharge to the peak rural one?

5. Why is there a higher discharge on the rural recessional curve than on the urban recessional curve?

RURAL LANDSCAPES: A COMPARISON OF FORESTED AND CLEAR-CUT WATERSHEDS

Human inhabitants modify rural landscapes, though the outcome is usually less dramatic than it is with an urbanized area.

This exercise deals with the effects of logging a forested watershed. When two watersheds, one with a forest cover and the other recently logged, are examined, it is found that the forested watershed will yield smaller volumes of total streamflow, the flood peaks will be smaller on the forested watershed than on the logged one, and the amount of sediment carried off the watershed will be inversely proportional to the vegetation cover. The forest manager, who must supervise logging of the land for which he is responsible, is often faced with the task of balancing demands that a watershed produce more water and that the land be kept with a forest cover for flood and erosion control. Environmental choices are rarely obvious or simple.

PROBLEMS

The hypothetical data in Table 31.2 show the effect of clear-cutting a watershed in 1947. Plot these data on Figure 31.3. Complete the graphs before answering the questions that follow.

6. Discuss the effects of clear-cutting the forest on water yield. What do these results imply about the management of forests for water supplies?

Table 31.2. Annual Precipitation, Annual Water Yield, and Annual Sediment Yield for a Forested Watershed

Year	Precipitation (in.)	Water Yield *runoff* (in.)	Sediment Yield (tons/acre/yr)
1940	47.1	4.5	5.3
1941	49.2	7.9	6.5
1942	48.9	5.6	6.1
1943	47.3	5.3	5.6
1944	48.3	5.7	6.3
1945	46.4	4.0	4.8
1946	48.1	5.3	6.2
1947	49.3	16.8	12.5
1948	47.4	19.4	25.8
1949	46.3	16.2	19.5
1950	48.4	16.9	17.4
1951	49.1	15.0	11.2
1952	46.1	10.1	9.8
1953	45.4	9.2	7.8
1954	47.3	9.3	8.2
1955	48.7	7.8	9.3
1956	46.4	9.1	7.1
1957	47.2	7.1	8.2
1958	46.3	6.3	7.2

7. It could be argued that the precipitation, rather than clear-cutting, is responsible for the increase in sediment yield. How would you check out this assertion with the data in Table 31.2?

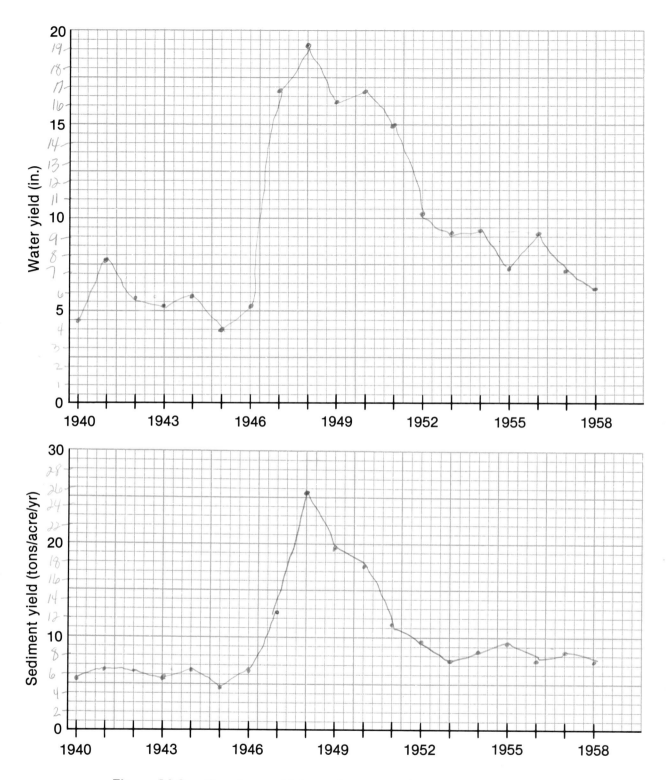

Figure 31.3. Graph on which to plot water yield and sediment yield

Exercise 32

THE FREQUENCY OF OCCURRENCE OF NATURAL EVENTS

One of the goals of the environmental sciences is to make accurate predictions about events such as floods (Figure 32.1), tornadoes, and extremely large rainfalls. However, the present level of understanding of these phenomena precludes precise prediction. It is simply not possible at this time to assert that a 6-in. rainfall will occur at a certain time and place.

The classical approach in science is to link every effect with its cause. This approach necessitates a thorough understanding of the processes at work, but for many, if not most, of the problems we encounter in geography this precise, deterministic approach cannot be used. The approach cannot be used because we have an inadequate understanding of the variables in a given problem and the interactions between them. Instead, physical geographers use probabilistic methods, such as the recurrence interval, for the analysis of natural events.

THE RECURRENCE INTERVAL

The *recurrence interval* (also called the return period) is the average interval of time within which a given flood will be equaled or exceeded once. A flood having a recurrence interval of 10 yr is one that has a 10% chance of recurring in any year, and one with a 100-yr recurrence interval (a 100-yr flood) has a 1% chance of recurring.

Table 32.1 is a listing of the highest flows that occurred on the Kyte River at Flagg Center, Illinois, for each year in the time period 1940–1950. A list of these annual, extreme flows is called the *annual series*.

Steps for calculating the recurrence interval for the data in Table 32.1 are as follows:
1. Rank the floods, giving the rank of 1 to the largest flood, and enter the results into column 3 of Table 32.1.
2. Calculate the recurrence interval for each flood, using the following formula:

$$T = \frac{n + 1}{m}$$

where T = recurrence interval (in years)
   n = number of years of record $= 11 + 1 = 12$ $\frac{12}{1} = 1$
   m = rank of the flood

Enter the results in Table 32.1 under column 4.

Figure 32.1   The flood of 12 March 1963 on the North Fork of the Kentucky River at Hazard, Kentucky. The recurrence interval of this flood was approximately 25 years. (From Louisville *Courier-Journal* 13 March 1963)

PROBLEMS

Plot each *T* value and its associated discharge on the graph paper in Figure 32.2, and fit a straight line through the data points. Use the completed graph to answer the following questions.

1.   In 1951 the peak flow of the river was found to be 2000 cfs. What is the recurrence interval of that flow? _____   *go to 2000 go over to line + that is recurrent.*

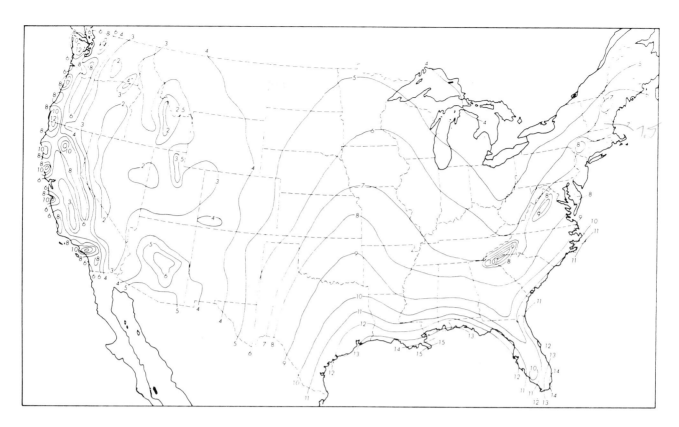

Figure 32.3. Map showing 24-hr rainfall with 100-yr recurrence interval. Rainfall amounts in inches; isopluvial interval varies. (U.S. Department of Commerce, Weather Bureau Technical Paper No. 40)

These pieces of information give dramatic evidence of the extremes of climatic conditions that can be expected. Not so spectacular are the extreme rainfalls of different durations that have been mapped for the United States and Canada in the following publications:

Bruce, J.P. 1968. *Atlas of rainfall intensity-duration frequency data for Canada.* Toronto: Department of Transport, Meteorological Branch Climatological Studies No. 8.

Hershfield, D.M. 1961. *Rainfall frequency atlas of the United Sates.* U.S. Weather Bureau Technical Paper No. 40.

These atlases have maps that show rainfalls of different durations (30 min, 1 hr, 2 hr, 3 hr, 24 hr, and so on) and different return periods. The great value of these maps is that they provide the user with extremes of rainfall for any location.

PROBLEMS

6. In which state, Florida or Minnesota, must the greatest care be taken in estimating precipitation for the construction of a reservoir? _____
Explain your answer.

7. Suggest a meteorological explanation for the very heavy rainfalls that occur along the Gulf coast.

8. From the isohyets, estimate the expected 100-yr 24-hr rainfall for your college's location. _____

9. The study of the impact of extreme geophysical events on human population is called natural-hazard research. List two natural hazards that have occurred in the last year in the vicinity of your college.
   a.
   b.

10. Droughts result in low streamflow. List three environmental impacts that result from unusually low flows and tell why you think they are a result of drought.

Name: _____

Laboratory Section: _____

Exercise 33

A CASE STUDY OF AN ENVIRONMENTAL HAZARD—LAND SUBSIDENCE IN LONG BEACH, CALIFORNIA

The subsidence of land is an environmental hazard caused by both human actions and natural processes; it varies in intensity from sudden drops in land elevation to movements so imperceptible that they can be sensed only by instruments. The effects of these ground-level changes on human activities, which can be severe, include

Flooding

Collapse of, or structural damage to, buildings

Buckling of roads and railroads

The shearing off of water and oil wells

This exercise examines the impact of oil-field development on Long Beach, California (Figure 33.1). Read over the whole exercise before you answer any of the questions.

Long Beach straddles part of a faulted, asymmetrical anticline that is the structure responsible for the oil reservoir forming the Wilmington Oil Field (Figure 33.2). Within 6 yr of the field's discovery in 1936, there were nearly 1000 producing wells; within the city limits the spacing of wells was so close that the density reached one well per 2.3 acres.

PROBLEMS

1. Plot the data in Table 33.1 on Figure 33.3. Connect the points with straight lines; use a colored pencil.

Land subsidence became evident as the oil field was intensely developed in the early 1940s (Table 33.2). Whereas at one time the land was above high-tide level, with subsidence parts of Terminal Island (Figure 33.1) were being inundated during high water. As the subsidence became more pronounced, diking and land-filling became necessary in conjunction with the structural raising of wharves and warehouses.

2. Using the graph (Figure 33.3) on which you have previously plotted oil production, insert the data from Table 33.2. You will find it advantageous to have a vertical scale such that the highest value will be below the oil-production line. Use a pencil of a different color for joining these.

The severity of the land subsidence problem required action, and in 1958 the city decided that the solution to the environmental problems lay with the restoration of pressure in the oil field. Consequently, a water-injection program was established with an injection rate of 750,000 barrels of salt water per day. Subsidence halted, and a few places even began rebounding.

Figure 33.1 Subsidence of the Wilmington Oil Field at Long Beach, California. Subsidence contours in ft. (Long Beach Department of Oil Properties)

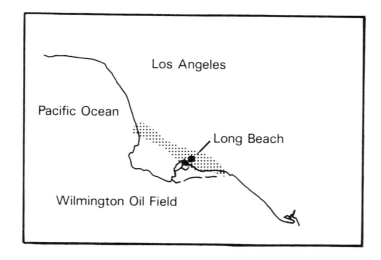

Figure 33.2. The Wilmington Oil Field, California

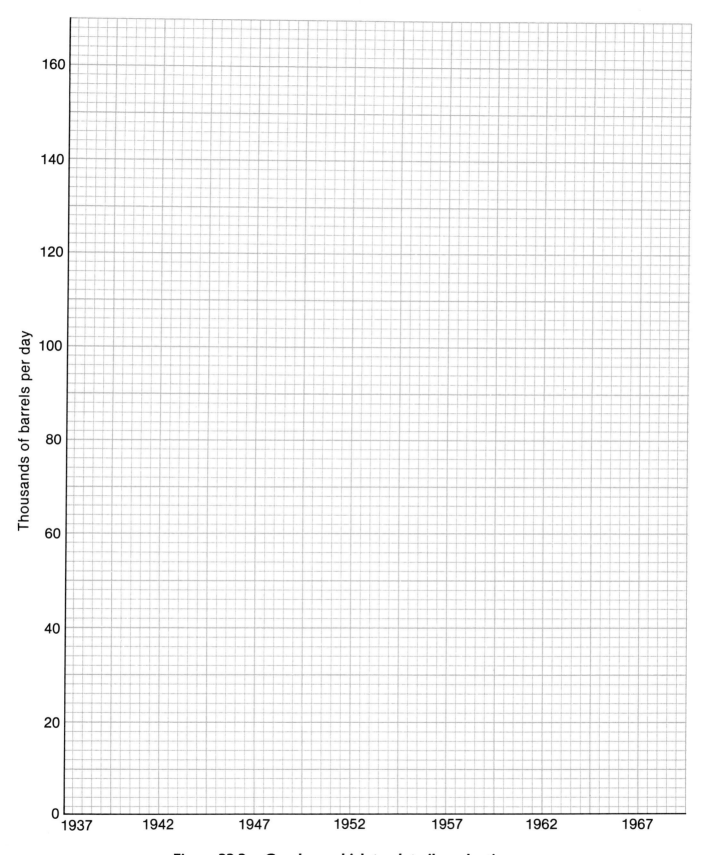

Figure 33.3.   Graph on which to plot oil production

Table 33.1. Oil Production in the Wilmington Oil Field: 1937–1968
(thousands of barrels/day)

1937	0	1945	99	1953	127	1961	76
1938	100	1946	93	1954	117	1962	82
1939	80	1947	117	1955	110	1963	90
1940	85	1948	136	1956	105	1964	97
1941	80	1949	127	1957	100	1965	97
1942	87	1950	110	1958	85	1966	102
1943	94	1951	142	1959	80	1967	150
1944	98	1952	133	1960	75	1968	167

Table 33.2. Subsidence Rate: 1947–1968
(in./yr)

1947	13.0	1953	24.0	1959	12.5	1965	2.5
1948	17.0	1954	20.0	1960	10.0	1966	3.0
1949	21.0	1955	17.5	1961	7.5	1967	0.5
1950	21.5	1956	18.3	1962	8.5	1968	0.5
1951	22.0	1957	15.0	1963	4.5		
1952	29.0	1958	14.0	1964	3.5		

3. You will now plot a third relationship on the graph: the information in Table 33.3. Join the points with a third colored pencil.

4. a. From 1947 until 1959 the oil-production rate and the rate of subsidence moved in tandem. Suggest an explanation for this.

   b. From 1959 onward, even though oil production increased, the rate of subsidence continued to fall. Explain this apparently contradictory outcome.

5. Suggest another type of land subsidence (other than in oil fields) where water injection might work to slow down or halt subsidence.

Table 33.3. Water Injection: 1958 –1968 (thousands of barrels/day)			
1958	35	1964	520
1959	160	1965	560
1960	250	1966	520
1961	290	1967	720
1962	360	1968	820
1963	440		

6. If you were the environmental manager of an area where oil was found close to the surface in relatively soft rocks, what measures would you take to monitor land subsidence?

7. On Figure 33.4, draw the profile X-Y from Figure 33.1, assuming a scale of 1 cm = 2000 m.

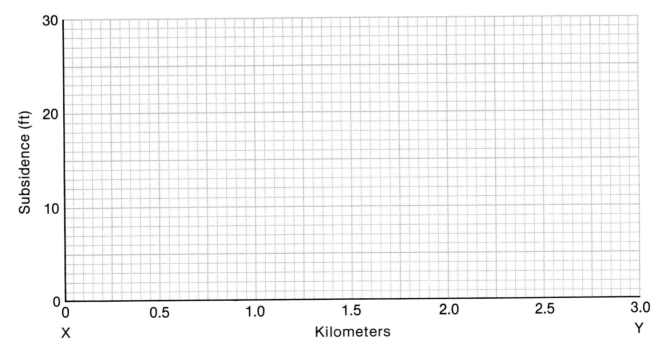

Figure 33.4. Graph on which to plot profile X-Y

Exercise 34

THE TIDES

Tides are a major fact of life along coastlines. The tides, which normally ebb and flow twice a day, are caused by several forces: the gravitational attraction of the moon, the gravitational attraction of the sun, and the centrifugal forces as the Earth-moon system revolves about the sun. The moon is far more important than the sun in determining the tides. The effect of the sun on the tides is such that it only modifies the lunar tide. The tides, although averaging twice a day, vary considerably with time and from place to place, but always in a predictable manner at a given location. This allows the tides to be predicted well in advance.

PROBLEMS

1. Using the data given in Table 34.1 complete Table 34.2.
2. What is the average time interval between high and low tides on October 14?

    _____

3. Explain why on some calendar days only one high tide or one low tide is indicated.

4. What is the mean tidal range (difference between high and low tide) for 14 and 15 October? _____
5. What is the mean tidal range for 21 and 22 October? _____
6. What is the time interval between high and low tides at Boston?_____
7. What is the earliest date following 22 October that the range again reaches or exceeds 13 ft.?

    _____

8. What is the time interval between the date of the highest tidal range in October and the highest tidal range in November?_____
9. Why are these tides higher than those in between?
10. On what date in December would you expect the spring tide to reach a maximum?

    _____

11. What is the maximum range on that date? _____
12. The range in the tide varies with location, largely because of the topography of the coastline. The range in tides is the lowest over the open ocean. Using the data in Table 34.3, determine the mean range of the spring tides at Chappaquiddick Island and at Nantucket Island.

    _____

Table 34.1 Times and Heights of High and Low Waters for Boston, Massachusetts, in 1981

October

Day	Time	ft	m	Day	Time	ft	m
1 Th	0051	9.6	2.9	16 F	0042	10.9	3.3
	0655	0.2	0.1		0648	-1.2	-0.4
	1307	9.8	3.0		1300	11.7	3.6
	1919	-0.1	0.0		1921	-2.0	-0.6
2 F	0132	9.2	2.8	17 Sa	0135	10.5	3.2
	0735	0.6	0.2		0738	-0.8	-0.2
	1346	9.6	2.9		1353	11.4	3.5
	2001	0.2	0.1		2013	-1.6	-0.5
3 Sa	0215	8.9	2.7	18 Su	0230	10.1	3.1
	0817	0.9	0.3		0832	-0.3	-0.1
	1428	9.3	2.8		1448	11.0	3.4
	2046	0.5	0.2		2110	-1.1	-0.3
4 Su	0259	8.5	2.6	19 M	0329	9.6	2.9
	0902	1.3	0.4		0931	0.2	0.1
	1515	9.0	2.7		1547	10.5	3.2
	2134	0.8	0.2		2211	-0.6	-0.2
5 M	0347	8.2	2.5	20 Tu	0430	9.2	2.8
	0951	1.6	0.5		1034	0.6	0.2
	1605	8.8	2.7		1652	10.0	3.0
	2227	1.0	0.3		2316	-0.2	-0.1
6 Tu	0440	8.0	2.4	21 W	0536	9.0	2.7
	1044	1.8	0.5		1139	0.8	0.2
	1658	8.7	2.7		1758	9.7	3.0
	2322	1.1	0.3				
7 W	0536	7.9	2.4	22 Th	0021	0.0	0.0
	1140	1.8	0.5		0642	9.0	2.7
	1753	8.8	2.7		1248	0.8	0.2
					1903	9.6	2.9
8 Th	0020	0.9	0.3	23 F	0125	0.0	0.0
	0632	8.1	2.5		0744	9.2	2.8
	1239	1.5	0.5		1349	0.6	0.2
	1848	9.0	2.7		2003	9.6	2.9
9 F	0114	0.6	0.2	24 Sa	0219	0.0	0.0
	0725	8.6	2.6		0839	9.4	2.9
	1334	1.0	0.3		1444	0.3	0.1
	1944	9.4	2.9		2058	9.6	2.9
10 Sa	0205	0.2	0.1	25 Su	0307	0.0	0.0
	0816	9.1	2.8		0924	9.7	3.0
	1426	0.4	0.1		1531	0.0	0.0
	2035	9.9	3.0		2145	9.6	2.9
11 Su	0253	-0.3	-0.1	26 M	0349	-0.1	0.0
	0904	9.8	3.0		1007	9.9	3.0
	1514	-0.3	-0.1		1615	-0.2	-0.1
	2125	10.4	3.2		2229	9.6	2.9
12 M	0340	-0.8	-0.2	27 Tu	0431	0.0	0.0
	0949	10.5	3.2		1044	10.0	3.0
	1604	-1.0	-0.3		1654	-0.4	-0.1
	2213	10.8	3.3		2308	9.5	2.9
13 Tu	0425	-1.2	-0.4	28 W	0507	0.1	0.0
	1036	11.1	3.4		1121	10.0	3.0
	1651	-1.6	-0.5		1733	-0.4	-0.1
	2302	11.0	3.4		2347	9.4	2.9
14 W	0511	-1.4	-0.4	29 Th	0546	0.3	0.1
	1124	11.5	3.5		1158	10.0	3.0
	1740	-2.0	-0.6		1812	-0.4	-0.1
	2351	11.0	3.4				
15 Th	0559	-1.4	-0.4	30 F	0026	9.2	2.8
	1211	11.7	3.6		0624	0.5	0.2
	1829	-2.1	-0.6		1235	9.8	3.0
					1851	-0.2	-0.1
				31 Sa	0103	9.0	2.7
					0703	0.7	0.2
					1314	9.6	2.9
					1932	0.0	0.0

November

Day	Time	ft	m	Day	Time	ft	m
1 Su	0145	8.7	2.7	16 M	0214	10.0	3.0
	0745	1.0	0.3		0813	-0.4	-0.1
	1356	9.4	2.9		1430	11.0	3.4
	2015	0.2	0.1		2052	-1.3	-0.4
2 M	0230	8.4	2.6	17 Tu	0312	9.6	2.9
	0828	1.3	0.4		0912	0.1	0.0
	1441	9.1	2.8		1529	10.4	3.2
	2102	0.5	0.2		2152	-0.7	-0.2
3 Tu	0318	8.2	2.5	18 W	0414	9.3	2.8
	0918	1.6	0.5		1014	0.6	0.2
	1528	8.9	2.7		1630	9.9	3.0
	2152	0.7	0.2		2255	-0.3	-0.1
4 W	0406	8.1	2.5	19 Th	0516	9.1	2.8
	1009	1.7	0.5		1119	0.8	0.2
	1620	8.8	2.7		1736	9.4	2.9
	2246	0.7	0.2		2356	0.1	0.0
5 Th	0459	8.2	2.5	20 F	0619	9.1	2.8
	1104	1.6	0.5		1224	0.8	0.2
	1715	8.8	2.7		1838	9.1	2.8
	2341	0.7	0.2				
6 F	0555	8.4	2.6	21 Sa	0055	0.3	0.1
	1202	1.3	0.4		0715	9.2	2.8
	1813	9.0	2.7		1324	0.6	0.2
					1942	9.0	2.7
7 Sa	0035	0.4	0.1	22 Su	0149	0.3	0.1
	0648	8.9	2.7		0809	9.4	2.9
	1300	0.8	0.2		1419	0.4	0.1
	1909	9.3	2.8		2033	9.0	2.7
8 Su	0128	0.0	0.0	23 M	0238	0.4	0.1
	0741	9.5	2.9		0855	9.6	2.9
	1355	0.1	0.0		1506	0.1	0.0
	2004	9.8	3.0		2122	9.0	2.7
9 M	0219	-0.4	-0.1	24 Tu	0319	0.4	0.1
	0832	10.3	3.1		0938	9.7	3.0
	1447	-0.7	-0.2		1551	-0.1	0.0
	2055	10.2	3.1		2204	9.0	2.7
10 Tu	0309	-0.9	-0.3	25 W	0401	0.4	0.1
	0919	11.0	3.4		1015	9.8	3.0
	1538	-1.4	-0.4		1631	-0.3	-0.1
	2148	10.5	3.2		2243	9.0	2.7
11 W	0357	-1.2	-0.4	26 Th	0441	0.4	0.1
	1009	11.5	3.5		1052	9.9	3.0
	1629	-2.0	-0.6		1710	-0.4	-0.1
	2239	10.8	3.3		2323	8.9	2.7
12 Th	0446	-1.4	-0.4	27 F	0518	0.5	0.2
	1058	11.9	3.6		1131	9.9	3.0
	1719	-2.4	-0.7		1748	-0.4	-0.1
	2332	10.8	3.3				
13 F	0535	-1.4	-0.4	28 Sa	0000	8.9	2.7
	1149	12.1	3.7		0557	0.6	0.2
	1810	-2.5	-0.8		1208	9.8	3.0
					1827	-0.4	-0.1
14 Sa	0023	10.7	3.3	29 Su	0039	8.8	2.7
	0625	-1.2	-0.4		0637	0.7	0.2
	1240	11.9	3.6		1246	9.7	3.0
	1902	-2.3	-0.7		1907	-0.3	-0.1
15 Su	0118	10.4	3.2	30 M	0120	8.6	2.6
	0718	-0.8	-0.2		0717	0.9	0.3
	1334	11.6	3.5		1329	9.5	2.9
	1956	-1.9	-0.6		1948	-0.1	0.0

December

Day	Time	ft	m	Day	Time	ft	m
1 Tu	0203	8.5	2.6	16 W	0251	9.7	3.0
	0801	1.1	0.3		0849	0.0	0.0
	1411	9.4	2.9		1507	10.3	3.1
	2034	0.1	0.0		2126	-0.8	-0.2
2 W	0248	8.4	2.6	17 Th	0349	9.4	2.9
	0848	1.2	0.4		0949	0.4	0.1
	1457	9.2	2.8		1606	9.7	3.0
	2121	0.2	0.1		2224	-0.3	-0.1
3 Th	0334	8.4	2.6	18 F	0445	9.1	2.8
	0937	1.3	0.4		1051	0.7	0.2
	1545	9.1	2.8		1705	9.1	2.8
	2211	0.3	0.1		2321	0.2	0.1
4 F	0427	8.5	2.6	19 Sa	0544	9.0	2.7
	1032	1.2	0.4		1153	0.8	0.2
	1643	9.0	2.7		1806	8.7	2.7
	2303	0.3	0.1				
5 Sa	0519	8.8	2.7	20 Su	0017	0.5	0.2
	1130	0.9	0.3		0639	9.0	2.7
	1739	9.1	2.8		1254	0.8	0.2
	2358	0.1	0.0		1903	8.4	2.6
6 Su	0612	9.3	2.8	21 M	0112	0.7	0.2
	1228	0.4	0.1		0731	9.1	2.8
	1836	9.2	2.8		1349	0.6	0.2
					1959	8.3	2.5
7 M	0053	-0.1	0.0	22 Tu	0202	0.8	0.2
	0707	9.9	3.0		0820	9.3	2.8
	1326	-0.2	-0.1		1439	0.4	0.1
	1933	9.5	2.9		2050	8.3	2.5
8 Tu	0146	-0.4	-0.1	23 W	0248	0.8	0.2
	0800	10.5	3.2		0904	9.4	2.9
	1422	-0.9	-0.3		1522	0.1	0.0
	2031	9.8	3.0		2135	8.4	2.6
9 W	0240	-0.8	-0.2	24 Th	0330	0.7	0.2
	0853	11.1	3.4		0945	9.6	2.9
	1516	-1.6	-0.5		1604	-0.1	0.0
	2126	10.1	3.1		2217	8.5	2.6
10 Th	0332	-1.0	-0.3	25 F	0412	0.7	0.2
	0945	11.6	3.5		1025	9.7	3.0
	1609	-2.1	-0.6		1645	-0.3	-0.1
	2220	10.3	3.1		2257	8.6	2.6
11 F	0423	-1.2	-0.4	26 Sa	0452	0.6	0.2
	1037	12.0	3.7		1105	9.8	3.0
	1702	-2.4	-0.7		1724	-0.4	-0.1
	2313	10.4	3.2		2336	8.6	2.6
12 Sa	0515	-1.3	-0.4	27 Su	0533	0.6	0.2
	1130	12.1	3.7		1143	9.8	3.0
	1753	-2.5	-0.8		1805	-0.5	-0.2
13 Su	0007	10.4	3.2	28 M	0015	8.7	2.7
	0607	-1.2	-0.4		0612	0.6	0.2
	1223	11.9	3.6		1223	9.8	3.0
	1845	-2.3	-0.7		1844	-0.5	-0.2
14 M	0101	10.2	3.1	29 Tu	0056	8.7	2.7
	0700	-0.9	-0.3		0653	0.6	0.2
	1316	11.5	3.5		1304	9.8	3.0
	1938	-1.9	-0.6		1924	-0.5	-0.2
15 Tu	0155	10.0	3.0	30 W	0137	8.8	2.7
	0753	-0.5	-0.2		0737	0.6	0.2
	1411	11.0	3.4		1346	9.7	3.0
	2032	-1.4	-0.4		2006	-0.4	-0.1
				31 Th	0220	8.8	2.7
					0823	0.6	0.2
					1432	9.5	2.9
					2052	-0.3	-0.1

Time meridian 75 degrees west. 0000 is midnight. 1200 is noon. Heights are referenced to mean low water.

Source: U.S. Department of Commerce. NOAA. Tide Tables, 1981. East coast of North America and South America, including Greenland.

13. What is the ratio of the range of the spring tide in Boston Harbor to that of Nantucket Island and Chappaquiddick Island? _____

14. Using a map of the Bay of Fundy area, explain the 43.6-ft range in the spring tides at Horton Bluff, Nova Scotia.

Table 34.2. Time and Height of Tides in Boston Harbor

	Time	Height	Time	Height	Time	Height	Time	Height
	14 October				**15–16 October**			
High	11:24	11.5	_____	_____	_____	_____	_____	_____
Low	05:11	− 1.4	_____	_____	_____	_____	_____	_____
Difference	6:13	12.9	_____	_____	_____	_____	_____	_____
	21 October				**22–23 October**			
High	_____	_____	_____	_____	_____	_____	_____	_____
Low	_____	_____	_____	_____	_____	_____	_____	_____
Difference	_____	_____	_____	_____	_____	_____	_____	_____

Table 34.3. Tidal Range and Mean Tidal Height for Selected Locations

Place	Tidal Range (ft) Mean	Spring	Mean Level of High Tide
Wasque Point, Chappaquiddick Island	1.1	1.4	0.6
Tom Nevers Head, Nantucket Island	1.2	1.4	0.6
New York City, the Battery	4.5	5.4	2.2
New York City, Coney Island	4.7	5.7	2.3
Boston Harbor	9.5	11.0	4.7
Steele Harbor Island, Maine	11.6	13.3	5.8
Eastport, Maine	18.2	20.7	9.1
Saint John, New Brunswick, Bay of Fundy, Nova Scotia	20.8	23.7	14.4
Spicer Cove, Chignecto Bay, Bay of Fundy, Nova Scotia	27.0	30.0	18.3
Spencers Island, Bay of Fundy, Nova Scotia	30.5	35.0	21.2
Horton Bluff, Avon River, Bay of Fundy, Nova Scotia	38.1	43.6	24.6

Exercise 35

SPATIAL DISTRIBUTION AND CONTROLS ON INDIVIDUAL PLANT SPECIES

This exercise and the one that follows are designed to show both the complexities and the regularities inherent in the geography of plants. Rather than starting off with the involved interactions of the ecosystem, these exercises will concentrate on the individual plant species.

SPECIES

"Although each plant is in some way morphologically unique, careful examination of a large number of plants reveals that these tend to fall into a number of fairly distinct categories on the basis of external appearance" (M. C. Kellman, 1980, *Plant geography,* 2nd ed., London: Methuen, p. 6). These categories based on morphological and physiological characteristics are called *species*. A species is a group of cross-pollinating individuals existing in a similar environment.

THE SPECIES AND THE ENVIRONMENT

The individual plant reflects the adaptation of a given species to its environment. For a plant to thrive, it must have a sufficient supply of nutrients and tolerable environmental conditions. The physical factors influencing plant growth include the following major ones:

Temperature	Solar radiation
Soil moisture	Atmospheric gases
Fire	Soil
Humidity	Wind

In evaluating these factors, note that plants *adapt* to the environment and *modify* it. Further, interaction with other plants can help a plant adapt to its surroundings.

THE RANGE OF A PLANT SPECIES

Given the limiting influence of nutrient and environmental factors, a plant will occur over a limited area. This region or spatial distribution is called the *range* of a species. Conceptually, the range of a plant has two aspects: *potential range* and *actual range*. The potential range of a plant is the area that a plant, given its physiological properties, should be able to grow in. However, the actual range of a plant is much less than its potential because of such constraints as the limited ability to the plant to migrate from its source area to all parts of the range. At the extremities of the range, the plant is exposed to greater variance in environmental conditions. Complicating the picture even further is the fact that a species adapts differently in different parts of the range. For example, the Douglas fir growing in central California is far more susceptible to frost (in its early years of growth) than the Douglas fir of central British Columbia.

PROBLEMS

Eastern Hemlock (*Tsuga canadensis*). Eastern hemlock is found in areas with humid, cool climates, though at the limits of the range, average annual precipitation is as low as 28 in. (711 mm). In the western and southern parts of the range, topography is a crucial factor, for hemlock is restricted to cool valleys and north-facing slopes.

1. What was the migration rate (meters per year) of hemlock between the locations X and Y in Figure 35.1? _____

2. In what part of the range is hemlock expanding? _____

3. Where is the range contracting? _____

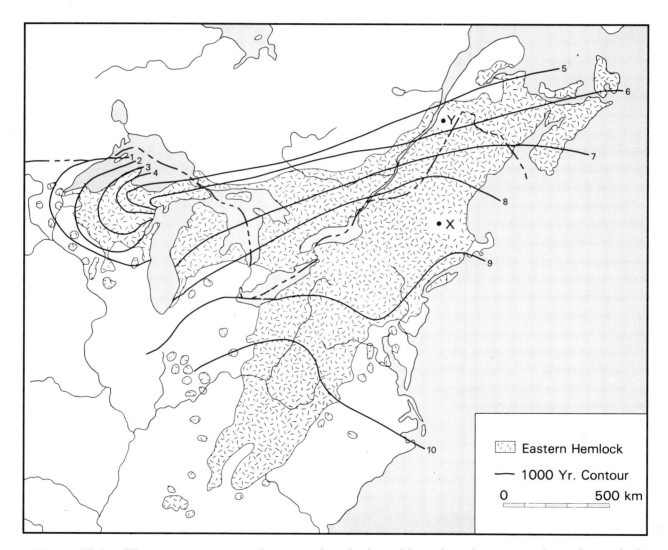

Figure 35.1. The present range of eastern hemlock and its migration route since the end of the last glaciation. Isochrons represent thousands of years before present. (Isochrons are derived from M. B. Davis, 1976, *Geoscience and man*, 13:13-26)

4. Examine the lines of hemlock migration and then answer the following questions:
   a. Did the eastern hemlock migrate more rapidly between 1000 and 2000 years ago or between 9000 and 10,000 years ago? _____

   b. The northern migration of eastern hemlock followed the retreat of _____.
   c. Place on Figure 35.1 a line marking the southern boundary of the Wisconsin ice at its maximum extent.
5. Suggest an explanation for the peninsula-shaped extension of eastern hemlock into the southeastern states.

Pollen Diagram Interpretation
6. What were the dominant species in the area of this lake (Figure 35.2) up until 6000 years before the present?

7. a. Spruce has a bimodal frequency distribution. Explain.

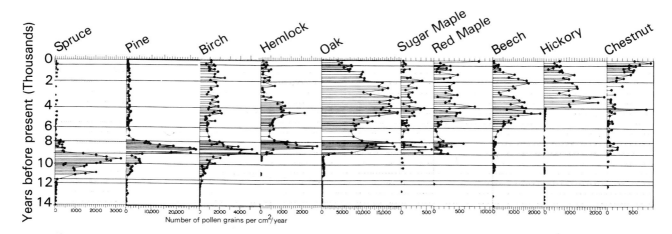

Figure 35.2. Accumulation of pollen in Rogers Lake, Connecticut (After M. B. Davis et al., 1973. *Quaternary plant ecology*. London: Blackwell)

b. Has spruce been declining or increasing in importance since 4000 years before the present?

8. Describe how Figure 35.2 shows the changing nature of the natural vegetation around this lake over a 14,000-year time span.

9. Using your textbook, compare and contrast the maps of climate and natural vegetation. With that general information in mind, examine Figure 35.2 and write a paragraph on the climatic implications of this data.

Geographical Scale and the Plant Species.

10. a. Which levels of the hierarchy (Figure 35.3) represent continuous distributions?

b. Which levels of the hierarchy represent point distributions?

c. At which level can you associate the occurrence of *Tetraphis* with a distinctive feature rather than just a point in space?

11. The levels of the range for *Tetraphis* (Figure 35.3) are governed by different environmental limiting factors. Insert the correct hierarchy level [*continent, cluster,* or *locality*] beside each limiting factor.

Limiting Factors	Hierarchy Level
Relative humidity	_____
Temperature, relative humidity, oceanic effects	_____
Shady conditions, pH variations	_____

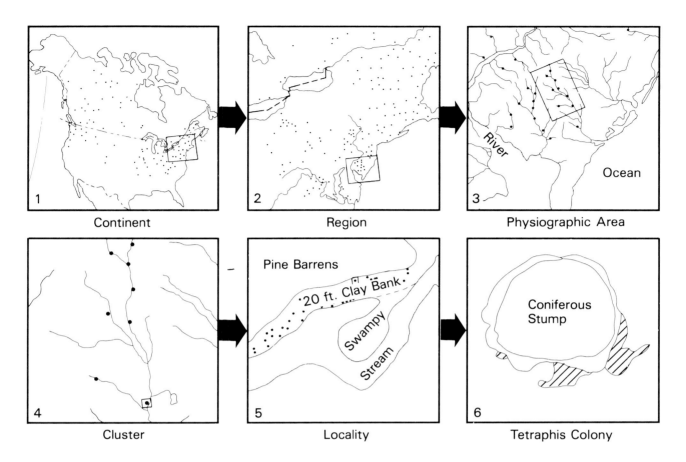

Figure 35.3. Maps of *Tetraphis* showing its spatial distribution at differing geographic scales (Adapted from R. T. T. Forman, 1964, *Ecological monographs*, 34: 1-25)

12. Discuss three different reasons why the theoretical and actual ranges of a plant species rarely coincide.

Exercise 36

THE VEGETATION OF A REGION

When a geographer examines the physical landscape of a region, the type and spatial pattern of the natural vegetation cover is of great importance. For it is this cover that can give insights into the potential and actual forest resources and agricultural activities of the region.

A biotic *community* is any grouping of plants and animals living in a limited area. It is mutually sustaining, with a close interdependence between the organic components that make it up. Communities range in size from a cluster of organisms on a decaying log to vegetation regions occupying a fifth of Canada. Most communities are influenced by one species or group of species called *dominants*.

Over time, regional climates and zonal soils will join to form large communities called *biomes*. This term applies to both plants and animals, but when the plant species are referred to alone, then *plant formation* is used by some biogeographers. In a biome the *climax vegetation* is uniform in appearance, though there can be variation in the dominant species in widely scattered parts of the biome. The boundaries between biomes are zones of change called *ecotones*.

PROBLEMS

1. Using Figure 36.1, name the biome your college town is situated in. _____

For the following questions, study Figure 36.1 and the maps of soils and climate of North America in your textbook.

2. Complete the following table:

Biome	Dominant Climate	Zonal Soils
Coniferous forest	_____	_____
Tropical rainforest	_____	_____
Summer-green deciduous forest	_____	_____
Desert (dry) scrub	_____	_____

3. a. What is the popular name used in Canada to identify the grassland biome?

   b. What is the popular name used in the United States to identify the grassland biome?

4. The map of biomes (Figure 36.1) shows a largely east-west trend in Canada but a north-south trend in the United States. How do you account for this?

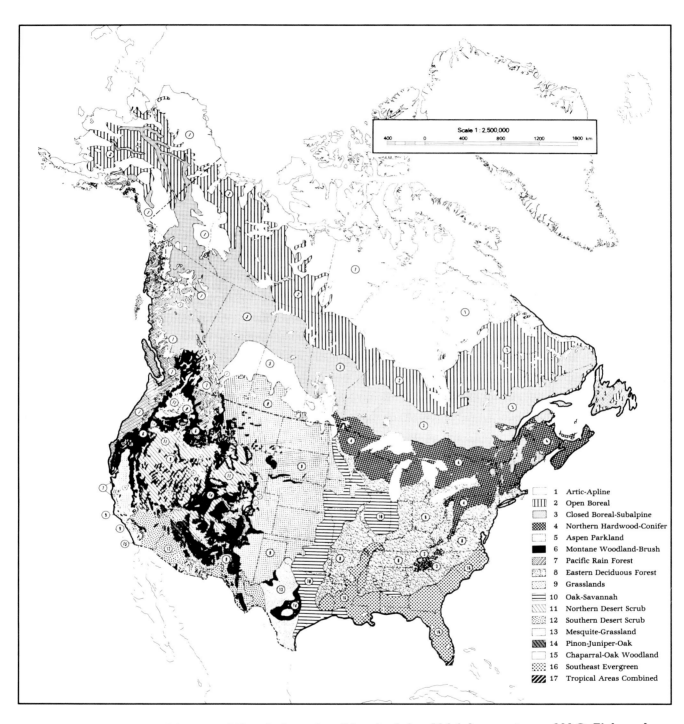

Figure 36.1. The biomes of North America (Map by John Aldrich, courtesy of U.S. Fish and Wildlife Service)

The legend of the map reads:

1 Artic-Apline
2 Open Boreal
3 Closed Boreal-Subalpine
4 Northern Hardwood-Conifer
5 Aspen Parkland
6 Montane Woodland-Brush
7 Pacific Rain Forest
8 Eastern Deciduous Forest
9 Grasslands
10 Oak-Savannah
11 Northern Desert Scrub
12 Southern Desert Scrub
13 Mesquite-Grassland
14 Pinon-Juniper-Oak
15 Chaparral-Oak Woodland
16 Southeast Evergreen
17 Tropical Areas Combined

Scale 1 : 2,500,000

5. The major grassland biome in North America (check your answers to question 3) stretches from the U.S.–Mexican border in Texas to central Saskatchewan. What are the *limiting factors* on its eastern, western, and northern boundaries?

6. The mountain chains of western North America show distinct vegetational zonation. Describe this zonation with the aid of a diagram.

7. South-central California is in the chaparral biome. A similar type of vegetation exists around the Mediterranean Sea. What are the reasons for the similarity between the two widely separated areas?

8. Figure 36.2B is a north–south transect across North America.
   a. What is the major climatic factor influencing this vegetational transect?

   b. Identify an ecotone. Clearly mark your answer on Figure 36.2.

   c. Where is oak-hickory forest located in North America (Figure 36.2)?

9. Define the following:
   a. Succession

   b. Xerophytes

Mesophytic forest Oak-hickory forest Oak woodland Prairie Dry grasslands Desert

(A)

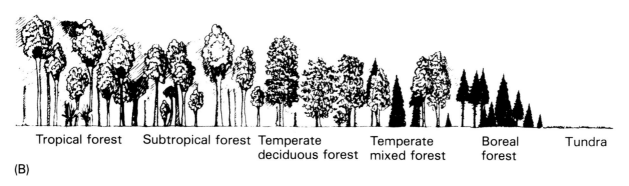

Tropical forest Subtropical forest Temperate deciduous forest Temperate mixed forest Boreal forest Tundra

(B)

Figure 36.2.   (A) An east–west transect across North America along the 35th parallel. (B) A north–south transect beginning in Mexico and ending at the Arctic Ocean (Figure 17.3, p. 538, in _Ecology and field biology_, 2nd ed., by Robert Leo Smith. Copyright 1966, 1974 by Robert Leo Smith. By permission of Harper and Row, publishers)

    c.   Tundra

    d.   Zonal soils

10.   Compare and contrast the vegetational base of the forest industry in western Canada and the Pacific Northwest with that of the southeastern states of the United States.

11.   The transect in Figure 36.2A is largely a function of precipitation. Explain.

Name: _____

Laboratory Section: _____

Exercise 37

SOIL—A REVIEW

One of the most critical parts of the physical landscape, at least as far as humans are concerned, is soil. This is the material that forms the outer "rind" of most of the world's land surfaces. Its relevance to us is evident in that this is the medium that ultimately determines much of our supply of food, shelter, and fiber. For the geographer who is interested in land-human relationships, knowledge of the soil is a must.

This exercise is designed to review the major properties of soil.

DEFINITION

For some people definitions hide more than they reveal, so we offer two definitions:

Soil is the collection of natural bodies occupying portions of the Earth's surface that supports plants and that has properties due to the integrated effect of climate and living matter, acting upon parent material, as conditioned by relief, over periods of time. (USDA, 1951, *Soil survey manual*, Agricultural Handbook No. 18, p. 8)

Soil is what plants grow in. (G. V. Jacks, 1954, *Soil*. London: Thomas Nelson and Sons, p. 1)

SOIL PROFILES

Every mature soil has a profile. This is revealed by the layering effect we can observe in road cuts, trenches, or quarries when we closely examine the makeup of the earth materials from the surface down. These layers, or *horizons,* can be used to distinguish one soil from another. They differ in various combinations of color, texture, structure, and permeability. Most soils, but not all, have three major horizons identified by the letters A, B, and C. These horizons are often subdivided, as for example: A_{00}, A_1, B_2.

A Hypothetical Soil Profile (Figure 37.1). The A horizon is that part of the soil profile containing the greatest quantity of organic matter. Water infiltrating into the soil will move through the A horizon removing (leaching) soluble material and clay particles. The leached material is deposited in the underlying B horizon. With its higher clay content, this horizon tends to be more compact and harder than either A or C horizons. Further, the B horizon is often intermediate in color between those above and below.

The C horizon is the decayed, broken-down rock material from which the overlying layers are formed. The frequently lighter-colored C horizon is the *parent material* of a given soil.

Simplified Soil Profiles. Figure 37.2 illustrates four soils found in many parts of the world. It is quite clear that the type and variety of horizons differ from soil to soil.

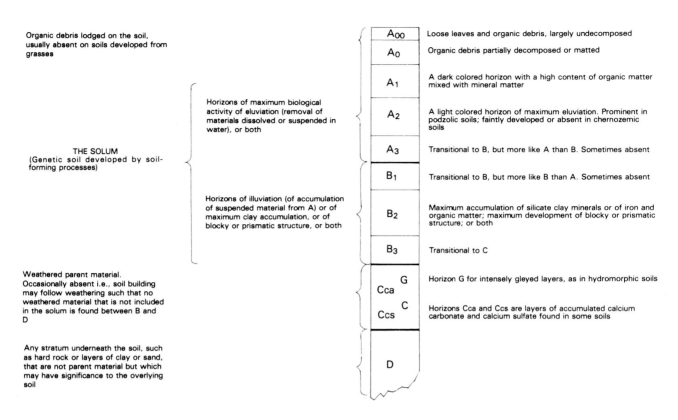

Figure 37.1. Hypothetical soil profile having all the principal horizons (USDA, 1951, *Soil survey manual*, Agricultural Handbook No. 18, p. 175)

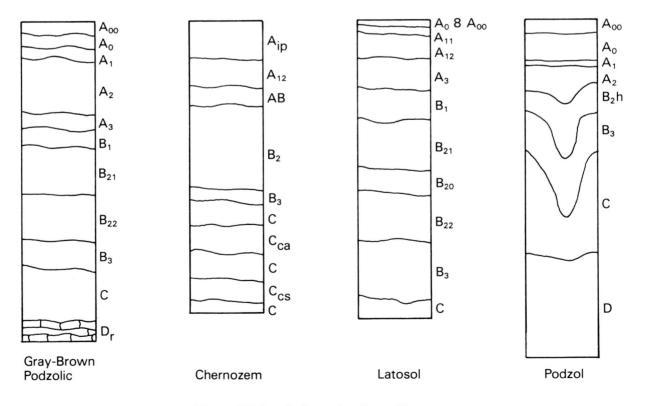

Figure 37.2. Selected soil profiles

THE U.S. SOIL CLASSIFICATION SYSTEM

The material in the previous sections of this exercise reflects the terminology of the old U.S. soil classification. This terminology is retained here because it still is widely used. It is found in the older soil reports, and it contains soil taxa terms used by the Food and Agriculture Organization of the United Nations and by the Canadian soil system.

The new soil classification (U.S. Department of Agriculture, Agricultural Handbook No. 436, 1975) has introduced a completely different terminology from that previously used. In this new approach emphasis is placed on the identification of two types of diagnostic soil horizons: first, the *epipedon*, which is formed in the upper part of the soil and contains an appreciable amount of organic matter; and second, the subsurface horizons (the names of these horizons are listed in Appendix C).

SOIL FORMATION

The formation of a soil is a complex process involving so many factors that it is extremely difficult to separate one from another. One writer has succinctly put it, "Soils are the product of their heredity and environment." Despite the difficulties of estimating their effects in an individual soil, it is possible to separate five major factors in soil formation: climate, living organisms, parent material, topography or landforms, and time.

Climate. The importance of climate to soil formation is clearly demonstrated by the way in which the world's major soil regions follow the distribution of climates. It is the interaction with temperature and precipitation that causes the breakdown of rock material.

Living organisms. The organic content of a soil is directly related to the activity of plants and animals. These, in turn, are functionally related to climate. For example, the luxuriant growth of the equatorial rainforest is a direct outcome of the high temperatures and precipitation of the equatorial climate.

Parent material. The weathering of bedrock reflects the composition of the actual rock material, so that some rocks break down rapidly and others exceedingly slowly. Some rocks, like limestone, have such distinctive characteristics that they are frequently associated with certain types of soil.

Topography (landforms). The surface of the earth is rarely completely flat. Hence, most soils are formed on sloping land. The position of a soil on a slope will greatly influence its drainage and erosion characteristics. The movement of water is rapid over and through soils on steep slopes, while there is a tendency for soils on flat areas to be badly drained. Topography, therefore, is a ubiquitous factor responsible for the minor fluctuations in soil.

Time. Soils do not form in a couple of days. Depending upon the nature of the other soil-forming properties, the time for a soil to be formed will vary. From fresh bedrock to several feet of soil is a process that requires time for weathering and time for the establishment of pioneering plant life.

SOIL PROPERTIES

When a soil is studied in the field, the observer will note certain rather obvious properties like color and texture; he will recognize that these vary from place to place. Knowledge of these characteristics will permit wise use and management of soils.

Color. This is one of the most noticeable features of a soil. A soil is rarely characterized by one color but by several, because the soil horizons usually have individual colors. In general, the colors of the upper horizons are darker than the lower horizons, for these (the upper) contain greater amounts of organic matter, which gives rise to black and brown colors. Red colors reflect unhydrated iron oxide and are typical of both well-drained locations and semiarid areas. Iron oxide also can give rise to yellow soils, though this color is often associated with higher rainfalls than the red.

Texture. The texture of a soil expresses the relative proportions of silt, sand, and clay. To express these three variables at one time, a triangular graph is used (Figures 37.3A and B). The corners of the

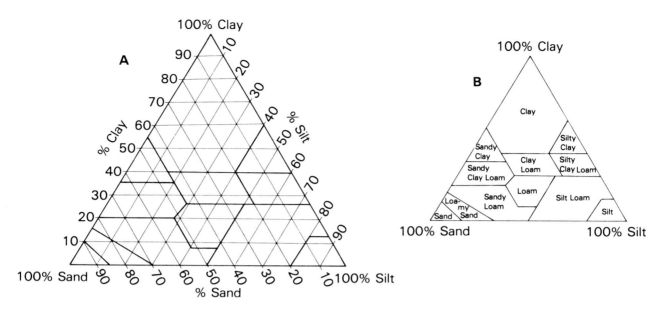

Figure 37.3.   Soil texture

triangle represent 100% silt, sand, and clay. The texture triangle (37.3B) is divided into units to which are applied names that make the comprehension of texture classes much easier.

Example: What is the textural class of a soil with 20% clay and 70% silt? (To read the texture triangle, follow the lines in accord with the tilt of the numbers.)

Answer: Silt loam.

Structure.   This property of a soil refers to shapes taken by clusters of soil particles. A *ped* is a naturally occurring cluster or aggregate of soil particles. Figure 37.4 illustrates some common types of soil structure. The usefulness of a soil with respect to crop production is largely a function of fertility and soil structure. Structure is one of the properties of soil having a direct bearing on the soil's moisture-retention capabilities. For example, where the soil peds are very loose, water will move through the soil too rapidly to be of use to the root systems of crops. Hence, these are considered droughty soils.

Air and water content.   A soil has its own atmosphere. For a soil to develop (in terms of both soil formation and plant growth), air must be held in the pore spaces. Many chemical and biological changes cannot take place without air. The volume of air in a soil is directly linked to its water content. The rate of percolation of water downward through the soil is a function of soil texture.

Organic content.   Though last in this list of soil properties, the organic content of the soil plays an important role in soil formation. When a soil is immature, it consists mainly of mineral particles derived from the parent material. Over time the organic content will increase as vegetation firmly establishes itself on the immature soil. Differences in the amount of organic matter in the vertical profile influence the degree of horizon differentiation.

PROBLEMS

1.   You have discovered that a soil has

Clay	10%
Silt	30%
Sand	60%

Name the soil in terms of a texture class. _____

Kind of Structure	Description		Horizon
Crumb 	Aggregates are small, porous, and weakly held together	Nearly spherical, with many irregular surfaces	Usually found in surface soil or A horizon
Platy 	Aggregates are flat or plate-like, with horizontal dimensions greater than the vertical. Plates overlap, usually causing slow permeability		Usually found in subsurface or A₂ horizon of timber and claypan soil
Angular Blocky or Cube-Like 	Aggregates have sides at nearly right angles, tend to overlap	Nearly block-like, with 6 or more sides. All 3 dimensions about the same	
Prismatic 	Without rounded caps	Prism-like with the vertical axis greater than the horizontal	Usually found in subsoil or B horizon
Columnar 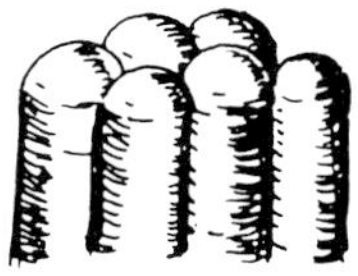	With rounded caps		
Structure Lacking, Single Grain	Soil particles exist individually (as in sand) and do not form aggregates		Usually found in substratum or C horizon
Massive	Soil material clings together in large uniform masses (as in loess)		

Figure 37.4. Selected soil structures

2. Suggest ways in which a soil profile may be truncated.

3. Name the common mineral most resistant to weathering. _____
4. What effect does the addition of organic matter (humus) have on a sandy soil?

5. What kind of soil (in terms of texture) would you expect in the following environments?
   Outwash plain _____
   Floodplains _____
   On limestone _____
6. Use a world soil map for the following questions.
   a. What soil type is most typical of steppes or prairies? _____
   b. What is the typical soil of the tropics? _____
   c. Where are podzols found?

   d. What is an alluvial soil and where is it found?

7. Of soil texture and soil structure, which can be most readily modified by farming?

8. The black soils of the prairies contain calcium carbonate ($CaCO_3$), but the occurrence of this mineral in soils of more humid areas is rare. Explain why. (The exercise on limestone landforms will be helpful here.)

9. In your textbook (or atlas), study the world maps of climate, soils, and vegetation. Then answer the following questions.
   a. What climates are associated with prairie or steppe soils?

   b. The coniferous forests that extend across the northern hemisphere correlate with which soil and climatic groups?

   c. Where are latosols (laterites) found?

   d. What is the great soil group of the area in which your college is located?

Exercise 38

SOILS AND THE LANDSCAPE

One of the most useful ways of summarizing soil information is in the form of a map. From the map it is possible to detect the spatial relationships between soils and the larger features of the landscape. This exercise is designed to show the relationship between soils and the landforms of a region.

SOURCES OF SOIL MAPS

Detailed soil maps of the United States are published on a county basis by the U.S. Department of Agriculture; these maps are accompanied by detailed soil descriptions and interpretations; this exercise will use the *Allen County, Indiana, soil survey report* (1969). The best way to check the availability of soil maps for a particular area is to contact the local county extension agent (USDA) or the agricultural experiment stations located at many land-grant universities. In Canada, soil maps can be obtained from the Soil Research Institute, Agriculture Canada, Ottawa, Ontario, Canada K1A 0C6.

THE GENERAL SOIL MAP

A USDA soil survey of a county will contain both a generalized map (see Figure 38.1) and a set of detailed maps. The detailed maps show the distribution of a *soil series,* which is a group of soils having similar soil horizons. To facilitate mapping, a soil series is usually subdivided into *soil types.*

For example, within a series, all the soils having a surface layer of the same texture belong to one soil type. Miami silt loam and the Miami loam are two soil types of the Blount Series, the differentiation within the series, therefore, being based on texture.

The detailed soil maps are valuable for the precise work dealing with conservation measures, land-capability studies, and the like, but it is the general soil that gives a person wanting an overall view of an area the most help. The *soil association* is a grouping of soils giving a greater degree of generalization than the soil-series maps. Grouping soils in this way reduces the complexity of the soil map, and the patterns of the soil groups become more obvious (often revealing a relationship to major physiographic features).

The relationships of two soil associations to the landforms (floodplains and terraces; rolling till uplands) of a part of Allen County are portrayed in Figure 38.2.

These diagrams are provided in the soil-survey reports to give a more detailed view of the topographic positions of the soil associations. The associations portrayed in Figure 38.2 are the Eel-Martinsville-Genesee Association and the Morley-Blount Association.

Eels-Martinsville-Genesee Association. This association consists of narrow bottomlands and fairly wide stream terraces. Eel and Genesee soils are on the bottomlands, and Martinsville soils are on the stream terraces. Eel soils make up about 45% of the acreage, Martinsville soils about 45%, and Genesee soils about 10%. The association occupies about 4% of the county.

Eel soils are nearly level and are moderately well drained. They have a surface layer of dark grayish brown loam or silt loam, underlain mostly by dark yellowish brown, mottled silty clay loam.

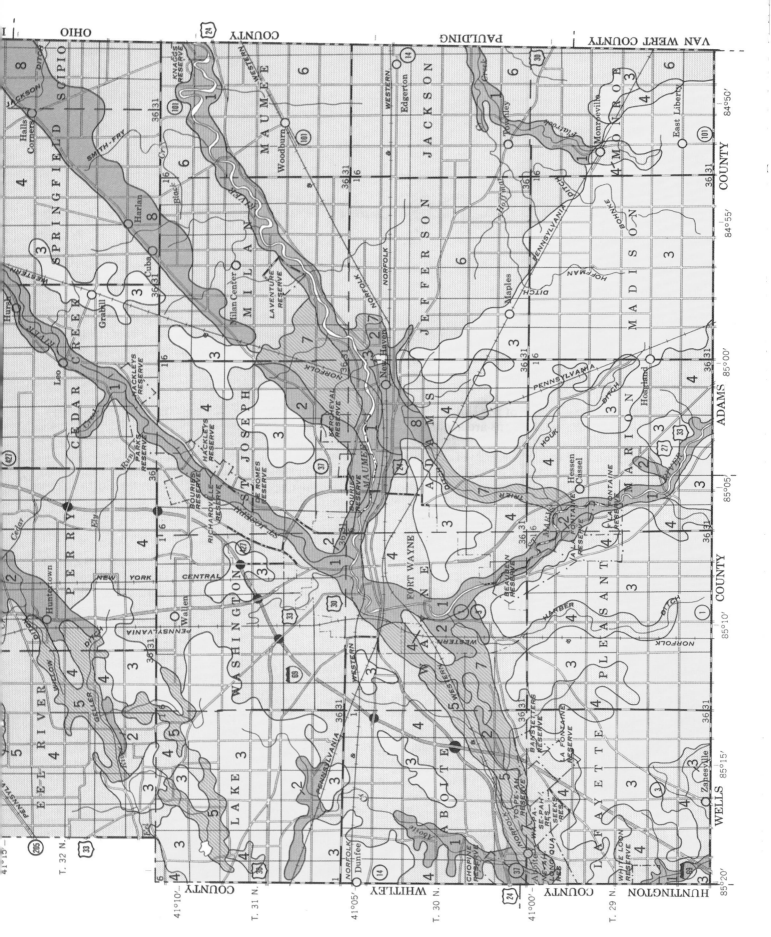

Figure 38.1. General soil map, Allen County, Indiana (USDA, Soil Conservation Service)

General Soil Map, Allen County, Indiana
Soil Associations

1   Eel-Martinsville-Genesee association: Deep, well-drained and moderately well drained, nearly level to moderately sloping, medium-textured and moderately fine textured soils on bottom lands and stream terraces

2   Martinsville-Belmore-Fox association: Deep, well-drained, nearly level to moderately sloping, medium-textured and moderately coarse textured soils on stream terraces and beach ridges

3   Blount-Pewamo association: Deep, somewhat poorly drained to very poorly drained, nearly level and gently sloping, medium-textured and moderately fine textured soils on uplands

4   Morley-Blount association: Deep, moderately well drained and somewhat poorly drained, nearly level to steep, medium-textured soils on uplands

5   Carlisle-Willette association: Deep, very poorly drained mucky soils in upland depressions

6   Hoytville-Nappanee association: Deep, somewhat poorly drained to very poorly drained, nearly level, medium-textured to fine-textured soils on uplands

7   Lenawee-Montgomery-Rensselaer association: Deep, very poorly drained, nearly level, medium-textured to fine-textured soils on uplands, in drainageways, and on stream terraces

8   Rensselaer-Whitaker association: Deep, somewhat poorly drained to very poorly drained, nearly level and gently sloping, moderately coarse textured to moderately fine textured soils on uplands and stream terraces

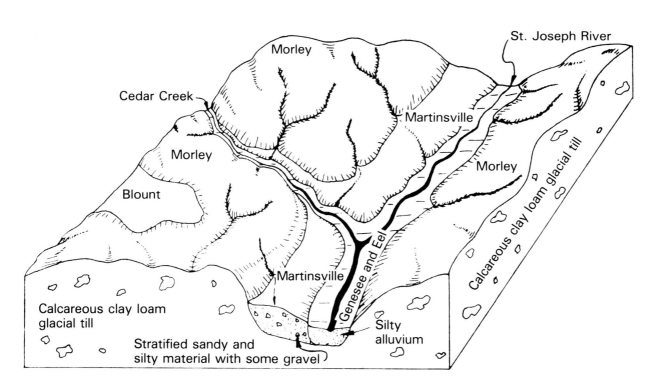

Figure 38.2. Topographic positions of the Eels-Martinsville-Genesee and the Morley-Blount associations (USDA, 1969, *Allen County, Indiana, soil survey report*, pp. 2-5)

Martinsville soils are nearly level to moderately sloping and are well drained. They have a surface layer of grayish brown and dark grayish brown loam or silt loam and a subsoil that is mostly yellowish brown and reddish brown sandy clay loam.

Genesee soils are nearly level and are well drained. They have a surface layer of dark grayish brown loam to silty clay loam underlain by dark yellowish brown and yellowish brown loam.

The soils in this association are well suited to meadow and to corn, soybeans, and small grain. Occasional flooding on the Eel and Genesee soils may destroy or severely damage small grain. The Martinsville soils are subject to erosion.

Morley-Blount Association. This association is in upland areas, mostly in the northern two thirds of the county but not on the Lake Maumee Plain. Morley soils make up about 50% of the acreage, and Blount soils about 40%. Small areas of Pewamo soils and of other soils make up the remaining 10%. This association occupies about 40% of the county.

Morley soils are gently sloping to steep and are moderately well drained. They have a surface layer of grayish brown and very dark grayish brown silt loam and a subsoil that is mostly dark yellowish brown and brown clay and is mottled in the lower part.

Blount soils are nearly level and gently sloping and are somewhat poorly drained. They have a surface layer of dark grayish brown and very dark grayish brown mottled silty clay and clay.

The more gently sloping soils in this association are suited to meadow crops and to corn, soybeans, and small grain, but the strongly sloping and steep soils are kept as permanent pasture or maintained in native vegetation. Erosion is a hazard, and wetness is a limitation. (USDA, 1969, *Allen County, Indiana, soil survey report,* pp. 2–5)

PROBLEMS

In preparation for answering the questions that follow, compare and study the distribution of soil associations and glacial landforms in Figure 38.1 and Figure 38.3.

1. Explain the reason for the lobate nature of the moraines in northeastern Indiana.

2. Why are there river valleys running parallel to the morainal ridges? Examine the branch of the Wabash River that runs parallel to the Salamonie Moraine in Huntington and Wells counties.

3. List the soil associations associated with the following landforms.
   a. Terminal moraine _____
   b. Till plain (ground moraine) _____
   c. Sites of former lakes _____
   d. Floodplains _____

4. Besides the nature of the sedimentary deposits, what other evidence is there that a lake existed east of Fort Wayne?

5. a. Why are the soils of the Hoytville-Nappanee association poorly drained?

   b. If you were instructed to make a map of the floodplains of the largest streams on the map, what association would you use as a guide? _____

   c. On the geology map there are strandlines (old beach deposits). What kind of texture would you expect of soils found on these features?

   d. Which soil association is most closely associated with a particular geologic feature on these maps? (That is, what soil and geologic features have the most similar patterns?)

6. What is the most frequently occurring soil problem in the area of the soil map?

7. What is the scale of the soil map (Figure 38.1)?

8. On a separate sheet of paper, draw a schematic cross section of the geology from Tipton (Tipton County) to Decatur (Adams County). Use Figure 38.3 for guidance.

9. Using the soil associations of Allen County as a guide, describe the probable soil conditions on the crest areas of the end moraine shown by the cross section in Problem 8.

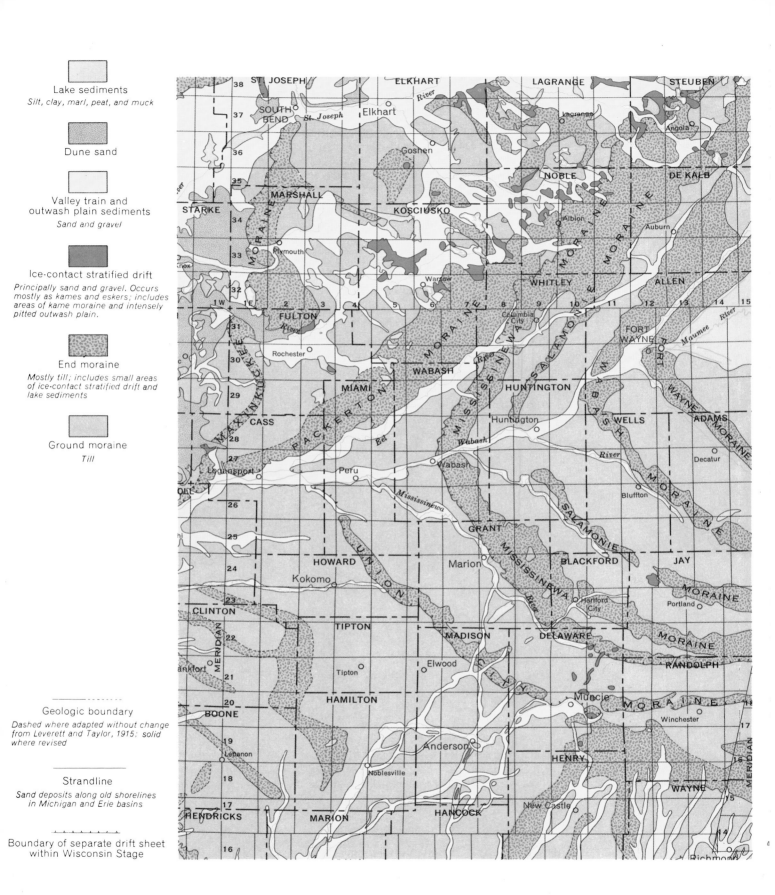

Figure 38.3.   Glacial geology of Indiana (Indiana Geological Survey, *Atlas of mineral resources of Indiana*, map 10)

Exercise 39

LAND USE AND SOIL EROSION

Soil erosion is a critical worldwide problem in the twentieth century. The continuing loss of topsoil to running water during rainstorms is reducing the productivity of land wherever agriculture is practiced. Clearing of forest land for agriculture, transportation systems, and urban expansion, along with overgrazing, produces the greatest amounts of soil erosion.

Four major variables affect the amount of soil loss from a given parcel of land. They are the extent of vegetation cover, soil type, frequency and intensity of precipitation, and the length and steepness of slope. A means of estimating soil loss from a parcel of land has been developed based upon these four variables, and is known as the universal soil loss equation (USLE). The soil loss equation yields an estimate of the amount of soil loss that occurs under different land-use conditions and different topographic conditions. The results can then be used to plan conservation measures to reduce soil erosion. The data used in this exercise were obtained in order to have a scientific basis for an erosion control plan in the Haw River Basin. The universal soil loss equation is

$$A = R \times K \times S \times C$$

where A = soil loss in tons per acre per year

R = rainfall index (R = 200 for the study area) ~Total rainfall – rainfall intensity~

K = soil erodibility index based upon soil type (K = 0.26 for the study area)

S = slope factor based on the length and steepness of the slope (table 39.1)

C = plant cover factor (table 39.2)

PROBLEMS

1. How does soil erosion change with the steepness of the slope? This can be determined by varying the slope angle in the equation and keeping the other variables constant. Calculate the difference in soil erosion on adjacent fields, one of which has slopes of 6% and the other slopes of 12%. Let C = .14 and slope length = 300 ft. Use Table 39.1 to determine the values of S and solve the equation; read down the left-hand column to 300 and read across the row to the column headed 6%, and then to the column headed 12%, to find S.

    a. $A = R \times K \times S \times C$ (for 6% slope) ~1.2~

    = ___200___ × ___.26___ × ___1.2___ × ___.14___

    = _____ tons/acre per year

    b. $A = R \times K \times S \times C$ (for 12% slope) ~3.1~

    = ___200___ × ___.26___ × ___3.12___ × ___.14___

    = _____ tons/acre per year   ~Divide B by A greater than 1.~

    c. What is ratio of soil erosion on the 12% slope to that on the land with 6% slope?

    _____

VIRGINIA

NORTH CAROLINA

ROCKINGHAM

CASWELL

REEDY FORK CREEK

HAW

GUILFORD

● GREENSBORO

RIVER

ORANGE

DURHAM

HAW RIVER BASIN
STUDY AREA

B. EVERETTE
JORDAN
LAKE

ALAMANCE

NORTH CAROLINA

HAW RIVER BASIN

NORTH CAROLINA

LEGEND

— — —   BASIN BOUNDARY
— · — ·   COUNTY BOUNDARY
- - - - -   SUB-BASIN BOUNDARY
———   STATE LINE
∿∿∿   RIVERS

10   0   10   20   30

SCALE   MILES

Figure 39.1.   The Haw River Basin of North Carolina and the Reedy Fork sub-basin

Table 39.1. Slope Factor (S) Based on Steepness and Length

Slope Length in Feet	Slope Steepness in Percent														
	4	6	8	10	12	14	16	18	20	25	30	35	40	45	50
50	.3	.5	.7	1.0	1.3	1.6	2.0	2.4	3.0	4.3	6.0	7.9	10.1	12.6	15.4
100	.4	.7	1.0	1.4	1.8	2.3	2.8	3.4	4.2	6.1	8.5	11.2	14.4	17.9	21.7
150	.5	.8	1.2	1.6	2.2	2.8	3.5	4.2	5.1	7.5	10.4	13.8	17.6	21.9	26.6
200	.6	.9	1.4	1.9	2.6	3.3	4.1	4.8	5.9	8.7	12.0	15.9	20.3	25.2	30.7
250	.7	1.0	1.6	2.2	2.9	3.7	4.5	5.4	6.6	9.7	13.4	17.8	22.7	28.2	34.4
300	.7	1.2	1.7	2.4	3.1	4.0	5.0	5.9	7.2	10.7	14.7	19.5	24.9	30.9	37.6
350	.8	1.2	1.8	2.6	3.4	4.3	5.4	6.4	7.8	11.5	15.9	21.0	26.9	33.4	40.6
400	.8	1.3	2.0	2.7	3.6	4.6	5.7	6.8	8.3	12.3	17.0	22.5	28.7	35.7	43.5
450	.9	1.4	2.1	2.9	3.8	4.9	6.1	7.2	8.9	13.1	18.0	23.8	30.5	37.9	46.1
500	.9	1.5	2.2	3.1	4.0	5.2	6.4	7.6	9.3	13.7	19.0	25.1	32.1	39.9	48.6
550	1.0	1.6	2.3	3.2	4.2	5.4	6.7	8.0	9.8	14.4	19.9	26.4	33.7	41.9	50.9
600	1.0	1.6	2.4	3.3	4.4	5.7	7.0	8.3	10.2	15.1	20.8	27.5	35.2	43.7	53.2
650	1.1	1.7	2.5	3.5	4.6	5.9	7.3	8.7	10.6	15.7	21.7	28.7	36.6	45.5	55.4
700	1.1	1.8	2.6	3.6	4.8	6.1	7.6	9.0	11.1	16.3	22.5	29.7	38.0	47.2	57.5
750	1.1	1.8	2.7	3.7	4.9	6.3	7.9	9.3	11.4	16.8	23.3	30.8	39.3	48.9	59.5
800	1.2	1.9	2.8	3.8	5.1	6.5	8.1	9.6	11.8	17.4	24.1	31.8	40.6	50.5	61.4
900	1.2	2.0	3.0	4.1	5.4	6.9	8.6	10.2	12.5	18.5	25.5	33.7	43.1	53.5	65.2
1000	1.3	2.1	3.1	4.3	5.7	7.3	9.1	10.8	13.2	19.5	26.9	35.5	45.4	56.4	68.7

2. How does soil erosion change with the length of slope? Calculate the difference in soil erosion on a slope 50 ft in length and on a slope 500 ft in length if the other variables are held constant. Let $C = .14$, and slope steepness = 6%.

   a. $A = R \times K \times S \times C$ (for 50 ft slope) ·5

      = ___200___ × __.26__ × ___.5___ × __.14__

      = _____ tons/acre per year

   b. $A = R \times K \times S \times C$ (for 500 ft slope) /.5

      = ___200___ × __.26__ × __1.5__ × __.14__

      = _____ tons/acre per year

   c. If the slope length is increased by a factor of 10, what is the ratio of increase in soil erosion? _____ to 1   ÷ larger by smaller,

3. How does soil erosion change with plant cover? Calculate soil losses from a forest area (75% canopy cover and 95–100% ground cover) and an adjacent field that is cleared and cultivated (no canopy cover or ground cover). Let $S = 7.2$. See Table 39.2 to determine C. Three variables are used to determine the value of C in Table 39.2. Go across the table to the column that

lower

Table 39.2. Vegetal Cover Factor (C)

Percent Canopy Cover	Percent of Ground Cover					
	0	20	40	60	80	95–100
0	.45[a]	.20	.10	.042	.013	.003
	.45	.20	.15	.09	.043	.011
25	.39	.18	.09	.039	.013	.003
	.39	.22	.14	.085	.042	.011
50	.39	.16	.08	.038	.012	.003
	.39	.19	.13	.080	.040	.011
75	.27	.10	.08	.035	.012	.003 *forest*
	.32	.18	.12	.080	.040	.011

[a] The upper number in each pair represents grass surface cover with turf or litter at least 2 in. deep, and the lower number represents broad-leafed herbs, such as weeds, with little turf or topsoil. *forest*

corresponds to percent ground cover; go down the row until you come to the row with the corresponding canopy cover; and then select the value of C depending on surface cover.

a. $A = R \times K \times S \times C$ (for forest land)

  $= \underline{200} \times \underline{.26} \times \underline{7.2} \times \underline{.003}$

  $= \underline{\hspace{2cm}}$ tons/acre per year

b. $A = R \times K \times S \times C$ (for bare ground)

  $= \underline{200} \times \underline{.26} \times \underline{7.2} \times \underline{.45}$

  $= \underline{\hspace{2cm}}$ tons/acre per year

c. What is the ratio of soil loss from the bare surface to that from the area with a forest canopy and ground cover? $\underline{\hspace{2cm}}$ to 1

d. While a direct comparison is not possible from these calculations, which variable—plant cover, slope length, or slope steepness—is the most important variable in soil erosion? $\underline{\hspace{2cm}}$ *Compare ratios – larger ratio is most important.*

    A study of soil erosion in the Haw River Basin of North Carolina was carried out in 1985. One of the sub-basins in the study is located in Guilford County and contains a mix of land-use types. There are a large urban area, including Greensboro with a population of some 160,000, considerable forest land, and some agricultural land.

4. Table 39.3 lists land-use types, soil erosion rates by groups, the mean of each group, and the number of acres in each group. Using the mean rate for each group, calculate the total soil loss for each category and the total for each type of land use. Place the results of your calculations in the column in the table headed total. When you complete this table, transfer your results to Table 39.4 and complete this table.

    a. Which type of land use has the highest average soil loss per acre? $\underline{\hspace{2cm}}$

    b. Which type of land use has the greatest total soil loss for the basin? $\underline{\hspace{2cm}}$

    c. What is the most prevalent type of land use in the basin? $\underline{\hspace{2cm}}$

Table 39.3. Land Use and Soil Loss in the Haw River Basin

Land Use[a]	Soil Loss by USLE Group (tons/acre/yr)	Mean Rate of Soil Loss (tons/acre/yr)	Area (acres)	Soil Loss (tons/year)
Cropland	0–5	2.5	1,613 *Multiply by AVG*	
	5–12	8.5	6,234	
	12–20	16.0	7,262	
	20+	20.0	4,399	
			19,508	*= 261,193.5*
Pasture/hayland	0–5	2.5	17,860	
Idle	0–5	2.5	1,567	*3917.5*
	5–12	8.5	185	*1572.50*
	12–20	16.0	0	0
	20+	20.0	56	*1120*
			1,808	*6610*
Urban/residential	0–5	2.5	42,147	*105,367.50*
	5–12	8.5	0	0
	12–20	16.0	0	0
	20+	20.0	191	*3570*
			42,338	*109,187.50*
Forest land	0–5	2.5	70,400	*176,000*
	5–12	8.5	40	*340*
			70,440	*176,340*
Other	0–5	2.5	4,367	*10,917.5*
	5–12	8.5	484	*4114*
	12–20	16.0	3,164	*50,624*
	20+	20.0	1,000	*20,000*
			9,015	*85,655.5*
Large lakes	0	0	3,263	0
			164,232	

[a]Soil loss computed from field data using the USLE.

Note: All data used in this exercise are from *Haw River Basin Erosion Study,* USDA, Soil Conservation Service, Forest Service, 1985.

d. What type of land use produces the greatest percentage of the total soil loss?

_____

e. Which three types of land use (other than lakes) have the least soil loss per acre?

_____

Table 39.4. Total, Mean, and Relative Soil Loss by land use

Land Use	Area (acres)	Total Loss (tons/year)	Mean Loss (tons/acre/yr)	Percent of Total Loss
Cropland	19,508	261,193.5	13.39	38.2
Pasture/hayland	17,860	44,650	2.5	_____
Idle	1,808	6,410	3.65	_____
Urban/residential	42,338	109,187.50	2.57	_____
Forest land	70,440	176,340	2.50	_____
Other	9,015	85,655.5	9.5	_____
Large lakes	3,263	–0–	_____	_____

From this study, and from many other studies, the evidence is clear. If agriculture is going to remain productive in the years ahead on this land and most other lands where agriculture is practiced, methods for greatly reducing soil erosion must be developed and utilized. Huge amounts of land are becoming unproductive each year because of soil loss. At a time when the human population is the greatest in history, loss of good soil is a disaster of major proportions.

#a Avg. Divide T.L. by # of Acres
#b Divide T.L. by Grand Total = 38.2 Cropland
do each one - Pasture

#e. mean loss
3 categories in last place

Name: _____

Laboratory Section: _____

Exercise 40

SATELLITE REMOTE SENSING AND IMAGE INTERPRETATION: VISUAL INTERPRETATION

SATELLITES AND IMAGING SYSTEMS

Aerial photography has been used extensively in the Earth sciences, as seen in Exercise 19 and in the aerial photographs that accompany Exercises 21–32. Aerial photographs have been used in physical geography since the turn of the twentieth century. The ongoing controversy over the origin of the mysterious "Carolina Bays" was initiated through examination of aerial photographs in 1930 and most subdisciplines within physical geography make use of aerial surveys for purposes as diverse as mapping topography, monitoring hazardous waste sites, and studying river channel changes.

Recently, images of the Earth taken from space have proven to be of tremendous value in a wide variety of applications. Hand-held cameras on board the Gemini and Apollo manned satellites indicated the potential of space-based imagery to provide a regional and global perspective on Earth resources issues in the 1960s; more systematic imaging was accomplished by the Skylab missions, and the first satellite devoted to observation of the land area on Earth (ERTS, now LANDSAT) was launched in 1972. Since that time, applications of satellite remote sensing have grown tremendously in breadth and in their capability to discriminate significant features at or near the Earth's surface.

Unlike aerial photographs, which differ from home photography only in the position from which they are taken, satellite images are not photographs at all. Rather, they are digital images recorded by instruments that are sensitive to reflected or emitted radiation over broad portions of the electromagnetic spectrum, including microwave and thermal infrared. These digital data are recorded on board the orbiting satellite and beamed to Earth receiving stations, where the data are recorded for later display, enhancement, and interpretation. While traditional photographs are recorded on film that is sensitive only to visible light or film that records visible and near-infrared light, satellite imaging systems are generally capable of recording energy emitted at any desired wavelengths. Terrestrial radiation carries a great deal of information that the eye cannot see and the ordinary camera cannot record. Digital images have the advantage of being computer compatible, which allows for machine processing of these huge data sets. They are thus easily manipulated, enhanced, and analyzed on computers. The following exercise provides examples of some of the procedures involved in the analysis of these digital images.

IMAGING SYSTEMS AND IMAGE CHARACTERISTICS

Most images used in the field of remote sensing have been obtained from three imaging systems: Landsat Multispectral Scanner (MSS), Landsat Thematic Mapper (TM), and the French SPOT system. The first of these, the Landsat MSS system (originally named ERTS-1), became operational in 1972.

Along with its successor satellites, the Landsat MSS system has been providing continuous coverage of the Earth for almost two decades. The MSS system orbits the Earth at such a height and velocity that each point on the planet's surface receives coverage every 18 days, with image data collected in the green and red visible portions of the spectrum, plus two parts of the near-infrared.

Since 1982, a second imaging system aboard the more recent Landsat satellites has been providing coverage concurrent with the MSS images. This is the newer Thematic Mapper or TM system, which records seven bands of data from the visible, near-, mid-, and far-infrared portions of the electromagnetic spectrum at a ground resolution of 30 m. This greatly improved spatial resolution allows the identification of far smaller objects and areas of interest on the Earth's surface. The latest commercial satellite is the French SPOT system, which provides up to 10-m resolution.

For viewing, digital images can be displayed on a computer screen or converted into a photographic paper product. The images may be viewed one band at a time through gray scale (black and white) reproduction, with the lowest reflectance values displayed as black, highest values as white, and intermediate values as various tones of gray. Alternatively, three bands of imagery may be displayed at one time to produce a color composite image. As illustrated in Figure 40.1 the images that accompany this exercise were produced by projecting the green visible satellite data values with blue light, the red visible with green light, and the near-infrared data with red light to produce a false-color composite. These three primary colors in combination are capable of producing all colors of the visible spectrum, such that a tremendous range of color values is possible.

THE IMAGES: YALWA, NIGERIA: 1973, 1986

Figures 40.2 and 40.3 are false-color LANDSAT MSS satellite images of the same area taken approximately 13 years apart. The area covered is in the northeastern portion of Nigeria, at approximately 10 degrees north, 5 degrees east. The water body is the Kainji Reservoir. Constructed in 1963, this impoundment on the Niger River has had chronic problems with sedimentation. The area is part of the Sahel region, the narrow strip of land between the verdant rainforest to the south and the severely arid Sahara desert to the north. Dependent on the vagaries of the migrating Inter-Tropical

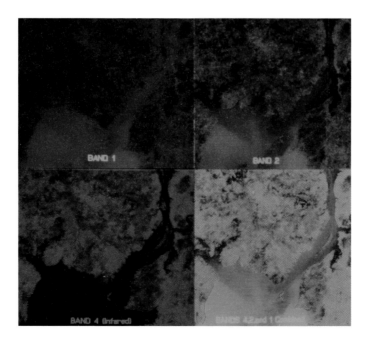

Figure 40.1.   Bands 1, 2, and 4 shown in blue. green, and infrared, respectively, and a false-color composite of bands 1, 3 and 4.

NORTH

EAST

Figure 40.2.   LANDSAT image taken in 1973 of the upper Kainji Reservoir in Nigeria and
vicinity. The river entering the reservoir is the Niger.

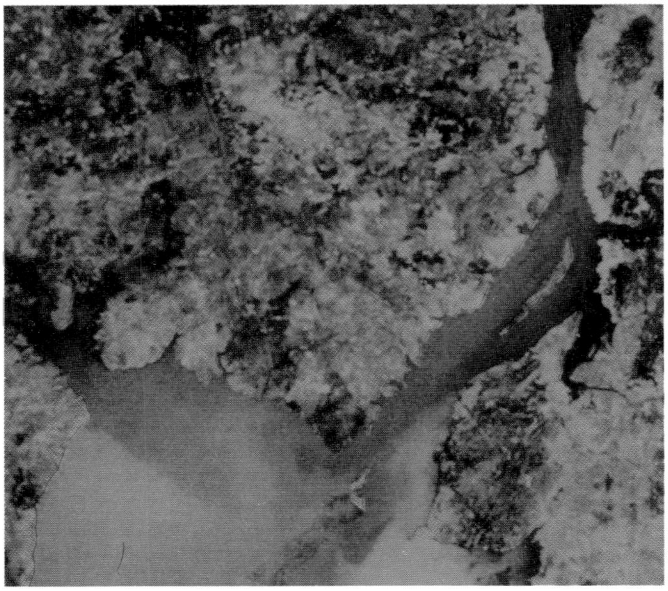

NORTH

EAST

Figure 40.3   LANDSAT image taken in 1986 of the upper Kainji Reservoir.

Convergence Zone (ITCZ) the area is subject to prolonged droughts, such as those of 1972–73 and 1986–87. The region is classified as an Aw climate with its typical savanna vegetation. The primary activity in the area is subsistence grazing; intensive grazing by sheep and goats has played an important role in desertification of the region. Fire is an important land management tool in the local farm economy. The inhabitants set fire to large tracts of land each fall season to burn off rough, thorny vegetation and promote the growth of edible shoots of greenery. Unfortunately, these fires occasionally get out of control and devastate large areas of rangeland and sometimes destroy villages.

Both of the images in this exercise are MSS images. The first image was obtained in October 1973, at the end of a drought that killed approximately 500,000 people throughout the Sahel. The second image was obtained in January 1986, during a drought that caused the deaths of over one million people. As mentioned previously, the images are color composites of the green and red visible light and the near-infrared. Because healthy vegetation reflects infrared radiation strongly, vegetation vigor is indicated by red tones—the darker the tone of red on the image, the healthier the vegetation.

PROBLEMS

1. a. On the 1986 image, what do the bright red areas in the channel of the Niger River represent?

   b. To what degree do these features appear in the 1973 image?

   c. What changes have occurred in the river channel that allowed so drastic a change from the 1973 scene to the 1986 scene?

2. a. Is there any evidence of sedimentation in the embayed tributaries at the western margin of the 1973 image?

   b. What about the 1986 image? Describe any changes in detail.

3. a. Is there any evidence of increased sedimentation in the main body of the reservoir between the two dates of coverage? If so, what is the evidence?

   b. What human and climatic factors have encouraged such rapid rates of sedimentation in the region?

4. a. What is the blackened area on the peninsula to the east of the Niger River on the 1973 image?

   b. Are there other areas on the image where the same feature can be found? Describe its abundance and distribution on this image.

   c. Where is the same feature found on the 1986 image? Describe the major differences in pattern and distribution between the two images.

5. Are the group of features which trend north-northwest to south-southeast in the central region of each image caused by land use patterns or by geologic structures? Explain your reasoning.

6. Can you find any manmade features on either image? If so, describe them.

Exercise 41

SATELLITE REMOTE SENSING AND IMAGE INTERPRETATION: NUMERICAL ANALYSIS

Exercise 40 was concerned primarily with *visual interpretation* of a pair of LANDSAT MSS images. This was accomplished in much the same manner as one would interpret aerial photographs. Visual analysis uses the unsurpassed abilities of the human mind to evaluate spatial patterns *qualitatively.* Today *quantitative* computer analysis of *digital* spectral data is becoming increasingly more common in a wide range of fields. It is important to note that computer analysis and visual analysis are complementary tools of the interpreter and are *not* redundant methods.

THE NATURE OF DIGITAL DATA

Imagine a grid placed over the Earth's surface, each cell of which is known as a *pixel.* A pixel is the basic data collection unit of a digital image. The average brightness or *radiance* of each pixel is measured electronically by a sensor located above the ground's surface (i.e., in a balloon, an aircraft, or a satellite). Some sensors can measure the ultraviolet energy being radiated by the pixel, or infrared energy, or the visible wavelengths. The LANDSAT MSS sensor used to create the images of the Kainji Reservoir used in Exercise 40 measures the amount of green light (.5 to .6 micrometer), red light (.6 to .7 micrometer), near infrared (.7 to .8 micrometer) and far infrared energy (.8 to 1.1 micrometer) being reflected by each pixel. Thus for each pixel four numeric values are recorded. For a comparison of the pixel size (*spatial resolution*) and the portions of the electromagnetic spectrum being recorded (*spectral resolution*) by the LANDSAT MSS, LANDSAT TM, and SPOT satellites, see Table 41.1 and Figure 41.1.

It is critical to recall that the sensor records only the *average* radiance of a pixel. For example, if an area of the Earth's surface, within a single pixel, was covered with pine trees the LANDSAT MSS satellite may record a brightness value of 30 (on a scale of 0 to 63) in the infrared energy band, while a pixel composed entirely of deep water may have a brightness value of only 10 in the far-infrared energy band. On the other hand, if our pixel happens to cover an area that is composed of half pine forest and half water, the brightness value will be approximately twenty. These *mixed pixels* present a challenge to any interpreter attempting to identify land-cover types from digital data.

MULTIPLE SPECTRAL SENSORS

The fact that many sensors are sensitive to more than one portion, or *band,* of the electromagnetic radiation spectrum makes the identification or classification of surface types significantly more reliable. For example, pixels comprised of pine trees may have a radiance value between 20 and 25 in bank 1 (the green portion of the spectrum) and a value between 15 and 21 in band 4 (the far-infrared portion of the spectrum), whereas pixels composed of wetland grass may have brightness values between 22 and

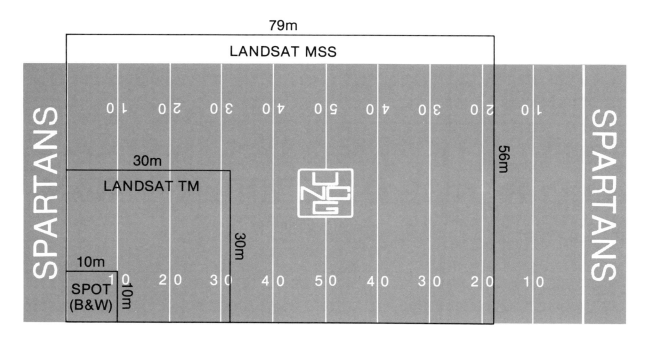

Figure 41.1.   Pixel size produced by three different environmental satellites

27 for band 1 and values between 9 and 14 for band 4. If one had only information from the green portion of the spectrum (band 1) it would be very difficult to distinguish between many of the pine tree areas and wetland grass areas.

PROBLEMS

1.   Table 41.2 provides the ranges of the radiance values for four land-cover types found on the LANDSAT MSS images of Nigeria used in Exercise 40. Using Table 41.2, identify pixels A to D in Table 41.3 according to which land-cover type they *most likely* represent. Place your answer in the column headed Land Cover.

Table 41.1.   Satellite Characteristics

Satellite	Pixel	No. of Spectral Bands	Orbit Time
LANDSAT MSS	79 m	4 (green, red, near-IR, far-IR)	18 days
LANDSAT TM	30 m	7 (blue, green, red, near-IR, two mid-IR, thermal IR)	16 days
SPOT	10 m	1 (Panchromatic B&W)	26 days
	20 m	3 (green, red, & near-IR)	a

[a] The optics of SPOT allow coverage as frequently as every day or every few days depending on the location of the area being monitored.

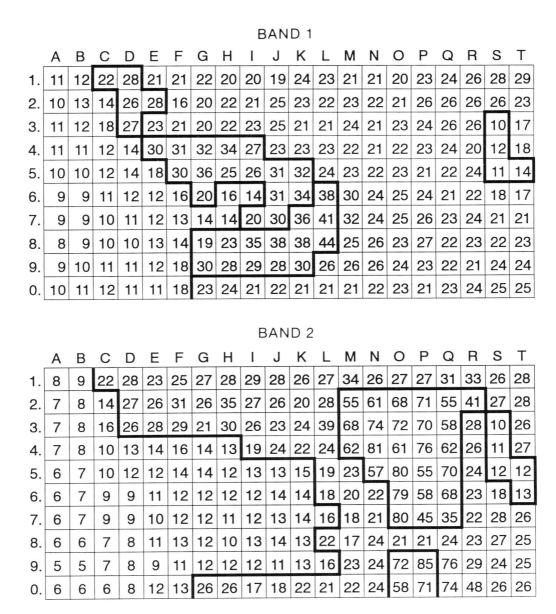

Figure 41.2. Band 1 and band 2 LANDSAT digital data for the greater Pixelville area

2. Again using Table 41.2, if it were necessary to separate all areas that were water from those areas that were not water, which *two* bands would you select to use and why?

Figure 41.2 contains two sets of LANDSAT TM raw data for the greater Pixelville area. The two sets of data are for bands 1 and 2. The two sets of data are in fact maps of the intensity of the reflected data. The data have been divided into classes based on the given reflectance value. Each class represents a land-use type.

Table 41.2. Ranges of Radiance Values for Selected Land-Use Types

	Band 1	Band 2	Band 3	Band 4
Water	38–50	36–58	12–18	4–14
Bare soil	45–51	33–61	29–33	32–37
Wetland grass	21–27	22–28	16–21	10–16
Burned-over areas	23–29	27–38	20–24	19–28

3. Note pixels C3 on band 1 and R0 on band 2. Why do you think they have values so different from the surrounding pixels?

4. Now, using the information in both bands 1 and 2, develop a land-cover system for greater Pixelville. Shade all pixels you believe are of the same land cover type with the same color.

5. After making your "educated guess" concerning the land types, you check your findings by using a statistical classification scheme on the data. The method chosen here is the minimum distance technique. In the first step of this method you sample four areas (see Figure 4.3) that you know to be water (sample #1), pine trees (sample #2), cornfields (sample #3), and urban (sample #4).

6. First calculate the mean reflectance for each sample for each band.

   a. Sample #1 Band 1 _____   c. Sample #3 Band 1 _____
      Sample #1 Band 2 _____   Sample #3 Band 2 _____
   b. Sample #2 Band 1 _____   d. Sample #4 Band 1 _____
      Sample #2 Band 2 _____   Sample #4 Band 2 _____

7. Plot all points in all samples on Figure 41.4. Use the following color scheme. Blue dots for water, green for pine trees, yellow for corn, and red for urban. In addition plot the mean value of each sample using black dots.

Table 41.3. Land Cover Classification by Radiance Value

Pixel	Band 1	Band 2	Band 3	Band 4	Land Cover
A	26	—	—	14	_____
B	—	37	—	34	_____
C	46	39	30	—	_____
D	23	27	20	—	_____

8. Using the graph you created for Problem 7, classify the following pixels, based on the minimum distance to mean method, as being water, pine, corn, or urban. Note that the minimum distance to mean is one of the most widely used algorithms for computer classification of digital imagery.

A1_____   B3_____   I6_____   P7_____   R1_____

M8_____   S4_____   T0_____   E5_____   Q1_____

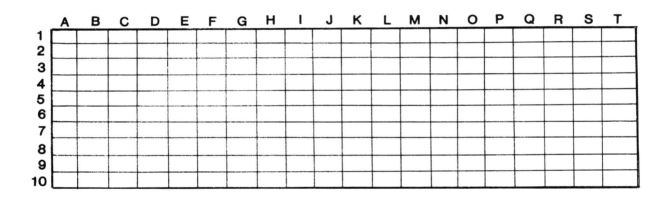

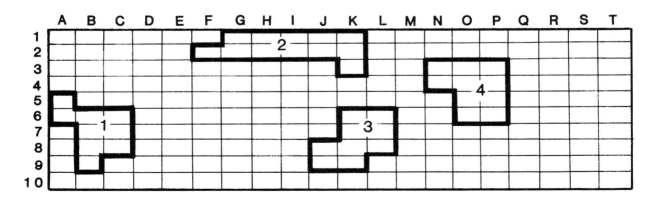

Figure 41.3.   Land classification—Pixelville, USA

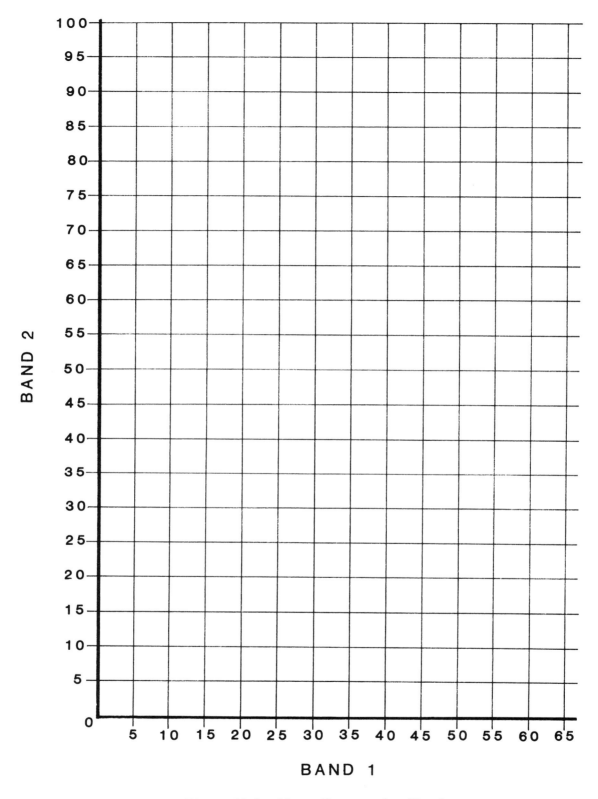

Figure 41.4.   Mean distance classification

Exercise 42

TIME

The measurement of time is a necessity of everyday life. Most of the activities of the human species are adjusted to two fundamental motions of the Earth. The time of year is related to the relative position of the Earth as it revolves around the sun. The succession of the four seasons of the midlatitudes and the wet and dry seasons of the tropics is a direct function of this relative location. The time of day is related to the rotation of the Earth on its axis. The eastward rotation of the Earth on its axis causes the sun to seem to make a westward movement across the sky each day and produces the alternation of daylight and darkness. A complete rotation through 360 degrees requires 24 hours. From this relationship the elements of Table 42.1, degrees(°), minutes, ('), and seconds ("), can be established. Local time, which is also referred to as sun time or solar time, actually differs for every point on a parallel of latitude.

PROBLEMS

1. On Figure 42.1, locate the boundaries of daylight when the sun's rays are vertical at 0 degrees latitude and 0 degrees longitude. For the purposes of this exercise, it is necessary to assume the vertical rays at the equator, as this is the only time of year when the circle of illumination is parallel to the meridians. On the map, label the meridian along which sunrise and sunset are occurring.

2. Complete the following based on the conditions specified in Figure 42.1.

    a. Time of sunset   _____
    b. Time of sunrise   _____
    c. Longitude of sunrise   _____
    d. Longitude of sunset   _____
    e. Local time at longitude 75 degrees west   _____
    f. Local time at longitude 75 degrees east   _____
    g. Local time at longitude 5 degrees west   _____
    h. Local time at longitude 15 degrees west   _____

Table 42.1.   Relation of Time to Longitudinal Arc

Time Interval	Longitudinal Arc
1 hr	15°
1 min	15′
1 sec	15″
4 min	1°
4 sec	1′
0.067 sec	1″

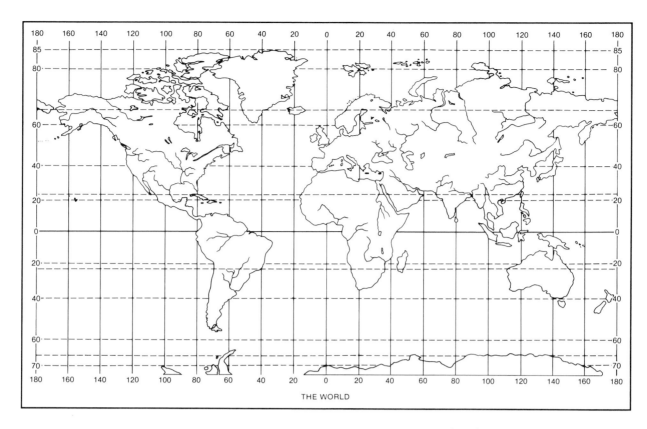

Figure 42.1. Mercator projection on which to plot the time zones

3. Now locate on the map the boundaries of daylight when the vertical rays of the sun have moved 6 hr to the west. Daylight exists from _____ longitude to _____ longitude.

Standard Time

If local sun time were used, then every place on an east-west line would have a different time. This was really no problem until rapid means of transportation came into existence. The development of railroads resulted in a need to standardize time to reduce confusion. The world was divided into standard time belts 15 degrees wide so that the difference in time between them is 1 hr; all places within a time zone accept the time of the center of the zone, or the standard meridian for that zone. In theory, the time belts extend a distance of 7.5 degrees on either side of the standard meridians, although there are many irregularities. Eastern standard time is based on the solar time of the meridian of 75 degrees west.

PROBLEMS

4. On Figure 42.2, draw in solid lines for the standard meridians for each of the time zones in the United States and southern Canada. Next, using dashed lines, draw in the boundary locations.
5. If the state of Texas uses central standard time, how much would the standard of El Paso (106 degrees 27 minutes west) differ from local sun time?

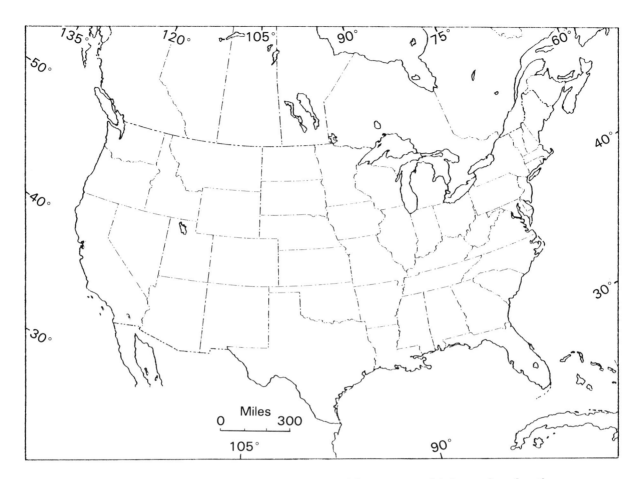

Figure 42.2. Polyconic projection of the United States on which to plot the time zones

DAYLIGHT SAVING TIME

Most people have daily routines that are not centered on the middle of the solar day, or noon. If 16 hr is the usual waking period, it is more likely to be from 7 A.M. to 11 P.M. than from 4 A.M. to 8 P.M. As a result, the average person does not take advantage of the early daylight hours and spends a substantial part of the evening hours in darkness, requiring the use of artificial light. The first use of daylight saving time, during World War I, had an energy-saving purpose. By setting the clock an hour ahead, most people gain an hour of daylight in the afternoon or evening, which in recent years has again served to save energy. Daylight saving time is seldom used in winter because of the shorter winter days when sunrise is rather late.

INTERNATIONAL DATE LINE

When the survivors of Magellan's voyage around the world returned to Spain, their records showed the date to be 6 September 1522. The local calendar indicated that the date was, in fact, 7 September 1522. By sailing westward, Magellan's expedition had gained an hour for each 15 degrees they traveled and hence, after making a full circle of 360 degrees, had picked up one full day.

By convention it is agreed that a day begins at midnight. At any given hour, clocks at the standard meridians point to each one of the 24 hr. The same day, however, can exist everywhere only when it is noon on the 0-degree meridian at Greenwich and midnight on the 180-degree meridian. There must

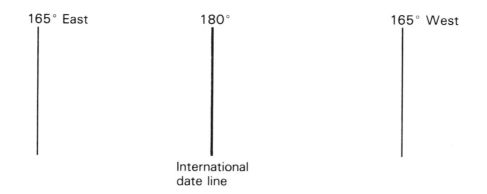

165° East   180°   165° West

International
date line

Figure 42.3.   International date line and adjacent time zones

Table 42.2.   Times at Different Longitudes

Location	Time	Location	Time
165° W	3 P.M. Sunday	175° W	_____
165° W	3 A.M. Sunday	175° W	_____
165° E	9 A.M. Sunday	170° E	_____
165° E	11 P.M. Sunday	165° W	_____

be a starting point for the calendar day. The 180-degree meridian has been arbitrarily chosen as the international date line. The actual international date line deviates from the 180-degree meridian at several points to place political units, such as the Aleutian Islands, in the same time zone. On crossing this date line, a person changes the calendar by one day-, advancing a day (Saturday becomes Sunday) when crossing westward and repeating a day (Sunday becomes Saturday) when crossing the line going eastward. In other words, to the west of the date line is the new day and on the east side of the line is the old day.

The solutions of time problems are easier for many people to understand when they use a globe or diagram. If you have difficulty, prepare a device as follows. Draw a circle about 2 in. in diameter to represent the globe with the North Pole at the center. Draw radii indicating meridians at 15-degree intervals, and label them 0 degrees to 180 degrees east and west inside the circumference; outside the circle write the hours of the day opposite each meridian. When you cut the circle out, you can rotate it to help solve time problems graphically.

PROBLEMS

6. On Figure 42.3, locate the boundaries of the time zones.
7. Basing your answers on the locations of the time zones and the international date line, complete Table 42.2.
8. What is the difference in hours between Chicago standard time and Madrid standard time? _____

9. What is the Chicago standard time when it's 7:30 A.M. in Madrid? _____

Appendix A

THE METRIC SYSTEM

Units of measurement used in different parts of the world have varied from time immemorial. Repeated efforts through history have gradually led to greater and greater standardization. As communications improved over the centuries and people and goods moved about ever more freely, a pressing need for uniformity developed. The imperial system of measurement, which utilizes the foot, pound, degree Fahrenheit, and mile, was widely disseminated by the British during the heyday of their empire.

In 1790, the French introduced the metric system, a system based upon decimalization. Initially, the spread of the metric system was aided by its adoption in a Europe dominated by Napoleonic France and by its use in the French colonies. The metric system has gained greater and greater favor among nations of the world so that by 1972 the only major industrialized nation not either fully using the metric system or in the process of adopting it was the United States. Several small countries not using the metric system are Ceylon, Gambia, Guyana, Jamaica, Liberia, Malawi, and Sierra Leone.

The advantages of the metric system are many, including near universality and the basic decimal character of the system. The system that is now being favored around the world is the "System International," or SI, which was adopted by an international committee in 1960 and has since been adopted as official by more than 30 countries. The advantages of the metric system led some sectors of the American economy to adopt this system long ago. The chemical industry is an example. If the United States is to play a major role in world affairs, it must adopt the system of measure used by the rest of the world. Most American scientific journals now require that the metric system of measurement be used either alone or in conjunction with the imperial system. The National Aeronautics and Space Administration (NASA) in November 1970 became the first official U.S. government agency to convert to the metric system. A bill was introduced in Congress in 1972 to have the SI adopted as the official system for the United States, but the bill did not pass. The Metric Conversion Act of 1975 made the change voluntary and thus has had little effect on everyday life. Yet there can be no doubt that the metric system will eventually be adopted here.

Table A.I.   Metric Prefixes and Symbols

	Basic Unit	Arabic Notation	Prefix	Symbol
Multiples	10^6	1,000,000	mega	M
	10^3	1000	kilo	k
	10^2	100	hecto	h
	10	10	deka	da
Fractions	10^{-1}	0.1	deci	d
	10^{-2}	0.01	centi	c
	10^{-3}	0.001	milli	m
	10^{-6}	0.000001	micro	μ

Note: Although fractions and multiples of 10 and 100 are shown in the table, the use of these units is discouraged. Multiples of 1000 are preferred.

Table A.2.   Conversion of Imperial Units to Metric Units

Physical Variable	Unit	SI Equivalent
Length	Inch	25.44 mm
	Foot	0.305 m
	Yard	0.914 m
	Mile	1.61 km
Area	Square inch	645.2 mm^2
	Square foot	0.093 m^2
	Square yard	0.836 m^2
	Acre	4047 m^2
	Square mile	2.59 km^2
Velocity	Foot/second	0.305 m/s^{-1}
	Mile/hour	0.447 m/s^{-1}
Mass	Pound	0.454 kg
Density	Pounds/cubic foot	16.02 kg/m^{-3}
Pressure	Standard atmosphere	101.3 kN/m^{-2}
	Pound/square inch	6895 N/m^{-2}
Temperature	Fahrenheit	$°F = (9/5) °C + 32$

Table A.3.   Conversion of Standard Metric Units to Imperial Units

	Standard Metric Unit	Imperial Equivalent
Length	Kilometer (km)	0.621 mile
	Meter (m)	1.094 yards
		39.370 inches
		3.281 feet
Area	Hectare (ha)	
	Square kilometer (km^2)	2.471 acres
	Square meter (m^2)	1.196 square yards
Volume	Cubic meter (m^3)	1.308 cubic yards
	Liter (l)	0.264 gallons
Velocity	Kilometers per hour (km/h)	0.621 miles per hour
	Meters per second (m/s)	3.281 feet per second
Mass	Kilogram (kg)	2.205 pounds
	Gram (g)	0.035 ounce

Table A.4. Proportional Parts for Degrees Celsius and Fahrenheit

°C	°F	°C	°F
.56	1	1	1.8
1.11	2	2	3.6
1.67	3	3	5.4
2.22	4	4	7.2
2.78	5	5	9.0
3.33	6	6	10.8
3.89	7	7	12.6
4.44	8	8	14.4
5.00	9	9	16.2

Appendix B

KEY TO WEATHER MAPS

TEMPERATURE MAP

Temperature data are entered from selected weather stations in the United States. The figures entered above the station dot denote maximum temperatures reported from these stations during the 24 hours ending 1:00 a.m., E.S.T.; the figures entered below the station dot denote minimum temperature during the 24 hours ending at 1:00 p.m., E.S.T., of the previous day. The letter "M" denotes missing data. Shaded areas labeled "HIGHER" or "LOWER" indicate the areas where temperatures recorded at 1:00 a.m., E.S.T., are at least 10° warmer or colder than 24 hours ago.

PRECIPITATION MAP

Precipitation data are entered from selected weather stations in the United States. When precipitation has occurred at any of these stations in the 24-hour period ending at 1:00 a.m., E.S.T., the total amount, in inches and hundredths, is entered above the station dot. When the figures for total precipitation have been compiled from incomplete data and entered on the map, the amount is underlined. "T" indicates a trace of precipitation, and the letter "M" denotes missing data. The geographical areas where precipitation has fallen during the 24 hours ending at 1:00 a.m., E.S.T., are shaded.

CONTINENTAL MAP

The insert map of nearly the entire North American continent shows the surface pressure pattern and frontal analysis twelve hours earlier than the principal map. Areas of precipitation at map time are shaded.

SURFACE FORECAST MAP

The insert map portrays surface pressure and frontal patterns expected at 7:00 p.m., E.S.T. today, or 18 hours after the principal map. Comparison of this map with the principal map will show forecast movements and changes in the surface pressure and frontal patterns.

500-MILLIBAR MAP

Contour lines, isotherms, and wind arrows are shown on the insert map for the 500-millibar contour level. Solid lines are drawn to show height above sea level and are labeled in feet. Dashed lines are drawn at 5 intervals of temperature, and labeled in degrees Celsius. A temperature conversion table is shown in block ⑬. True wind direction is shown by "arrows" which are plotted as flying with the wind. The wind speed is shown by flags and feathers, each flag representing 50 knots, each full feather 10 knots, and each half-feather 5 knots. For conversion to miles per hour, refer to block ⑨.

INQUIRIES

Inquiries regarding these maps may be addressed to Chief, U. S. Weather Bureau, Washington, D. C., 20235.

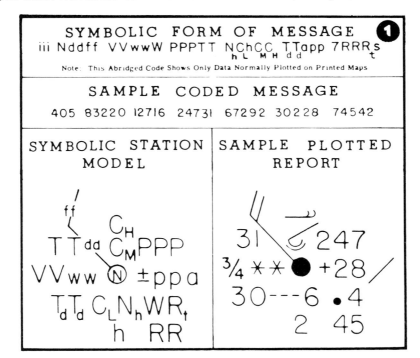

EXPLANATION OF SYMBOLS AND MAP ENTRIES

②

Symbols in order as they appear in the message	Explanation of symbols and decode of example above	Remarks on coding and plotting
iii	Station number 405 = Washington	Usually printed on manuscript maps below station circle. Omitted on Daily Weather Map in favor of printed station names.
N	Total amount of cloud 8 = completely covered	Observed in tenths of cloud cover and coded in Oktas (eighths) according to code table in block ❻. Plotted in symbols shown in same table.
dd	True direction from which wind is blowing 32 = 320° = NW	Coded in tens of degrees and plotted as the shaft of an arrow extending from the station circle toward the direction from which the wind is blowing.
ff	Wind speed in knots 20 = 20 knots	Coded in knots (nautical miles per hour) and plotted as feathers and half-feathers representing 10 and 5 knots, respectively, on the shaft of the wind direction arrow. See block ❷.
VV	Visibility in miles and fractions 12 = 12/16 or 3/4 miles	Decoded and plotted in miles and fractions up to 3 1/8 miles. Visibilities above 3 1/8 miles but less than 10 miles are plotted to the nearest whole mile. Values higher than 10 miles are omitted from the map.
ww	Present weather 71 = continuous slight snow	Coded in figures taken from the "ww" table (block ❾) and plotted in the corresponding symbols same block. Entries for code figures 00, 01, 02, and 03 are omitted from this map.
W	Past weather 6 = rain	Coded in figures taken from the "W" table (block ⑪) and plotted in the corresponding symbols same block. No entry made for code figures 0, 1, or 2.
ppp	Barometric Pressure (in millibars) reduced to sea-level 247 = 1024.7 mb.	Coded and plotted in tens, units, and tenths of millibars. The initial 9 or 10 and the decimal point are omitted. See block ⑫.
TT	Current air temperature 31 = 31° F.	Coded and plotted in actual value in whole degrees F. See block ⑪.
Nh	Fraction of sky covered by low or middle cloud 6 = 7 or 8 tenths	Observed and coded in tenths of cloud cover. Plotted on map as code figure in message. See block ❼.
C_L	Cloud type 7 = Fractostratus and/or Fractocumulus of bad weather (scud)	Predominating clouds of types in C_L table (block ❽) are coded from that table and plotted in corresponding symbols.
h	Height of base of cloud 2 = 300 to 599 feet	Observed in feet and coded and plotted as code figures according to code table in block ❺.
C_M	Cloud type 9 = Altocumulus of chaotic sky	See C_M table in block ❾.
C_H	Cloud type 2 = Dense cirrus in patches	See C_H table in block ❿.
$T_d T_d$	Temperature of dewpoint 30 = 30° F.	Coded and plotted in actual value in whole degrees F.
a	Characteristic of barograph trace 2 = rising steadily or unsteadily	Coded according to table in block ❿ and plotted in corresponding symbols.
pp	Pressure change in 3 hours preceding observation 28 - 2.8 millibars	Coded and plotted in units and tenths of millibars.
7	Indicator figure	Not plotted.
RR	Amount of precipitation 45 = 0.45 inches	Coded and plotted in inches to the nearest hundredth of an inch.
R_t	Time precipitation began or ended 4 = 3 to 4 hours ago	Coded and plotted in figures from table in block ❹.
s	Depth of snow on ground	Not plotted.

Cloud Codes

CLOUD ABBREVIATION	C_L	DESCRIPTION (Abridged From W M O Code)
St or Fs—Stratus or Fractostratus	1	Cu of fair weather, little vertical development and seemingly flattened
Ci—Cirrus	2	Cu of considerable development, generally towering, with or without other Cu or Sc bases all at same level
Cs—Cirrostratus	3	Cb with tops lacking clear-cut outlines, but distinctly not cirriform or anvil-shaped; with or without Cu, Sc, or St
Cc—Cirrocumulus	4	Sc formed by spreading out of Cu; Cu often present also
Ac—Altocumulus	5	Sc not formed by spreading out of Cu
As—Altostratus	6	St or Fs or both, but no Fs of bad weather
Sc—Stratocumulus	7	Fs and/or Fc of bad weather (scud)
Ns—Nimbostratus	8	Cu and Sc (not formed by spreading out of Cu) with bases at different levels
Cu or Fc—Cumulus or Fractocumulus	9	Cb having a clearly fibrous (cirriform) top, often anvil-shaped, with or without Cu, Sc, St, or scud
Cb—Cumulonimbus		

③ C_M — DESCRIPTION (Abridged From W M O Code)

C_M	DESCRIPTION
1	Thin As (most of cloud layer semi-transparent)
2	Thick As, greater part sufficiently dense to hide sun (or moon), or Ns
3	Thin Ac, mostly semi-transparent; cloud elements not changing much and at a single level
4	Thin Ac in patches; cloud elements continually changing and/or occurring at more than one level
5	Thin Ac in bands or in a layer gradually spreading over sky and usually thickening as a whole
6	Ac formed by the spreading out of Cu
7	Double-layered Ac, or a thick layer of Ac, not increasing, or Ac with As and/or Ns
8	Ac in the form of Cu-shaped tufts or Ac with turrets
9	Ac of a chaotic sky, usually at different levels; patches of dense Ci are usually present also

③ C_H — DESCRIPTION (Abridged From W M O Code)

C_H	DESCRIPTION
1	Filaments of Ci, or "mares tails," scattered and not increasing
2	Dense Ci in patches or twisted sheaves, usually not increasing, sometimes like remains of Cb, or towers or tufts
3	Dense Ci, often anvil-shaped, derived from or associated with Cb
4	Ci, often hook-shaped, gradually spreading over the sky and usually thickening as a whole
5	Ci and Cs, often in converging bands, or Cs alone; generally overspreading and growing denser; the continuous layer not reaching 45° altitude
6	Ci and Cs, often in converging bands, or Cs alone, generally overspreading and growing denser; the continuous layer exceeding 45° altitude
7	Veil of Cs covering the entire sky
8	Cs not increasing and not covering entire sky
9	Cc alone or Cc with some Ci or Cs, but the Cc being the main cirriform cloud

⑦ N_h — SKY COVERAGE (Low And/Or Middle Clouds)

N_h	
0	No clouds
1	Less than one-tenth or one-tenth
2	Two-tenths or three-tenths
3	Four-tenths
4	Five-tenths
5	Six-tenths
6	Seven-tenths or eight-tenths
7	Nine-tenths or over-cast with openings
8	Completely overcast
9	Sky obscured

⑥ N — SKY COVERAGE (Total Amount)

N	
0	No clouds
1	Less than one-tenth or one-tenth
2	Two-tenths or three-tenths
3	Four-tenths
4	Five-tenths
5	Six-tenths
6	Seven-tenths or eight-tenths
7	Nine-tenths or over-cast with openings
8	Completely overcast
9	Sky obscured

⑤ h — HEIGHT

h	HEIGHT IN FEET (Rounded Off)	HEIGHT IN METERS (Approximate)
0	0 – 149	0 – 49
1	150 – 299	50 – 99
2	300 – 599	100 – 199
3	600 – 999	200 – 299
4	1,000 – 1,999	300 – 599
5	2,000 – 3,499	600 – 999
6	3,500 – 4,999	1,000 – 1,499
7	5,000 – 6,499	1,500 – 1,999
8	6,500 – 7,999	2,000 – 2,499
9	At or above 8,000, or no clouds	At or above 2,500, or no clouds

④ R_t — TIME OF PRECIPITATION

R_t	
0	No Precipitation
1	Less than 1 hour ago
2	1 to 2 hours ago
3	2 to 3 hours ago
4	3 to 4 hours ago
5	4 to 5 hours ago
6	5 to 6 hours ago
7	6 to 12 hours ago
8	More than 12 hours ago
9	Unknown

	0	**1**	**2**	**3**	**4**
00	Cloud development NOT observed or NOT observable during past hour	Clouds generally dissolving or becoming less developed during past hour	State of sky on the whole unchanged during past hour	Clouds generally forming or developing during past hour	Visibility reduced by smoke
10	Light fog	Patches of shallow fog at station, NOT deeper than 6 feet on land	More or less continuous shallow fog at station, NOT deeper than 6 feet on land	Lightning visible, no thunder heard	Precipitation within sight, but NOT reaching the ground
20	Drizzle (NOT freezing and NOT falling as showers) during past hour, but NOT at time of observation	Rain (NOT freezing and NOT falling as showers) during past hour, but NOT at time of observation	Snow (NOT falling as showers) during past hour, but NOT at time of observation	Rain and snow (NOT falling as showers) during past hour, but NOT at time of observation	Freezing drizzle or freezing rain (NOT falling as showers) during past hour, but NOT at time of observation
30	Slight or moderate dust storm or sand storm, has decreased during past hour	Slight or moderate dust storm or sand storm, no appreciable change during past hour	Slight or moderate dust storm or sand storm, has increased during past hour	Severe dust storm or sand storm, has decreased during past hour	Severe dust storm or sand storm, no appreciable change during past hour
40	Fog at distance at time of observation, but NOT at station during past hour	Fog in patches	Fog, sky discernible, has become thinner during past hour	Fog, sky NOT discernible, has become thinner during past hour	Fog, sky discernible, no appreciable change during past hour
50	Intermittent drizzle (NOT freezing) slight at time of observation	Continuous drizzle (NOT freezing) slight at time of observation	Intermittent drizzle (NOT freezing) moderate at time of observation	Continuous drizzle (NOT freezing), moderate at time of observation	Intermittent drizzle (NOT freezing), thick at time of observation
60	Intermittent rain (NOT freezing), slight at time of observation	Continuous rain (NOT freezing), slight at time of observation	Intermittent rain (NOT freezing) moderate at time of obs.	Continuous rain (NOT freezing), moderate at time of observation	Intermittent rain (NOT freezing), heavy at time of observation
70	Intermittent fall of snow flakes, slight at time of observation	Continuous fall of snow-flakes, slight at time of observation	Intermittent fall of snow-flakes, moderate at time of observation	Continuous fall of snow-flakes, moderate at time of observation	Intermittent fall of snowflakes, heavy at time of observation
80	Slight rain shower(s)	Moderate or heavy rain shower(s)	Violent rain shower(s)	Slight shower(s) of rain and snow mixed	Moderate or heavy shower(s) of rain and snow mixed
90	Moderate or heavy shower(s) of hail, with or without rain or rain and snow mixed, not associated with thunder	Slight rain at time of observation, thunderstorm during past hour, but NOT at time of observation	Moderate or heavy rain at time of observation; thunderstorm during past hour, but NOT at time of observation	Slight snow or rain and snow mixed or hail at time of observation; thunderstorm during past hour, but not at time of observation	Moderate or heavy snow, or rain and snow mixed or hail at time of observation; thunderstorm during past hour, but NOT at time of obs.

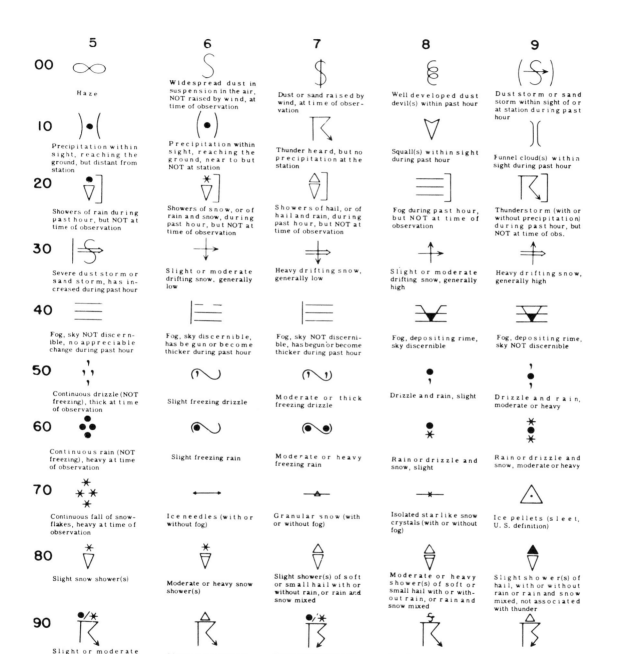

	5	**6**	**7**	**8**	**9**
00	Haze	Widespread dust in suspension in the air, NOT raised by wind, at time of observation	Dust or sand raised by wind, at time of observation	Well developed dust devil(s) within past hour	Dust storm or sand storm within sight of or at station during past hour
10	Precipitation within sight, reaching the ground, but distant from station	Precipitation within sight, reaching the ground, near to but NOT at station	Thunder heard, but no precipitation at the station	Squall(s) within sight during past hour	Funnel cloud(s) within sight during past hour
20	Showers of rain during past hour, but NOT at time of observation	Showers of snow, or of rain and snow, during past hour, but NOT at time of observation	Showers of hail, or of hail and rain, during past hour, but NOT at time of observation	Fog during past hour, but NOT at time of observation	Thunderstorm (with or without precipitation) during past hour, but NOT at time of obs.
30	Severe dust storm or sand storm, has increased during past hour	Slight or moderate drifting snow, generally low	Heavy drifting snow, generally low	Slight or moderate drifting snow, generally high	Heavy drifting snow, generally high
40	Fog, sky NOT discernible, no appreciable change during past hour	Fog, sky discernible, has begun or become thicker during past hour	Fog, sky NOT discernible, has begun or become thicker during past hour	Fog, depositing rime, sky discernible	Fog, depositing rime, sky NOT discernible
50	Continuous drizzle (NOT freezing), thick at time of observation	Slight freezing drizzle	Moderate or thick freezing drizzle	Drizzle and rain, slight	Drizzle and rain, moderate or heavy
60	Continuous rain (NOT freezing), heavy at time of observation	Slight freezing rain	Moderate or heavy freezing rain	Rain or drizzle and snow, slight	Rain or drizzle and snow, moderate or heavy
70	Continuous fall of snowflakes, heavy at time of observation	Ice needles (with or without fog)	Granular snow (with or without fog)	Isolated starlike snow crystals (with or without fog)	Ice pellets (sleet, U. S. definition)
80	Slight snow shower(s)	Moderate or heavy snow shower(s)	Slight shower(s) of soft or small hail with or without rain, or rain and snow mixed	Moderate or heavy shower(s) of soft or small hail with or without rain, or rain and snow mixed	Slight shower(s) of hail, with or without rain or rain and snow mixed, not associated with thunder
90	Slight or moderate thunderstorm without hail, but with rain and/or snow at time of obs.	Slight or moderate thunderstorm, with hail at time of observation	Heavy thunderstorm, without hail, but with rain and/or snow at time of observation	Thunderstorm combined with dust storm or sand storm at time of obs.	Heavy thunderstorm with hail at time of observation

Wind Speed (ff) — 9

ff	(MILES) (Statute) Per Hour	KNOTS
Calm	Calm	Calm
	1 - 2	1 - 2
	3 - 8	3 - 7
	9 - 14	8 - 12
	15 - 20	13 - 17
	21 - 25	18 - 22
	26 - 31	23 - 27
	32 - 37	28 - 32
	38 - 43	33 - 37
	44 - 49	38 - 42
	50 - 54	43 - 47
	55 - 60	48 - 52
	61 - 66	53 - 57
	67 - 71	58 - 62
	72 - 77	63 - 67
	78 - 83	68 - 72
	84 - 89	73 - 77
	119 - 123	103 - 107

BAROMETRIC TENDENCY — 10

Code Number	a	BAROMETRIC TENDENCY
0		Rising, then falling
1		Rising, then steady; or rising, then rising more slowly
2		Rising steadily, or unsteadily
3		Falling or steady, then rising; or rising, then rising more quickly

Barometer now higher than 3 hours ago (codes 1, 2, 3)

Code Number	a	BAROMETRIC TENDENCY
4		Steady, same as 3 hours ago
5		Falling, then rising, same or lower than 3 hours ago
6		Falling, then steady; or falling, then falling more slowly
7		Falling steadily, or unsteadily
8		Steady or rising, then falling; or falling, then falling more quickly

Barometer now lower than 3 hours ago (codes 5, 6, 7, 8)

PAST WEATHER — 11

Code Number	W	PAST WEATHER
0		Clear or few clouds
1		Partly cloudy (scattered) or variable sky
2		Cloudy (broken) or overcast

Not Plotted (codes 0, 1, 2)

Code Number	W	PAST WEATHER
3		Sandstorm or dust-storm, or drifting or blowing snow
4		Fog, or smoke, or thick dust haze
5		Drizzle
6		Rain
7		Snow, or rain and snow mixed, or ice pellets (sleet)
8		Shower(s)
9		Thunderstorm, with or without precipitation

258

Appendix C

SOIL CLASSIFICATION

Table C.1. A List of Diagnostic Horizons Used for the Differentiation of Orders in U.S. Soil Classification

Epidedons	
Mollic epipedon	Histic epipedon
Anthropic epipedon	Plaggen epipedon
Umbric epipedon	Ochric epipedon

Subsurface Horizons	
Argillic horizon	Fragipan
Agric horizon	Albic horizon
Natric horizon	Calcic and ca horizon
Sombric horizon	Gypsic horizon
Spodic horizon	Petrocalcic horizon
Placic horizon	Petrogypsic horizon
Cambic horizon	Salic horizon
Oxic horizon	Sulfuric horizon
Duripan	

Source: USDA, 1975, Agricultural Handbook No. 436.

Table C.2.   U.S. Soil Classification (orders)

Alfisols	Soils with clay accumulation in subsurface horizons.
Aridisols	Soils of arid climates (desert soils).
Entisols	Soils lacking diagnostic horizons.
Histosols	Organic soils usually formed from peat in places with high water tables.
Inceptisols	Weakly developed or absent soil horizons; has soil moisture available for plant growth for a minimum of 3 months a year; little accumulation of translocated materials.
Mollisols	Soils with dark, organic-rich surface horizons; significant amounts of calcium; typically associated with grasslands.
Oxisols	Soils with significant weathering of all minerals of the quartz; occur in tropical or subtropical areas.
Spodosols	The B horizon has an accumulation of black-red amorphous materials, above which is a light-colored (albic) horizon. Associated with forests in cool, moist climates.
Ultisols	Heavily leached soils with horizons of clay accumulation.
Vertisols	Soils with clays that swell when wet and develop cracks during dry seasons.

Source: USDA, 1975, Agricultural Handbook No. 436.

Table C.3.   Soil Classification of Canada (orders)

Chernozemic	Dark-colored A horizons with high organic content; accumulation of lime carbonate in a lower part of the soil.
Solonetzic	Mineral soils with salinization (presence of alkaline salts); often with a clayey B horizon.
Luvisolic	Leached soils produced in a forest environment; concentration of clays in the B horizon; light-colored Ae horizon.
Podsolic	Distinguished by the accumulation of soluble organic matters and mobile compounds of aluminum of iron in the B horizon. Often have light-colored Ae horizon.
Brunisolic	A broad category of soils with a brown-colored Bm horizon differentiated by color, structure and composition from the A and C horizons.
Regosolic	A weakly developed soil profile though often with an organic surface layer. These soils reflect the parent materials from which they are formed.
Gleysolic	Poorly drained soils; reducing conditions leading to gleyed horizons with greenish-bluish colors.
Organic	Soil derived from organic deposits (e.g., peats).

Source: Agriculture Canada, 1977, Soils of Canada, Vol. 1. This report and the U.S. Department of Agriculture Agricultural Handbook No. 436 contain tables correlating the U.S. and Canadian soil classification systems.

Name: _____

Laboratory Section: _____

Appendix D

AERIAL PHOTOGRAPHS: ADDITIONAL EXAMPLES

In the previous exercises the aerial photographs selected for analysis have been assembled into stereo pairs, a technique that aids beginning interpreters. However, when one is working with aerial photographs as a field or laboratory tool, complete photographs are used, not stereo pairs.

The ideal way to use the complete photographs is with a mirror stereoscope (Figure D.1). This instrument permits easier manipulation of the photographs and brings the entire area of overlap into stereoscopic vision. Each figure in this appendix is composed of two photographs; they are best removed from the manual for use with the mirror stereoscope.

The bedrock of the area shown in Figure D.2 has been folded into a distinctive dome. Erosion reveals the pattern of the sedimentary beds and an intricate drainage pattern.

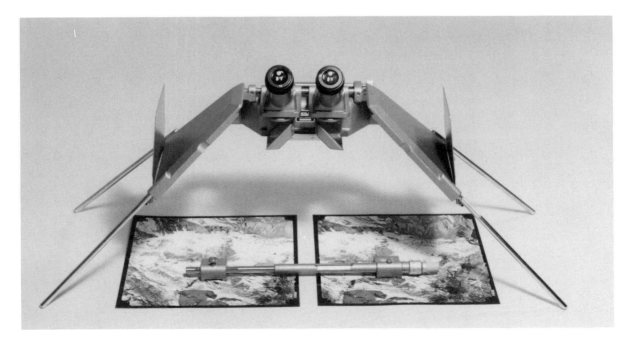

Figure D.1. Mirror stereoscope with photographs in position for analysis (Courtesy Wild Heerbrugg Instruments, Inc.)

Figure D.2.a.   Isachsen Dome (Geological Survey of Canada A16192—20 and 21)

PROBLEMS

1. Place six arrows around the dome (use a colored pencil); the arrows should point down the dip.

2. Compare the rocks on the outside of the dome with the ones in the center.

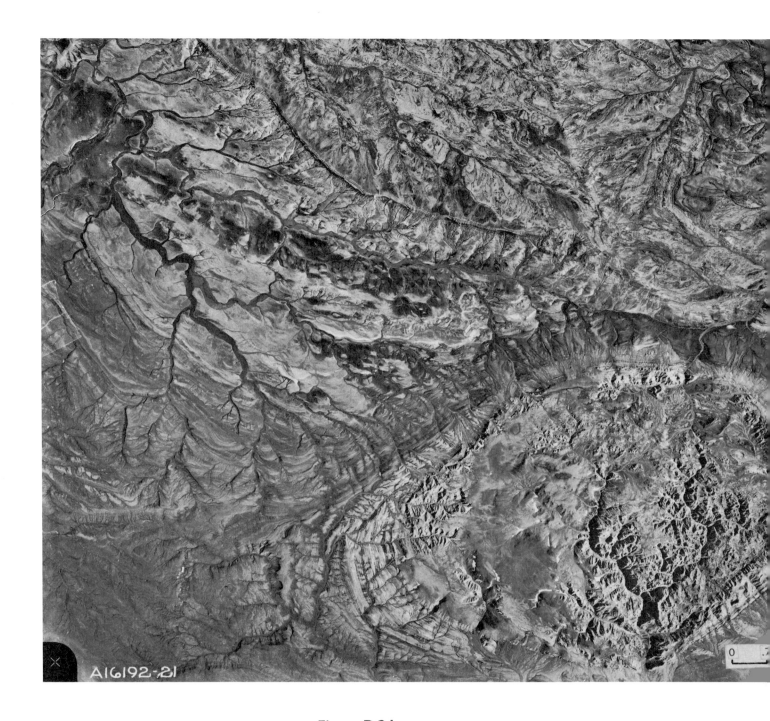

Figure D.2.b.

3. Draw a schematic (simplified) cross section across the dome.

4. Using your textbook, list three other examples of domes.

The viscous nature of lava formed from obsidian is quite evident in the photographs in Figure D.3. The steep front and edges of the flow are visible, as are the parallel ridges reflecting the flow of the lava.

PROBLEMS

5. Show the flow paths of the lava from the main vent by inserting arrows on the photographs.
6. Trending northwest to southeast there is a line of small cones.
    a. Provide a possible explanation for the linear trend of the cones.

    b. Are these cones younger or older than the steep-fronted lava flow found to the southeast?

7. Is there evidence on these photographs of earlier lava flows?

PROBLEMS

8. Is the terminus of the Kaskawulsh Glacier active or stagnant?

9. Give reasons for your answer to Problem 8.

Figure D.4.a shows a wide variety of spectacular features of glaciation.

10. Make a sketch map of the glacier in the space below. Identify on your map the following: terminal, lateral and medial moraines, braided streams, and alluvial fans.

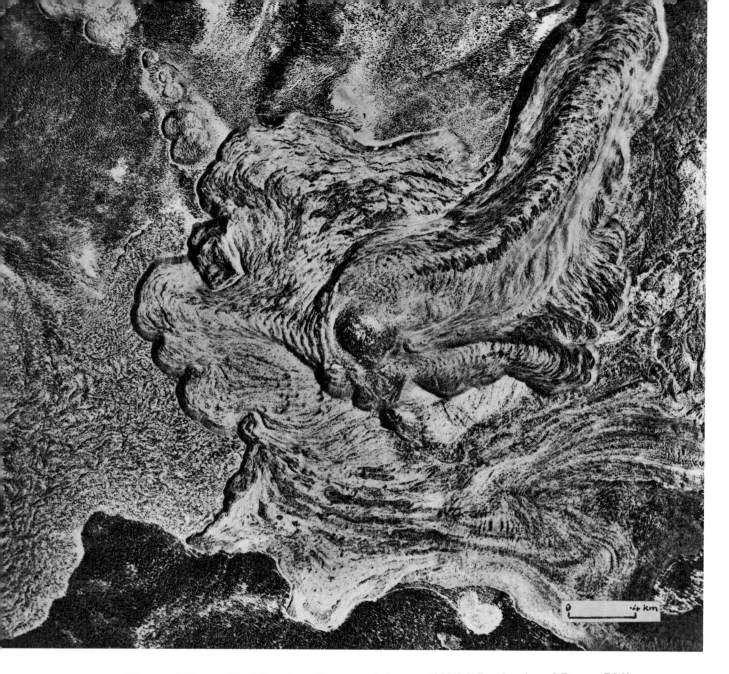

Figure D.3.a.   Obsidian lava flows and domes (USGS Professional Paper 590)

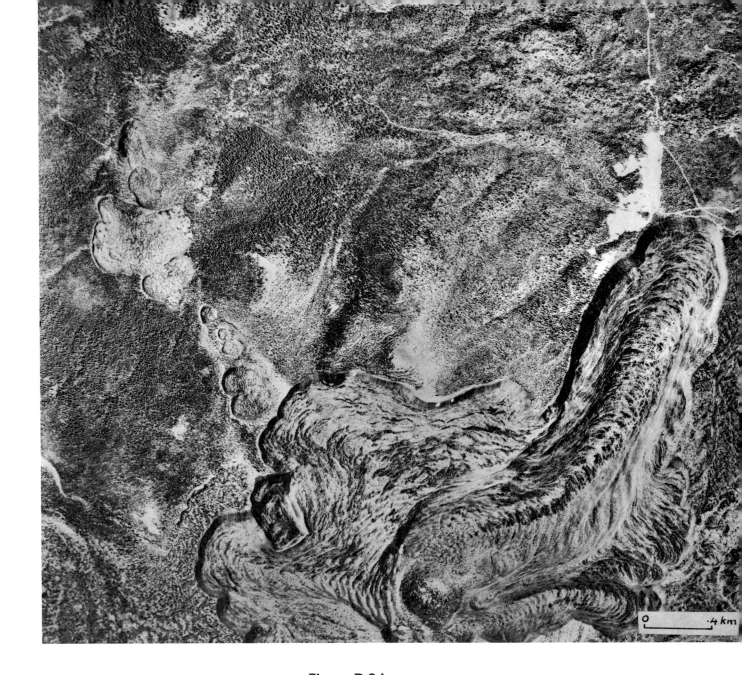

Figure D.3.b.

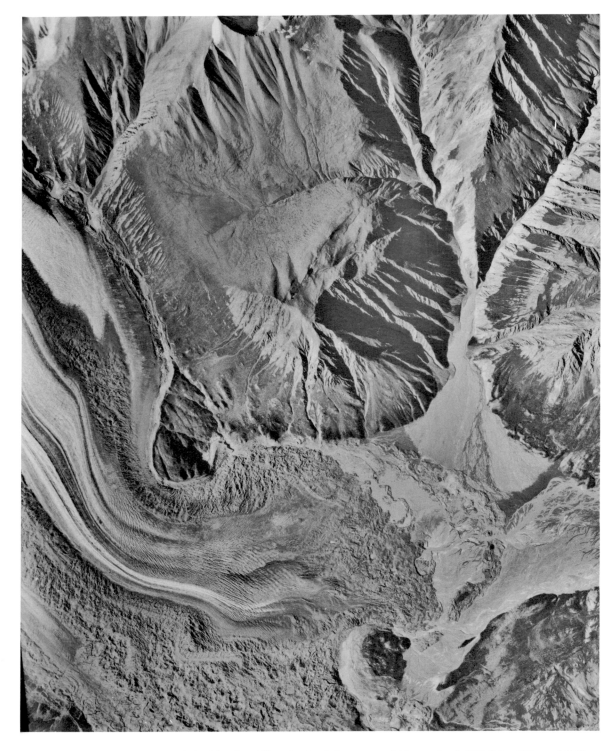

Figure D.4.a.   Kaskawulsh Glacier (Geological Survey of Canada A15517—20 and 21)

Figure D.4.b.